The End of the Peasantry

GERARDO OTERO

SEPTIEMBRE 2001

NEW ORLEANS

PITT LATIN AMERICAN SERIES

Billie R. DeWalt, *Editor*

G. Reid Andrews, Carmen Diana Deere,

Jorge I. Domínguez, *Associate Editors*

The

END OF THE PEASANTRY

THE RURAL LABOR MOVEMENT
IN NORTHEAST BRAZIL, 1961–1988

Anthony W. Pereira

UNIVERSITY OF PITTSBURGH PRESS

Published by the University of Pittsburgh Press, Pittsburgh, Pa.
15260
Copyright © 1997, University of Pittsburgh Press
Manufactured in the United States of America
Printed on acid-free paper

10 9 8 7 6 5 4 3 2 1

Pereira, Anthony W.
    The end of the peasantry ; the rural labor movement in northeast
Brazil, 1961–1988 / Anthony W. Pereira.
        p.   cm. — (Pitt Latin American series)
    Includes bibliographical references and index.
    ISBN 0-8229-3964-9 (cloth : acid-free paper). — ISBN 0-8229-5618-7
(pbk. : acid-free paper)
        1. Trade-unions—Agricultural laborers—Brazil, Northeast—History.
2. Peasantry—Brazil, Northeast—History.   3. Land reform—Brazil, Northeast—History.   I. Title.   II. Series.
    HD6614.A29P47   1997
    331.88'13'09813—dc21   96-45889
                                                                CIP

A CIP catalog record for this book is available from the British Library.

To my parents,
para todo o amor e carinho,
and for teaching me about *hwyl* and *saudades*

CONTENTS

TABLES

ACRONYMS

AFCPE   Associação dos Plantadores de Cana de Pernambuco (Pernambuco Association of Cane Planters). Cane growers' association without formal status in annual wage bargain.

AIFLD   American Institute for Free Labor Development (Instituto Americano para o Desenvolvimento do Sindicalismo Livre) AFL-CIO institute that promoted U.S.-style business unionism in Latin America.

ARENA   Aliança Renovadora Nacional (National Renovatory Alliance). Ruling party during much of military era; created by military in 1965.

CGT   Confederação Geral dos Trabalhadores (General Confederation of Workers). One of three labor centrals in Brazil.

CONTAG   Confederação Nacional dos Trabalhadores na Agricultura (Confederation of Agricultural Workers). National body composed of state federations of agricultural workers; created 1963.

CPT   Comissão Pastoral da Terra (Pastoral Land Commission). Church organization active in land issues; created 1975.

DRT   Delegacia Regional do Trabalho (Regional Labor Delegation). Office of Labor Ministry in the state.

CUT   Central Única dos Trabalhadores (Unified Workers' Central). One of three labor centrals in Brazil.

FETAPE   Federação dos Trabalhadores na Agricultura de Pernambuco (Federation of Agricultural Workers of Pernambuco). State body composed of 153 local unions; 45 of these sign the annual contract in the sugar zone; created 1962.

FUNRURAL   Fundo de Assistência ao Trabalhador Rural (Fund for the Assistance of the Rural Worker). Rural health program administered by trade unions; established in the early 1970s.

IAA   Instituto do Açúcar e Álcool (Sugar and Alcohol Institute). Federal agency that sets prices for sugar and related products, regulates the industry.

INCRA   Instituto Nacional de Colonização e Reforma Agrária (National Institute of Colonization and Agrarian Reform). Created by military government to administer agrarian reform.

MDB   Movimento Democrático Brasileiro (Brazilian Democratic Move-
                ment). Opposition to ARENA during military rule; created in 1965.
MIRAD   Ministério de Reforma Agrária e Desenvolvimento (Ministry of
                Agrarian Reform and Development). Second ministry responsible
                for agrarian reform. Abolished in 1990.
MST   Movimento dos Trabalhadores Rurais Sem Terra (Movement of
                Landless Rural Workers). Organization representing landless work-
                ers that organizes land occupations; formed 1985.
PDS   Partido Democrático Social (Democratic Socialist Party). Ruling
                party in early 1980s, outgrowth of ARENA.
PFL   Partido Frente Liberal (Liberal Front Party). Conservative party
                based mainly in northeast; outgrowth of the PDS.
PMDB   Partido do Movimento Democrático Brasileiro (Brazilian Demo-
                cratic Movement Party). Outgrowth of MDB, became ruling party
                in Pernambuco in 1986.
PSB   Partido Socialista Brasileiro (Brazilian Socialist Party). Miguel
                Arraes and his followers joined this party when they left the PMDB
                in 1989.
PT   Partido dos Trabalhadores (Workers' Party). Opposition party
                formed in São Paulo in 1980.
SFC   Sindicato dos Forneçedores da Cana (Cane Planters' Union). One
                of two cane planters' groups in Pernambuco, with formal rights to
                participate in the annual wage negotiations.
SINDACUÇAR Sindicato do Açúcar e Álcool (Sugar and Alcohol Union). Pernam-
                buco producers' association of mill and distillery owners.
STR   Sindicato dos Trabalhadores Rurais (Rural Workers' Union). Local
                unions which exist in almost every *município* in the Pernambuco
                sugar zone.
TRT   Tribunal Regional do Trabalho (Regional Labor Court). Settles dis-
                putes between workers and owners by issuing a collective labor
                contract.
TST   Tribunal Superior do Trabalho (Supreme Labor Court). Court of
                appeals above the TRT.
UDR   União Democrático Ruralista (Democratic Rural Union).
                Landowners' association formed in 1985 to oppose the govern-
                ment's proposed land reform.

ACKNOWLEDGMENTS

This book is the result of a long journey. It reflects the ideas, support, and inspiration of many people. The first inspiration was the United Farm Workers of America (UFW), the union whose marchers arrived in my hometown of Sacramento, California, after a 250-mile walk from Delano one balmy day in April 1966. The walk was to protest the refusal of grape growers to sign contracts with the union and to publicize the nationwide consumer boycott of California grapes that the union had initiated. The UFW was my first exposure to the power of rural workers' collective action.

As an undergraduate, I was introduced to the study of agrarian politics by my tutors at the School of African and Asian Studies at the University of Sussex, U.K. While I was in graduate school, many people were generous with their knowledge and time, including Robert Fishman, John French, Merilee Grindle, Frances Hagopian, James Ito-Adler, Joseph Thome, John Womack Jr., and especially Jorge Domínguez. The financial support of the Organization of American States, the Inter-American Foundation, the Tinker Foundation, and Harvard's Committee for Latin American and Iberian Studies was essential to the conduct of my field work.

In Brazil, I was helped by many. I am especially grateful to all the trade union officials and rural workers whom I talked to. They were polite if bemused by my initial approaches, listened patiently to my questions, and drew deeply from their experience in order to tell me how they saw events in the countryside. If the picture I present in this book is inadequate, it is not for any lack of cooperation from them. I especially benefited from the guidance of the then president of the union in Nazaré da Mata, José Patrocínio Gomes, and his secretary (and later, founder of the town's association of women), Eliane Rodrigues de Andrade Ferreira.

At the Federal University of Pernambuco in Recife, an extraordinary group of people helped to make my visit exciting and productive. Without Roberto Aguiar, Fernando Azevêdo, Terry Groth and Loussia Mousse Felix, Jorge Jatobá, Cecília Mariz, Marcus Mclo, Eliana Souza de Melo, Maria José dos Santos, Parry Scott, Alexandrina Sobreira de Moura, Claudio and Solange Souto, and Jorge and Popy Ventura de Morais, I never would have completed my research project. Outside of the university, Jandyra Guerra e Silva, Brian Honeyball, José Lauryston, Marisol Oliveira de Sousa, Silvana Olimpo de Siqueira, Lia Pandolfi, Melquisedec Pastor do Nascimento, and Maristela Vasconcelos helped with the research in important ways. Elsewhere in Brazil, Anita Brumer, Eduardo Gomes, Michael Hall, Zander Navarro, Paulo and Severino Manuel Soares, and João Gabriel Teixeira made my trips outside Recife memorable and stimulating.

At the Graduate Faculty of the New School for Social Research, many people were supportive and helpful. I am especially indebted to members of the New School's Proseminar on State Formation and Collective Action, including Edwin Amenta, Guy Baldwin, Richard Bensel, Vivianne Brachet-Marques, Perry Chang, Richard Ford, Elaine Fuller, Carmenza Gallo, Jeff Goodwin, Michael Hanagan, Roy Licklider, Fred Murphy, Marifeli Pérez-Stable, Wayne Te Brake, and Charles Tilly, who offered much-appreciated comments on, criticisms of, and encouragement about parts of this book. Among my Political Science Department colleagues, Victoria Hattam made helpful comments on a presentation based on the manuscript, and Aristide Zolberg's periodic reminders to "get it out" kept me focused on the importance of finishing, rather than compulsively revising, this work. Valuable assistance in producing this book was also furnished by Linda Allegro, Indran Amirthanayagam, Augusto Barcelos, Lauro Bueno, Teófilo Spencer Carvalho, Michael Diamond, Dean Graber, Andrew Jack, Caitlin McGrath, Maria de Fátima Monteiro, Lynne Perry, and Sonia Salas.

I also appreciate the careful comments of William Nylen and Cliff Welch on various drafts of the manuscript, as well as the thoughtful evaluations of the two anonymous reviewers for the University of Pittsburgh Press. I thank the director of the press, Cynthia Miller, acquisitions editor Catherine Marshall, and managing editor Kathleen McLaughlin for their assistance and professionalism. And I owe a deep debt of gratitude to my parents, Herbert and Mavis Perry, whose love and support have meant so much to me over the years.

While all of these people offered me a hand in my long journey, they must be absolved of blame for the remaining errors and omissions in this book. For these, I reluctantly shoulder all responsibility. It is fitting that the final "thank you" should go to my confidante and counsel throughout this project, my wife Rita Gordon Pereira. Rita, you and our daughter, Bela Wynne, have the heart of my heart.

✑ *Introduction* ✑

Fui até o campo com grandes propósitos.
Mas lá encontrei só ervas e árvores,
E quando havia gente era igual a outra.

(I went even to the countryside with grand designs.
But there I found only grasses and trees,
And when there were people they were the same as others.)

—Fernando Pessoa, "Tabacaria" (1928)

This book grew out of my interest in a social movement that no longer exists. The Peasant Leagues were organizations of peasants and rural workers that inflamed the northeast of Brazil, one of the poorest regions of Latin America, between 1955 and 1964. They organized marches that brought cane cutters and cowhands onto city streets, occupied plantations, confronted landlords, demanded the immediate redistribution of land to cultivators, and, in so doing, symbolically threw off the yoke of four centuries of the peasantry's oppression, exploitation, and silence.

However, the Peasant Leagues were abolished by a military regime that came to power in 1964 and were never resurrected. They were part of an agrarian Latin America that no longer exists. In its place are increasingly complex urban societies that juxtapose high-technology industries with subsistence agriculture, great wealth with total destitution, tight security with unchecked violence. This new Latin America is also a place of dramatic political change. With the possible exception of Eastern and Central Europe, no region in the world has recently experienced so many democratic transitions in so short a time.

While the authenticity of the new democracies is open to question, few would argue that their construction has involved the emergence, and in some cases the reemergence, of political movements long controlled and repressed by the various kinds of dictatorship that ruled in the 1960s and 1970s. Yet very few studies of the transitions in Latin America have looked outside the region's cities to study rural social movements—the spiritual, and sometimes literal, descendants of the members of the Peasant Leagues.

This book is one such effort. It analyzes the historical trajectory of the rural labor movement in Brazil, where one-third of the entire Latin American population lives, and where a democratic transition—or rather, a series of transitions—occurred in the 1970s and 1980s. During that time, the Brazilian rural trade union movement emerged as a powerful political force, representing millions of rural workers, small farmers, and, to a lesser extent, landless cultivators and other rural poor displaced by agricultural modernization. It organized strikes, pressured state institutions for agrarian reform, and opposed state agricultural and labor policies long geared to the interests of large estates. It was an important part of the popular mobilization that led eventually to the end of military rule in 1985, the creation of a new constitution in 1988, and direct elections for president in 1989.

The emergence of this movement is surprising. First, it has no parallel in Brazil's southern cone neighbors, nor, with the possible exception of Colombia and parts of Central America, in the rest of Latin America. In Chile the Pinochet regime of 1973–1990 decimated the ranks of organized labor in the countryside.[1] The rural labor movement also declined in membership and political strength under the military regime in Argentina (1976–1983). Of these three countries, only in Brazil did rural trade union membership expand under the authoritarian regime, and only there did rural unions play a significant role in the popular mobilizations for democratic reform in the 1980s.

Second, Brazil is a country with a conservative political history. It has never experienced a revolutionary break with the past in the countryside, where large landowners continue to dominate the agrarian social order. The 1964 military coup was directed, in part, against Peasant Leagues and rural unions that threatened the power of large landlords. The regime subsequently used state controls to replace most union leaders and keep those organizations weak and politically quiescent.

Third, the rural unions in Brazil were reactivated at a time when economic policies worked against most of their members. Brazil's agricultural policies promoted a process of modernization that favored large agribusiness and the transnationalization of production, leading to concentration of land, greater mechanization, increased use of expensive inputs, and the removal of tenants and smallholders from the land. This in turn led to huge streams of migrants to cities, frontiers, and sites of seasonal rural employment, as well as a general abundance of cheap labor. Representing an impoverished and scattered membership base, the rural unions faced formidable barriers to collective action.

How was this trade union movement created under a military regime notorious for its "demobilization" of labor? Why were the Peasant Leagues and their demands for land redistribution replaced by a union movement that primarily represented wage workers and small farmers? What was the relationship between the struggle of these rural trade unions and the transition to democracy that took place in Brazil in the late 1970s and 1980s?

In answering these questions, I offer evidence from a detailed case study of part of the rural labor movement in one region, rather than the rural labor movement as a whole. The Pernambuco rural labor movement was chosen, in part, not only because it was the birthplace of the Peasant Leagues and a center of early rural unionization, but because substantial documentary evidence and a secondary literature allows it to be analyzed closely over a long period. The rural unions in Pernambuco's sugar zone were also prominent in the later democratic transition and engaged in frequent and broad forms of collective action. Finally, they constituted a bedrock of support for the national rural workers' confederation in the 1980s, which held up their strikes as a model of union organizing that could be emulated elsewhere. Pernambuco's rural unions thus by no means constitute a "typical" case (no union could be in a country as vastly heterogeneous as Brazil), but they are especially closely intertwined both with the democratic transition and with the fortunes of the national rural workers' movement. And, as I shall argue later, the opportunities of and constraints on its rural labor movement stem from economic and institutional changes that occurred throughout Brazil.

At the end of the 1970s and throughout the 1980s, rural unions in Pernambuco seized the opportunity offered by the democratic transition in Brazil to engage in large-scale strikes, representing a quarter of a million workers, against employers almost every year. Furthermore, they forced the federal government, before military rule had even formally ended, to include them in a system of centralized negotiations with employers that strongly resembled the kind of social democratic mechanisms in place in many advanced capitalist countries. The unions' achievements are thus significant, but they were obtained at a price and still did not benefit a large portion of workers in the region; it was this awareness that led me to the questions that animate this book.

In seeking to answer those questions, I encountered some of the limits of the literature on transitions to democracy. That literature has been concerned with classifying the different types of transition, analyzing the interaction between elite representatives of forces within and outside the old regimes, charting subsequent institutional changes, and assessing the prospects of the new regimes. It has thus provided persuasive accounts of how the political opportunities facing social movements have changed, sometimes quite quickly. What it has *not* done is help to understand how the interests represented by, and the capacities for action of, social movements change over time—why social movements have played the role in transitions that they have. This book therefore spends less time on the dynamics of the transition itself and more on gradual, long-term processes that took place below the surface of national politics to shape the rural labor movement. This local realm is where we should look to understand how the movement was created and sustained, and how its members' and leaders' demands, ideologies, and aspirations were shaped by their interests, environment, and experiences.

In accounting for the rural labor movement's trajectory, I came back again and again to two "great transformations": the development of capitalism in agriculture, with accompanying changes in economic structure and class relations, and the expansion of the power of the central state, in this case in the form of new institutions that offered welfare benefits to a wide spectrum of previously excluded citizens. This book therefore deals with the interaction of two processes normally studied in isolation from one another. The first is the conservative modernization of agricultural production, the shift from labor-intensive smallholder agriculture to agro-industry. Part of the history of the West, and well known to economists and agronomists, the political implications of this shift where it is still occurring in developing countries is too little understood. The second process is the expansion of the power of the central state, and the movement in the countryside from a system of "dispersed domination" in which landlord power over subordinate classes is direct and unmediated, to one of "integrated domination," in which landlord power is mediated through state institutions (Migdal 1994, 9).

This book's theoretical approach is therefore neither society- nor state-centered. The state is a crucial factor in the case analyzed here, but to assume a priori in Latin America that the state is always central to political conflict is dangerous (Migdal 1994, 18). The state in Latin America is large but ramshackle, and, as O'Donnell (1993) points out, there are some regions and some people in many of its nations for whom the state is virtually nonexistent. As I will argue in the conclusion of the book, the role of the state in the representation of rural labor is itself an issue of intense conflict in the Brazilian countryside.

The book thus avoids reducing Brazil's democratic transition to one of two ideal types: the resurrection of a unified civil society against a despotic state (an extreme society-centered argument), and a controlled liberalization from above by agents within the state (an equally strong state-centered account) (Hagopian 1994, 38). Instead, it sees the transition as involving political struggles in multiple arenas of domination both inside and outside the state, a state that is less cohesive and unified than it looks from a distance, and does not assume a priori that either social forces or the state are dominant. This corresponds with the "state-in-society" approach advocated by Migdal (1994, 2–9). Thus I find that state power in the countryside grew, and increasingly "caged" social forces over time (Mann 1993), but that there were still many areas of rural social life unregulated by state institutions. I also argue that state officials, acting in tandem with powerful social interests, deeply transformed Brazilian agriculture and rural social reality, but not always in ways that they intended.

The title of this book is meant to convey a double meaning.[2] The end of the peasantry, first of all, suggests how the salience of peasant politics and land distribution issues can be reduced in a newly industrializing country. Agricultural modernization and the growth of the central state can combine, as they do in this case, to marginalize peasants both economically and as political actors. Peasant subsistence farming is not encouraged by the state, nor is the expression of a peasant political identity, and millions of rural people lose access to land and their traditional way of life. This outcome, it is important to emphasize, is not the result of an ineluctable "modernity"; while strong global pressures help to induce it, in the final analysis it is the product of political choice. The second part of this book examines Pernambuco's trade unions as an embodiment of the end of the peasantry in this sense, despite the prevalence of land hunger in the northeast.

The title also refers to another meaning. While capitalist development in agriculture marginalizes the peasantry, it creates new categories of individuals—rural workers, farmers, migrants, the landless—with new, divergent, and sometimes conflicting political demands. How these demands—the political "ends" of former peasants—are made and processed depends in large measure on certain institutions: the political organizations that represent the rural lower classes (unions, but also political parties and new social movements), and the links between those organizations and the state. These representative organizations inevitably privilege some interests over others. After the democratic transition, even the rural trade union movement could not fully represent the diverse interests of all the rural poor. The third part of this book is thus an analysis of how the political demands of the rural lower classes in Pernambuco influenced and were shaped by the institutions—both state and societal— that affected them, how these institutions related to one another, and how the local was connected politically to the national.

This book draws upon four types of sources. First, I conducted a survey of over fifty trade union officials representing every trade union in the Pernambuco sugar zone in 1987–88, asking them about their attitudes toward the national political regime, their union activities, and their relationships with local politicians and institutions. The account I extracted from these interviews certainly has its biases. However, such biases are exactly what is important for understanding the strengths and weaknesses of the unions' political linkages and alliances, and the relationship between the unions' local conflicts and democratic transition at the national level.

Second, I drew upon archival sources to reconstruct the history of rural unionism in Pernambuco, the local political economy in which that history unfolded, and the national political scene of which Pernambuco was a part. (Descriptions of both the survey and archival sources can be found in the appendixes.) Third, I interviewed individuals involved in Pernambuco's rural politics: Church activists, sugar industry and landlord representatives, government officials, party activists, and so on. Finally, I drew on an abundance of secondary sources, including Brazilian master's theses, dissertations, articles, and books.

This book is organized both chronologically and analytically. Chapter 1 introduces the topic, states the main questions of the study, and reviews theoretical approaches to those questions. Chapter 2 gives some necessary historical background, showing that the political domination of sugar producers remained unchallenged in Pernambuco until the mobilization of rural labor in the 1950s. Part II (chapters 3 and 4) deals with the 1964–1979 period, explaining why the Pernambuco rural trade unions reemerged as a political force in 1979, and why they had been transformed in the preceding 15 years. Part III treats the period between 1979 and 1988, dealing with the unions' relationship to, respectively, the union structure (chapter 5), the coercive power of landowners (chapter 6), political parties (chapter 7), and the struggle for agrarian reform (chapter 8). The analysis culminates with the creation of Brazil's 1988 constitution, because that document signified the political victory of antipeasant forces. In taking the possibility of large-scale land redistribution off the political agenda, it ratified the new rural order dominated by agribusiness. The concluding chapter covers tensions in rural interest representation in Pernambuco and Brazil since the 1988 watershed, pointing out how Brazil's present trade union structure impedes the representation of some interests in the countryside. It also highlights some conclusions about the role of labor in democratic transitions, and the potential political impacts of social movements, that can be derived from this study.

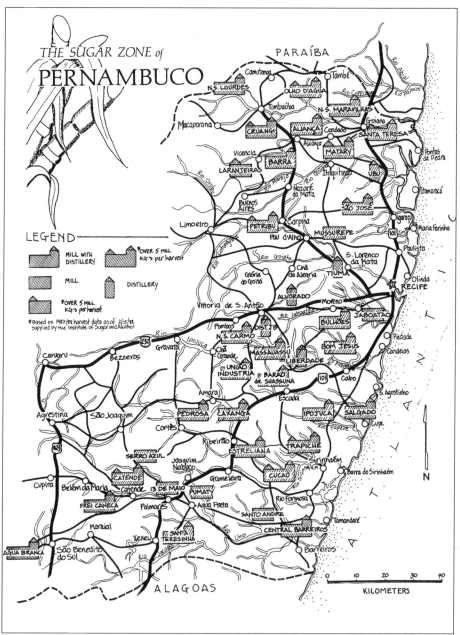

THE SUGAR ZONE of
PERNAMBUCO

PARAÍBA

LEGEND

MILL WITH DISTILLERY

*OVER 5 MILL. KG's per harvest

MILL

DISTILLERY

*OVER 5 MILL. KG's per harvest

*Based on 1987/88 harvest data as of 2/5/88 supplied by the Institute of Sugar and Alcohol

N.S. LOURDES
Camutanga
També
OLHO D'AGUA
Timbaúba
N.S. MARAVILHAS
Macaparana
CRUANGI
ALIANÇA
Condado
Goiana
SANTA TERESA
Aliança
Vicencia
MATARY
Pontas de Pedra
LARANJEIRAS
BARRA
Itaquitinga
UBÚ
Nazaré da Mata
Itamaracá
Buenos Aires
SÃO JOSÉ
Limoeiro
PETRIBU
Carpina
MUSSUREPE
Igaraçú
Maria Farinha
Pau d'Alho
IOLI
Paulista
Rio Croata
S. Lorenço da Mata
Glória do Goitá
Chã da Alegria
TIUMA
Olinda
RECIFE
ALVORADO
Vittoria de S. Antão
Moreno
Pombos
DISTΙΒ
BULHÕES
JABOATÃO
N.S. CARMO
Rio Jaboatão
Piedade
Chã Grande
MASSUASSU
LIBERDADE
Candeias
UNIÃO INDUSTRIA
BARÃO de Suassuna
BOM JESUS
Cabo
Canaru
Bezerros
Gravatá
Amaraji
Escada
S. Agostinho
Agrestina
São Joaquim
PEDROSA
TICHA
IPOJUCA
SALGADO
Cupe
Cortés
Ribeirão
STRELIANA
TRAPICHE
SERRO AZUL
Joaquim Nabuco
Gameleira
Barra do Sirinhaém
CATENDE
CUCAÚ
Sirinhaém
Cupira
Belém da Maria
Catende
13 DE MAIO
PUMATY
Rio Formosa
FREI CANECA
Palmares
Agua Preta
SANTO ANDRE
Tamandaré
Maraial
Yexeu
SANTA TERESINHA
CENTRAL BARREIROS
AGUA BRANCA
São Benedito do Sul
Barreiros

ALAGOAS

0   10   20   30   40
KILOMETERS

N

LYNNE PERRY

The Awakening of
the Unions

~ 1 ~

From Peasant Leagues to Unions in Rural Brazil

round 8:00 A.M. on 15 October 1988, a pickup truck filled with about fifteen striking rural workers arrived at the entrance of a sugar plantation near the town of Nazaré da Mata, Pernambuco. Led by José Patrocínio Gomes, then president of the local rural workers' union, the strikers clambered out of the pickup and came face-to-face with the plantation owner and his administrator. While many strikers clutched a cutting implement (foice) used in the fields, the administrator, a stout, dark man in a blue safari jacket and porkpie hat, brandished a double-barreled shotgun. Gomes explained to the owner and the administrator that the strikers wanted to enter the plantation and talk to the workers in the fields, in an effort to persuade them to stop work. The owner would have none of it.

A tense standoff ensued. Cowed by the shotgun, the strikers huddled by the side of the pickup as Gomes complained about the weapon. Several strikers shouted for everyone to calm down. A striker grabbed the union's megaphone and spoke to the workers, saying that he didn't want violence and that the strike committee only wanted to talk to them as comrades (companheiros). Slowly, the strikers formed a semicircle around the owner and the administrator, who issued threats in a low, tense voice. After several minutes, the situation slowly shifted. The strikers became angry. One said, "Well, he can kill one of us, but then we will certainly kill him." A young striker in a red hat and blue jacket quipped, "Who's afraid of a shotgun?" A heated discussion with the owner ensued, with much shouting and anger on the part of the workers. The owner insisted that the strike, then in its sixth day, was not obligatory and that anyone who wanted to work for him would work. On several occasions Gomes raised his arms and asked for silence so that he could negotiate with the owner, but the

3

shouting continued. Almost unnoticed, the administrator and his shotgun began retreating, first by edging behind the owner, then by facing the group further down the road, and finally by turning his back on the assembly and walking away.

With the departure of the administrator, the plantation belonged to the workers. Led by Gomes, the strikers strode past the owner and into the fields, getting the strikebreaking cane cutters—many of them children—to stop work. They handed out leaflets that explained why they were on strike. The man with the megaphone made a short speech in favor of the strike, saying that he and his comrades were not there to pit worker against worker but to gain a better salary for all, and that it was better for them to go home and come back after the strike, when they could be assured of better wages and working conditions. With calls of "go home" to the workers in the fields, the strikers drove away in their pickup.[1]

The incident at the plantation near Nazaré da Mata was part of an annual war of maneuver between landowners and labor in Pernambuco's sugar zone. It reflected the ability of local unions to defy the armed force of the landowners through organization, a little courage, and the power of numbers. And it reflected how the sugar workers' unions were able to force themselves back onto the local political stage after years of military rule in which such bold actions would not have been permitted. The strikers were thus capitalizing on the democratic transition, but they were also part of the transition—their actions were taken into account, if not always appreciated, by landlords, state officials, and other powerful figures involved in the regime change.

The unionists of Nazaré da Mata were part of a labor movement that represented a quarter of a million workers in Pernambuco's sugar zone (also called the forested zone or *zona da mata*). This strike was the eighth since their path-breaking action of 1979, when they became the first rural unions in the country to challenge the military regime with a strike. During the 1980s, their repeated mobilizations and strikes formed part of the great surge of popular pressure that influenced the Brazilian military's decision to abandon direct control over the executive in 1985. Together with the metalworkers and bank employees, they formed one of the pillars of the revitalized Brazilian labor movement whose militancy helped to democratize politics in the 1980s.

How was this militant labor movement created, despite the vigilance and repression of the Brazilian military regime? Why was it primarily a working-class rather than a peasant movement? What was the relationship between the rural trade unions and the transition to democracy that took place in Brazil in the 1980s? This book sets out to answer these questions.

The most significant characteristic of Brazil's new rural trade union-ism was that it was primarily a movement of workers and small farmers rather than peasants. Thus it was fundamentally different from the agrar-ian movement of Brazil's preauthoritarian period. In the early 1960s, under a populist regime, rapid and intense mobilization of the rural labor force in the Brazilian northeast had alarmed landowners, political leaders, and the U.S. government. The initial mobilization had been conducted by Peasant Leagues, organizations of the rural poor that invoked the image of the Cuban revolution, engaged in direct actions such as land occupation, and demanded a redistribution of land "by law or by force," without com-pensation to large landowners. This mobilization made the agrarian ques-tion, especially in the northeast, one of the most important national issues of the day.

The Peasant Leagues were voluntary organizations with no formal link to the state; a large repertoire of collective action; many urban, middle-class leaders; and a multiclass membership with little or no central coor-dination of what were essentially local struggles. In response to the Leagues, trade unions concerned primarily with wage increases were founded by activists from the Communist Party and the Catholic Church. The actions of both the Leagues and the unions were condemned as sub-versive and unacceptable by most landowners, who supported the post-1964 military regime's policy of abolishing the Peasant Leagues and purg-ing and repressing the trade unions.

The rural labor movement that reemerged as a political force in the 1980s was very different from its 1960s counterpart. It was formally included within the state's corporatist labor structure, had a narrow reper-toire of collective action, was led mainly by professional union officials with peasant and worker backgrounds, and was centrally coordinated at the national level by CONTAG (Confederação Nacional dos Trabalhadores na Agricultura), the National Confederation of Agricultural Workers, and at the state level by state federations. While some CONTAG advisors had backgrounds in the Communist Party, the role of that party as an orga-nized force within the movement was relatively small. The influence of the Church, on the other hand, which had been a major force in rural unionism in the 1960s, was now strongest outside the official union struc-ture in the new social movements of the landless.[2]

In the 1980s, CONTAG mobilized thousands of workers in legal strikes every year, including those organized by the Federation of Agricultural Workers of Pernambuco, FETAPE (Federação dos Trabalhadores na Agri-cultura de Pernambuco). It did pressure the federal government for land reform, but by parliamentary means. In 1988 CONTAG was the largest confederation in the Brazilian labor system, with twenty-two state federations, 2,747 unions, and almost 10 million members on its books.[3] This is significant growth for an organization that was founded only in 1963 by a few hundred newly formed unions. In Pernambuco, the number of unions in the sugar zone increased from thirty-two in 1964 (Price 1964) to forty-five in 1988.

An adequate analysis of the Brazilian rural labor movement must therefore try to account both for the movement's reemergence in the 1980s, and for the changes in its form, size, capacities, and activities. In addition, it must explain the decline in the importance of "peasant" questions, and the emergence of new conflicts centered on the demands of rural workers and small farmers.[4]

Rather than try to analyze the movement in toto—a very difficult task in a continent-sized country such as Brazil, with vastly heterogeneous conditions in agriculture—this book focuses on unions in Pernambuco, one of the leading segments of Brazil's rural labor movement. Pernambuco is significant because its 1979 strike made its federation an "initiator" that many other state rural labor federations later copied.[5] Pernambuco unions also created a dynasty within the national confederation, CONTAG, in much the same way that metalworkers' unions from the ABC region of São Paulo dominated the national labor central, the CUT (Central Única dos Trabalhadores, or Unified Workers' Central).[6] This dynasty is symbolized by the fact that from 1968 to 1989, the president of CONTAG was José Francisco da Silva, a leader from Pernambuco's sugarcane fields. Da Silva and other CONTAG leaders directly coordinated the eight strikes in the Pernambuco sugar zone between 1979 and 1988, proclaiming that the strikes were a model for rural unionists around the country. Pernambuco thus represents an "exemplary" rural labor movement whose high degree of organizational capacity calls for explanation.

Rural Labor and Democratic Transitions

Authoritarian regimes in almost fifty countries around the world have collapsed or been reformed since 1970 (Schmitter 1993, 1). These transitions have resulted in democracy when the new regime, at the very least, conducts regular, open, and competitive elections of top government officials; makes bureaucratic agencies of the state responsible to the elected parliament and/or chief executive; and guarantees a minimum of civil liberties to its citizens.[7] The literature on democratic transitions and their consolidation is primarily concerned with explaining why and how, at the macro level, the institutional reforms necessary for democracy are brought about and preserved.[8]

Another aspect of regime transition has been undertheorized in this literature. That is: as regime change takes place, how do citizens at the local level claim the rights embodied by the new national institutions? Seen from this angle, transitions cannot adequately be reduced to single, holistic narratives that homogenize the political experience of citizens within national territories (Rubin 1994). The historical reality is that both formal and effective democratic rights are usually extended variably—by gender, race, ethnicity, economic sector, region, and so on—within a nation over time. Of particular relevance to this study, the democratic rights most important to labor—to freely organize unions, bargain collectively, and strike—are not explicitly included in many macroanalyses of democratic change. They form part of a broad array of popular demands that inevitably accompany the macroinstitutional reforms of regime transition.

Because of their concern with national institutional reform, many scholars share a rather narrow view of the role of popular pressures in democratic transitions. Either popular organizations and movements are seen as unimportant, or their only relevance is their capacity and inclination to upset the carefully constructed transition, once it has been installed from above.[9] Thus Przeworski writes (in O'Donnell, Schmitter, and Whitehead 1986, 63): "It seems as if an almost complete docility and patience on the part of organized workers are needed for a democratic transformation to succeed." In a similar vein, Terry Karl asserts:

> No stable political democracy has resulted from regime transitions in which mass actors have gained control, even momentarily, over traditional ruling classes. . . . Thus far, the most frequently encountered types of transition, and the ones which have most often resulted in the implantation of a political democracy, are "transitions from above." (1990, 8)

These and other similar comments prompted Charles Tilly to decry the "top-down models, instrumental and constructivist approaches to democratization, and short-run analyses" that currently prevail in the literature (1995, 365).

One reason for discounting the role of popular pressures in regime change in this literature is that the time frame analyzed is usually very short. Most studies using the notion of a democratic transition implicitly assume that the main causes of democratic change can be found in events occurring immediately before the establishment of a new regime. The focus is thus on elite bargains and pacts, the institutional compromises of high national politics, fissures within the authoritarian regime, and the like. Explanations of the formation of democratic regimes that concentrate on these events tend to stress rational-actor models and the individual decisions of the most powerful members of society (O'Donnell, Schmitter, and Whitehead 1986). The notion of "contingency"—in which outcomes "depend less on objective conditions than subjective rules surrounding strategic choices" (Karl 1990, 6) is a key component of these explanations.

Transitions to democracy within this perspective are seen primarily as the result of a series of conscious, planned, strategic actions. A previous generation of scholars' "bottom-up, deterministic, long-term theories" of democracy (Tilly 1995, 365), with their focus on history, culture, and economic and political structures have been laid to one side. What really seems to count in contemporary analysis is the inclination of political elites to make pacts; in Samuel Huntington's words, "Whether democracy in fact falters or is sustained will depend primarily on the extent to which political leaders wish to maintain it and are willing to pay the costs of doing so" (1991, 279).

Such an approach is one-sided. Popular organizations that have been shaped, at least in part, by long-term structural and institutional change have often played a significant role in the collapse or reformation of authoritarian regimes. In turn, regime change has sometimes involved concessions to popular movements. In the case of trade unions, authoritarian governments are said to "demobilize" labor, while civilian ones are expected to allow for labor's "remobilization." Institutions previously barred to workers' representatives are frequently opened up to them; some decentralization of decision making can take place; and labor's demands have occupied a more prominent place on some post-transition government agendas. Yet the role of labor in regime transitions has not won the attention that it deserves (Buchanan 1995, xv).

However, acknowledging that labor can play an important role in democratic transitions and that authoritarian regimes "demobilize" labor, while democratic ones allow for its "remobilization," is only a starting point—and a corrective to the elitism and lack of historical perspective in much theorizing about transitions. The demobilization-remobilization dichotomy oversimplifies state-labor relations. In fact, controlled labor mobilization of some type was allowed by most Latin American authoritarian regimes except in the most repressive periods. The dichotomy draws attention away from continuous political processes across and within regimes. It does little to help us understand changes in the organizational capacities and demands of labor movements, or how these might vary regionally, sectorally, and over time.

Regarding the case of rural labor in Brazil, therefore, the social science literature seems to contain two major gaps. The first is in theorizing about the relationship between rural labor and transitions. The vast literature on the role of the peasantry in revolution has not generated an equally rich body of work on the role of peasants (and other rural actors) in negotiated changes of regime. The second gap lies in historical approaches that look at long-term change, not just short-term interactions; these are rather thin on the ground. As Karl comments, what is needed is a

> path-dependent approach which clarifies how broad structural changes shape particular regime transitions in ways that may be especially conducive to (or especially obstructive of) democratization . . . [and how] such structural changes become embodied in political institutions and rules which subsequently mold the preferences and capacities of individuals during and after regime changes. (1990, 7)

Some scholars have adopted such an approach, showing, for example, how state practices and capabilities changed over a long period, whether during the authoritarian regime or before its foundation, to shape the contours of the democratic transition (Cavarozzi 1992; Hagopian 1993; Munck 1994; Remmer 1989). This book shares this perspective, arguing that the political institutions regulating rural labor during the Brazilian regime transition embodied a massive structural change: the decline of the peasantry.

How did this change occur? In Latin America, the rural working class did grow in agro-export regions, but much more slowly than in either manufacturing or mining sectors. This is because plantations had previously coexisted uneasily with peasant plots. Plantation owners in northeast Brazil and elsewhere extracted labor first from indigenous people, then from African slaves, and then from the "reconstituted peasantries" that formed in and around the plantations after the abolition of slavery (Mintz 1974b, 132–33). Peasant labor was extracted through sharecropping and other nonmonetary arrangements; wage labor tended to come quite late, if at all, in the process of capitalist development. When it did come, wage labor was frequently mixed with precapitalist relations of production, creating a "peasantariat," or labor force with mixed peasant and proletarian characteristics.[10]

To the extent that a rural working class emerged free of dependent relations with landlords involving land, this new class was likely to demand inclusion in the political system. The rural working class has a strong interest in gaining the democratic rights to assemble, speak out, bargain collectively, go on strike, and vote, because with these rights it has a much better chance of being able to improve wages and working conditions. Rural workers are also, in many cases, much better able to act on this desire for political freedom than peasants, tied as the latter often are to landlords. However, when rural workers surmount the high barriers to collective action in the countryside and engage in autonomous organization, they face the likelihood of employer repression. According to a recent comparative study of democratization, in the cases reviewed "the landed upper classes which were dependent on a large supply of cheap labor were the most consistently anti-democratic force" (Rueschemeyer, Stephens, and Stephens 1992, 8). In turn, landlord repression may engender a messianic or maximalist political orientation among rural workers, as was the case with Brazil's Peasant Leagues. In the context of labor-intensive agriculture and incipient working-class formation, therefore, mobilization from below is likely to lead in the short term to revolutionary or authoritarian violence rather than to democracy.

The tensions generated by agricultural modernization, however, can enhance the prospects for agrarian democracy. This dynamic is analyzed clearly by Paige. When hacienda agriculture undergoes capitalist transformation, he argues, labor declines as a percentage of landowners' costs, making it easier for landlords to accept bargaining with labor organizations and the possibility of wage increases.[11] Rural workers, for their part, begin to resemble their industrial counterparts. As patron-client ties are replaced by the cash nexus of the marketplace, workers move away from the plantation and the supervision of the landlord and break out of their former isolation. Their scope for organization increases, and in the absence of repression they do not adopt maximalist positions. Eventually, they will lose their peasant attachments to land and tend to develop a militant but reformist labor movement that negotiates for higher wages and better working conditions.[12] A democratic class pact, rather than revolution or authoritarianism, is likely to emerge. Rural workers will join their urban counterparts in pushing for democratic political inclusion (Rueschemeyer, Stephens, and Stephens 1992, 8).

However, such an outcome is not guaranteed—Paige's analysis should be interpreted probabilistically rather than as a universal law. The structure of landholding, the history of past conflicts, and the cultural predispositions ("frames") of the local population (Tarrow 1994, 6), among other factors, influence the likelihood of a democratic class pact in the countryside. More specifically, the organization of agricultural production also varies significantly from one crop to another. Therefore, this book draws on an eclectic variety of works in political economy that focus on the distinctiveness of collective action within economic sectors (Frieden 1991; Shafer 1990). Understanding the sector—in this case, sugar—within which the unions are embedded is very important, because the sector imposes additional, specific structural constraints on unions' collective action aside from those that exist in the broader social setting.

My argument is that something like the trajectory from hacienda to capitalist agriculture described by Paige occurred in the Pernambuco sugar zone in the 1960s and 1970s, and that this facilitated the emergence of a labor movement capable of negotiating a local democratic class pact during the national regime transition of the 1980s. Brazil as a whole evolved from a rural to an urban nation in this period; while the majority of the population lived in the countryside in 1960, by 1980 almost 70 percent was urban. Pernambuco urbanized as well. In its sugar zone, traditional landlord-peasant arrangements such as tenancy, sharecropping, and *moradía* (in which peasants had the right to cultivate a small plot on the landlord's estate in return for several days of labor per week) declined. Meanwhile, larger, more efficient mills increasingly dominated production, leading to a reduction in the total number of mills. Wage employment increased, as did the size of the rural working class. In pursuit of their own interests, rural labor organizations played a vital role in demanding the inclusion of all those excluded by policies of conservative modernization in the countryside. Agrarian transformation laid the basis for local acceptance of the democratic transition in the 1980s.

Rural Labor in Brazil

To understand Brazil's rural unionism, we need to distinguish among the movement's four different facets, which are not always sufficiently disentangled: (1) opportunities for action, (2) capacities to act, (3) ideology and program, and (4) strategy. The argument made here is that opportunities for action are explained mainly by macropolitical factors at the level of the national regime; capacities to act are influenced primarily by large historical processes—changes in social structure and the institutional form of representative institutions; and ideology and strategy are explained by the members', and especially the leaders', learning through experience and through local traditions and institutions. Part II of this book mainly concerns the capacity to act, while Part III covers ideology and strategy. Some background information on opportunities for action is given throughout the text.

An account of Brazil's rural unionism inevitably confronts the state's central involvement to the unions' operations. State agriculture policies influence the kinds of popular protest that arise in the countryside. Reciprocally, the state's responses to popular protest determine the political consequences of that protest (Davis 1994, 381). More specifically, all Brazilian trade unions operate within a structure highly controlled by the central state, a structure that has not been fundamentally reformed since the 1930s, despite several changes of national regime (Sandoval 1993). The key features of this union structure, discussed in more detail in chapter 5, are a unitary system of representation or *unicidade* (only one union allowed per category of worker in a given territory); a mandatory union tax (*imposto sindical* or *contribuição sindical*) deducted from employees' pay and passed on to unions by the state; and a hierarchy of union organizations, ranging from the local union in a *município* (equivalent to a county) through state federations and national confederations. Like most other Latin American union structures, Brazil's is a mandatory closed shop enforced through a state-controlled, hierarchical, corporatist, and bureaucratic structure. Thus, the political opportunities available to unions fluctuate with changes in the composition of the national regime. Furthermore, rural unions operate in agriculture, a portion of the economy highly regulated by the state in Brazil, as it is in many other countries.

The state in Brazil and in Latin America more generally has promoted the modernization of agriculture, which has contributed to some of the most important structural changes in the region over the last forty years. Agricultural modernization refers to the application of scientific knowledge and capitalist rationality to the ancient art of farming. It involves the transformation of agriculture from a subsistence activity or a productive system in which profits derive primarily from land and labor to one in which profits accrue mainly from capital investment and in which land or labor productivity, or both, are increased through the use of new inputs.[13]

The most dramatic increase in agricultural modernization in the advanced capitalist countries took place after World War II. There, rural labor became relatively scarce, due to the growth of urban industry. This forced agricultural producers to adopt capital-intensive forms of production. Chemical fertilizers and pesticides, new planting and harvesting machines, and genetically engineered plants facilitated a quantum leap in agricultural productivity. These new technologies caused relatively little social dislocation because they were introduced in societies whose rural labor force had already become largely urban.[14]

In many parts of the Third World, these new agricultural technologies were rapidly adopted in very different social environments. The new technology spread, despite the relative scarcity of capital and abundance of labor. This occurred for various reasons, including transnational pressures, state subsidies to large estates and skewed prices, a highly unequal distribution of land, the desire of large farmers to insulate themselves from rural union organizing, and the prestige associated with "modern" forms of agriculture. Unlike the case in advanced capitalist countries, the labor surplus often produced by high-technology, capital-intensive agriculture in the Third World could not readily be absorbed by the industrial and service sectors. The agricultural revolution in the Third World thus contributed to, rather than mitigated, social strains. Peasants were uprooted from the land without a corresponding increase in available urban employment.[15]

The modernization of agriculture has been part of the larger transformation of rural societies into predominantly urban ones in Latin America (see table 1.1). This change has been rapid and dramatic: a process that took half a century in many advanced capitalist countries occurred in much of Latin America in a mere twenty years. The traditional Latin American large estate *(latifúndio)* has become, in many places, a capital-intensive enterprise. At the same time, the peasantry has been greatly reduced, while a large class has emerged of mostly seasonal rural workers and small farmers, alongside an even larger class of former peasants in the cities who are self-employed or employed in the informal sector.

This de-peasantization is an economic, political, and cultural phenomenon. *De-peasantization* is a more accurate term than *proletarianization* because not all former peasants become full-time wage earners.[16] In the economic sphere, rural and urban labor markets become more tightly integrated, and increased transportation and communication links bridge the urban-rural gap. Politically, de-peasantization is usually accompanied by the incorporation of former peasants by the state, but not as subsistence cultivators. Culturally, the distance between the rural and urban areas is reduced by the spread of schooling and literacy, television and radio, frequent migration from rural areas to cities and other rural areas and back again, and the relocation of many large landowners to cities.

The structural change induced by agricultural modernization did not lead invariably to the formation of only two, highly polarized classes. Agrarian growth may produce the immiseration of all but a handful of rich farmers (Lenin 1982), but if applied indiscriminately and mechanically as a kind of universal law of capitalist development in agriculture, this formula misses important, subtle forms of differentiation in the countryside. Even in the Brazilian northeast, a region considered economically backward, expansion and improved production techniques in the 1970s led not just to the dislocation of many, but to increased opportunities for small

Table 1.1 Agriculture's Share of Gross Domestic Product, the Labor Force, and Rural Population in Selected Latin American Countries, 1990–1992

	Share of GDP		% of Labor Force		Rural Population (as % of Total)	
	1960[a]	1992[b]	1965	1990–92	1960	1992
Argentina	17	6	18	13	26	13
Bolivia	29	23	54	47	61	48
Brazil	28	10	49	25	55	23
Chile	12	9	27	19	32	15
Colombia	35	16	45	10	52	29
Costa Rica	33	18	47	25	64	52
Cuba	n.a.	n.a.	33	24	45	25
Dominican Republic	27	18	59	46	70	38
Ecuador	37	13	55	33	66	42
El Salvador	32	9	58	11	62	55
Guatemala	30	25	64	50	68	60
Honduras	44	22	68	38	77	55
Mexico	19	8	49	23	49	26
Nicaragua	37	30	56	46	60	39
Panama	25	10	46	27	61	46
Paraguay	36	22	54	48	63	51
Peru	22	13	49	35	54	29
Uruguay	19	10	20	5	21	11
Venezuela	7	5	30	13	33	9
Average	27	15	46	28	54	35

Source: United Nations Development Programme 1995, 172, 176, 184.

a. Data from *United Nations Statistical Yearbook 1966*, 563–69.

b. Data for Bolivia, Chile, and Peru are for 1988 (Twomey and Helwege 1991, 2); data for Brazil, Panama, and Paraguay are for 1991 (United Nations Development Programme 1994, 154).

landowners (and an expansion in their numbers), more permanent jobs for laborers, and the growth of an intermediate strata of technical and supervisory personnel such as agronomists, chemists, economists, and machine operators. These various categories of people had divergent interests. Development in agriculture can thus lead to complex patterns of differentiation that are not as simple as class polarization between a small group of capitalists and a mass of destitute workers.

This study argues that it is precisely because the rural labor force was not a mass, but rather a highly heterogeneous and changing collection of interests and identities, that the challenges faced by the rural labor movement during the democratic transition were so complex.[17] While capitalist modernization mainly benefited large landowners and was detrimental to the poor, many of whom lost access to land, people who fell between these two poles in the production system frequently benefited from change as well. In the process, trade unions that had been organized around the single identity of the "rural worker" became arenas of contention between small farmers, wage laborers, and a declining number of subsistence cultivators.

The complexity of structural change in the countryside is related to the unions' problems of representation. Structural change can lead to conditions that favor union formation. But the types of collective action that unions engage in, the ideologies they espouse, and the demands they make, are not necessarily determined by social structure. For these issues, cultural and political factors—local cultural frames, the background of the leadership, its alliances and values, political opportunities, the nature of state institutions—may have significant weight. Disentangling union foundation, capacity, strategy, and ideology seems crucial if one is to avoid teleological reasoning that attaches inevitable political consequences to economic change (Eckstein 1989, 55).

With these distinctions in mind, we can see that CONTAG's claim to represent all progressive forces in the countryside was problematic. The confederation could not be all things to all its members, and a stable, national political consensus did not exist within its member unions. Given the great heterogeneity of interests represented by the unions, and the shifting opportunities they faced, it was not always clear what a "progressive" political line was at any point. There were certainly internal debates about this. For example, the labor central CUT (Central Única dos Trabalhadores, or Unified Workers' Central), founded in 1983, frequently clashed with CONTAG leaders over the confederation's leadership style, position on union reform, and tactics on the land question.[18] There were also criticisms of the unions from without, on the part of new social movements of the landless such as the Church's Pastoral Land Commission (CPT, Comissão Pastoral da Terra) and the Landless Workers' Movement (MST, Movimento dos Trabalhadores Rurais Sem Terra). All of these organizations claimed to speak for the rural poor against the large landholders and existing state policies, but their analyses and tactics differed markedly, revealing the contested nature of representation in this period.[19]

The Pernambuco Case

A cartoon in a Recife newspaper reflected the surprise with which many middle-class city dwellers regarded the strikes in the Pernambuco sugar zone. In it, a reporter says to a rural worker, "Tell me something ...

how did all of you, so malnourished and stunted, manage to stage such a well-organized strike?" The rural worker, gesturing with outstretched arms from beneath a straw hat, responds, "Sir, we are stunted, but we have a unity that is *this* big!" (*Jornal de Comércio*, 3 October 1979, 2). This book chronicles the construction of that unity, focusing in particular on the causes of renewed rural union mobilization and its role in the local workings of a new, more democratic regime.

The Pernambuco sugar zone forms one of the economic poles of the northeast. The Brazilian northeast, home to about 40 million people, is the largest concentration of mass poverty in the western hemisphere and is known for its hunger, misery, recurring droughts, and hugely inegalitarian agrarian system.[20] United Nations statistics show that the northeast lags behind the south of Brazil in almost every indicator of social development, with an average life expectancy seventeen years shorter, adult literacy 33 percent lower, and gross domestic product per capita 40 percent lower than that of the south (United Nations Development Programme 1994, 99).

Popular movements that sought to change the inegalitarian structures that perpetuate poverty in the northeast have dotted the region's history. The labor movement of Peasant Leagues and unions that arose in Pernambuco in the late 1950s and early 1960s, under a populist regime, is one of the most important. It was the most renowned rural labor movement in the whole of Brazil during the Second Republic (1945–1964). At that time, rural workers' political rights were curtailed because of a suffrage limitation that excluded the majority of the rural population: only literates could vote, a restriction that lasted until 1985. Landowners effectively controlled electoral politics in the countryside.

However, the expansion of sugar production, and the subsequent conversion of many peasants into wage laborers, brought rural workers into politics in a new, more active role. Recife, the capital of Pernambuco and the second-largest city in the northeast, had an extensive middle and working class, and it was votes from these sectors that propelled a politician drawing on the support of the rural labor movement, Miguel Arraes, to the governorship in 1962. The unions established in the sugar zone at this time, supported by Arraes and aided by the sponsorship of the federal government, began demanding workers' rights that had previously been enjoyed only by urban workers. The Peasant Leagues, for their part, pressured for land reform. The unions enjoyed an unprecedented victory in August 1963, when Arraes brokered a labor accord that recognized the unions' right to bargain collectively, granted a major wage increase to workers, and codified working conditions. The wage increase was gained by workers only after a stunning, massive, and successful strike in November in which, for the first and last time in the region, mill workers joined forces with cane workers in the fields and virtually shut down the state's sugar production.

The military coup and subsequent establishment of a military regime in April 1964 wiped out almost all the gains of this early period of union organizing. The brief democratic modus vivendi engineered by the Arraes government was never successfully consolidated. Arraes himself was deposed in the coup, imprisoned, and later sent into exile. The Peasant Leagues were abolished, while many League and union activists were violently purged from the movement. Unions were allowed to continue functioning but were subject to numerous restrictions. Many workers' rights (crucially, the right to strike and to negotiate over wages) were eliminated in practice. So also were many political rights, including union support for parties; and the political system itself was drastically reduced to two official parties in 1965. The provision of legal services on an individual basis became the only permitted activity of union officials, who became in effect part of the state's bureaucratic apparatus. In the economic realm, production of sugar continued to expand while the demand for labor remained constant, due to the introduction of labor-saving technology.

This was the situation until 1979, when liberalization at the national level gave the unions space to organize and negotiate wages once again. The 1979 strike brought the labor unions back to life in Pernambuco, and in subsequent years other rural unions followed the Pernambuco example and engaged in strikes. In Pernambuco, between 1979 and 1990 strikes were held almost every year in late September and early October, at the peak of the sugar harvest. These mobilizations involved large numbers of workers as union organizational capacity increased, and by 1988 the union federation, FETAPE, represented almost a quarter of a million wage earners in its negotiations with mill owners and sugarcane planters. During the 1980s, the right to vote for the highest offices in the country was also gradually restored to workers. In the sugar zone, important worker rights were recognized by the state. The rural unions played a vital role in the region's democratization.

However, the rural trade union leaders interviewed as part of this research had reasons to worry about their and their members' access to the benefits of the new democratic regime. They were mostly black and mulatto in a country dominated by whites. They lived in the poorest region of Brazil, a region that produced large numbers of migrants who often faced discrimination in other parts of the country. They represented rural laborers in a former slave society in which an aristocratic disdain for manual labor, particularly agricultural labor, stigmatized rural workers. Finally, they formed part of the majority of poor people in a country with a strongly oligarchic political system in which economic inequalities had markedly increased in recent decades.

This study finds that the political emergence of rural workers' organizations strengthened democracy in the region. The mobilization of wage workers in labor disputes created a counterweight to the entrenched power of landlords and their manipulation of clients among the lower class. The state federation was thus instrumental in forging a new, more democratic modus vivendi in the sugar zone. Yet it did not represent everyone squeezed by agricultural modernization. In particular, it was relatively uninvolved in the struggles of smallholders and displaced peasants to retain and acquire land.

The key to understanding the trajectory of the rural labor movement in Pernambuco, and in much of the rest of Brazil, lies in recognizing key changes in economic structure and political institutions. The first of these is the de-peasantization of the rural population and an increase in union resources that greatly enhanced the political capacity of rural unions, so that when regime liberalization created an opportunity for pressure from below in 1979, the unions were part of that pressure. Second, the "peasant" orientation of the unions disappeared both because peasants themselves were marginalized by capitalist development (transformed into wage workers, self-employed petty capitalists, or small farmers), and because state policies recognized and rewarded "worker" identities but not "peasant" ones. Third, both the success and failure of the unions to effect political change can best be understood in terms of their articulation with other political institutions, especially those of the state and of political parties.

Before we analyze why the union movement reemerged as a political force in 1979 (the task of chapters 3 and 4), some historical background is necessary. Only by understanding the nature of the landowners' historical power in Pernambuco can one grasp the significance of the contemporary union movement's winning of citizenship rights. Only in the last two decades have workers had the right to participate in negotiations over the fate of an industry based on their labor. The unchallenged despotism of Pernambuco's landed oligarchy lasted for almost 450 years.

~ 2 ~

The Past as Prologue

he Pernambuco rural workers' strike of October 1979 ended a fifteen-year period in which public collective resistance to the military regime was suppressed in the Brazilian countryside. The 1979 strike transformed everyday struggles at the local level into a collective, public, overtly political conflict. In James Scott's terms, it revealed the "hidden transcripts" of rural labor and demonstrated that the harmony imposed by the military regime had been an illusion.[1]

But the strike, and the right to collective bargaining that the unions won through it, was not created overnight. Its success was the outcome of a long history of prior attempts at organization, defeats, and reorganization, as well as gradual structural and institutional change in the sugar zone. While chapters 3 and 4 deal with the latter topic, this chapter summarizes the history of labor resistance and political change in the Pernambuco sugar zone before the 1979 strike. Only by understanding how workers' previous attempts to challenge the political control of the landed oligarchy were prevented and defeated, can one fully appreciate the significance of the strike.

The history of Pernambuco can be summarized as the interconnection between three processes: the changing form of the state, agricultural modernization, and the development of a rural working class. None of these processes developed in a unilinear fashion, and none is complete. In the first, what Mann (1993, 59) calls the infrastructural power of the state—its capacity to coordinate social actors so as to enforce its policies within a given territory—expanded, so that the state increasingly replaced private power centers as the locus of binding authority. In Migdal's terms, dispersed domination was gradually supplanted by a more integrated domination (1994, 9). The state's claim to a monopoly of the means of coercion was more tightly enforced, although by no means was this monopoly fully established. In the early 1960s, the state replaced the private power of landlords by incorporating rural labor.

In the second process, sugar production was modernized and became more capital-intensive, with milling capacity increasingly concentrated in fewer hands and the whole coming to look increasingly industrial. Depeasantization accelerated, labor decreased as a proportion of total costs, and workers became more productive as a result of increased capital investment.

Finally, workers themselves were transformed by the changes in production processes. Rural cultivators who had once relied on access to land for subsistence agriculture increasingly became full proletarians, living in towns and becoming entirely dependent on wages and the cash economy. In the early 1960s, they founded their own unions, linked to the state, outside the direct control of landlords. However, the development of a purely working-class consciousness is incomplete, and the vestiges of a peasant identity are still strong in the sugar zone, as I argue in chapter 4.

Of the relationship between these two processes, we can say that the rural working class emerged partly as a result of changes in the production process. One clearly helped to create the other. With regard to the changing form of the state and agricultural modernization, however, the relationship is more complex, as they developed together. Agricultural modernization would have been impossible without state support; surpluses derived from sugar production, on the other hand, were used by state managers for their own purposes. Rather than saying that one clearly caused the other, we can say that they developed symbiotically.

Sugar, Slavery, and the State

Sugar was an integral part of Spanish and Portuguese imperialism in the Americas, an instrument for financing colonial expansion as well as an incentive for appropriating more territory (Galloway 1989, 49). Production of sugar in Pernambuco is as old as Portuguese settlement itself (Burns 1966, 34; Schwartz 1985, 15–22), and has dominated the economy of the state for over 450 years, linking it with the centers of the world economy in Europe and, later, North America as well.[2] Duarte Coelho, who received the captaincy of Pernambuco from the Portuguese crown in 1534, consciously developed the sugar industry by attracting Portuguese investors and bringing in specialists in sugar from Portugal, Galicia, and the Canary Islands (Schwartz 1985, 18). In 1575 the son of Duarte Coelho was the wealthiest man in Brazil, exporting more than fifty shiploads of sugar a year to Portugal (Burns 1966, 34). In that period, Pernambuco was the leading sugar producer in Brazil and, according to one historian, the richest plantation economy in the world (Carvalho 1994, 1). Ironically, Pernambuco today is at the center of one of the poorest regions in the developing world—the Brazilian northeast.

Sugar plantations in Pernambuco and the rest of the northeast first relied on the labor of local indigenous people. Indians comprised the bulk of the labor force until about the 1580s, but for various reasons were eventually replaced by black African slaves.[3] The union of black slavery and sugarcane developed first in the Atlantic islands of Madeira, the Canaries, Cape Verde, and São Tomé and was brought to Brazil by the Portuguese from there (Schwartz 1985, 6–10). Sugar harvesting is a labor-intensive business. By 1819, on the eve of Brazilian independence in 1822, 368,465 people were living in Pernambuco, and 97,633 (26 percent) of them were slaves, most of them engaged in sugar production (Carvalho 1994, 1).

The Portuguese in Brazil attempted to create a political system in the image of their own absolutist state. However, the state that emerged in Brazil in the nineteenth century was far weaker, and attempted to rule over a much larger territory, than its European progenitor. It was often hard pressed even to maintain the loyalty of the various regional elites within the nation. In the first half of the nineteenth century, there were three major liberal rebellions in Pernambuco (1817, 1824, and 1848), in which local elites made unsuccessful attempts to secede from the central state. These interelite conflicts gave subordinate groups some opportunities for escape and resistance. Some slaves were able to flee the plantations and establish settlements (quilombos) in the forests surrounding the sugar zone.[4] The runaway slaves sometimes used the settlements as a base from which to attack plantations.[5] A major peasant rebellion, the Cabanada, also took place in the southern sugar zone in 1832–1835 (Carvalho 1994). The contemporary rural labor movement in Brazil traces its roots to these kinds of popular uprisings (CONTAG 1993b, 5).

However, there were severe limits on popular resistance to ruling-class domination in Brazil. Unlike all other Latin American countries, Brazil gained its independence without severing ties to the European monarchy of the colonizing power; hence, lower-class mobilization against the colonial power was also limited. In 1808, during the Napoleonic wars, the Portuguese crown transferred its court to Brazil. In 1821, the court was reestablished in Portugal with the return of King João VI, but his son, Dom Pedro I, remained in Brazil and declared the country independent in 1822, arranging his coronation as emperor of Brazil that same year. The country, an independent monarchy, remained an anomaly in Latin America for most of the rest of the century (Bushnell and Macaulay 1994, 147–53).

In the northeast, local governing institutions clearly reflected the long history of dominance by the sugar-producing oligarchy.[6] However, the role of sugar in the world economy has declined dramatically over the last two centuries. Once a highly prized and profitable luxury good, sugar has become a very common, overproduced commodity whose relative value has steadily decreased (Goldszal 1992). Thus in the 1980s Pernambuco produced 1,000 times more sugar, with more efficient technology, than it had 140 years earlier, but its relative poverty vis-à-vis the core of the capitalist world economy was more severe than ever before.[7] The decline was long and gradual. Within Brazil, sugar was replaced by coffee as the principal export crop in the 1830s. After this, the sugar-producing northeast never recovered the economic and political influence of the previous era.

Between 1822 and 1850, slavers brought some 70,000 Africans into Pernambuco's capital city and principal port, Recife. Although the slave trade was declared illegal by the Brazilian government in 1831, it was not effectively repressed until 1850. The availability of new supplies of African slaves, combined with increased sugar production for export, meant that the treatment of slaves on many plantations deteriorated during this time.

As elsewhere in Brazil, the manumission of slaves was relatively common in Pernambuco in the nineteenth century. Combined with the presence of runaway slaves, this resulted in a large free nonwhite population. Free blacks and mulattoes accounted for about 10 to 15 percent of the Brazilian population around 1800, and probably much more by 1850. For this reason, attempts to abolish the slave trade sat uneasily with many free nonwhites. In 1826, when Brazil signed a treaty with Britain agreeing to make the slave trade illegal within three years, many in Pernambuco's free colored population interpreted this as signifying the government's intention to reenslave *pardos* (mulattoes) and *pretos forros* (freed blacks). Crowds of angry nonwhites invaded churches in several places in the sugar zone to demand the reading of the document that supposedly enslaved nonwhites (Carvalho 1994, 5–7).

While slavery in Brazil, as elsewhere, was highly repressive, it did allow some opportunities for solidarity and resistance.[8] Slaves on the plantations often formed networks of *malungos*. Of African origin, *malungo* means companion or comrade and was applied to men who had come to the New World on the same slave ship. It finds an echo today in the common use of the term *companheiro* to refer to fellow workers within the rural trade union movement. Another form of resistance by slaves to oppression was to arrange their "theft" by another owner. The theft of slaves was quite common in Pernambuco in the nineteenth century, often with the willing participation of slaves anxious to find better working conditions on other plantations. According to Carvalho, being stolen was "a metaphor for choosing another master through illegal means" (1994, 9).

Brazil's involvement in the War of the Triple Alliance (1864–1870)—in which Brazil, Argentina, and Uruguay, backed by British capital, dismembered Paraguay—greatly strengthened Brazil's central state. The military was expanded and professionalized during and after the war (Graham 1969, 76–93). Brazil's various regions were tied more closely together in what can now be seen as a prelude to the significant changes of the last quarter of the nineteenth century.

Free Labor and Modernization

The late nineteenth century saw the development of two interrelated processes in Pernambuco: accelerated capitalist development and the beginnings of a modern state. The abolition of slavery in 1888 (Brazil was the last country in the Western Hemisphere to take this step) and the end of the monarchy in 1889 were two of the most significant moments in the gradual development of these two larger processes.

Capitalist development in the countryside resulted in agricultural modernization. Modernization does not imply that new techniques in agricultural production were always more "rational" than those they replaced, nor that these innovations were clearly and unambiguously improvements from the workers' point of view. In addition, the use of the term does not suggest that these changes were inevitable or irreversible— rather, they were consciously adopted by landowners in response to their environment. In the history of agriculture, labor-saving machinery, for example, may be abandoned by landowners when labor costs decline sufficiently (Krissman 1994).

The abolition of slavery was part of the process of agricultural modernization in Brazil. Its impact was not large in Pernambuco, because the transition to free, or more accurately, partly free, labor had been going on for some time prior to abolition. This is because planters had found it profitable to sell their slaves to São Paulo coffee estates. Slave labor was replaced by labor that was practically free: migrant workers from the interior could be induced to work in the cane fields in exchange for the right to cultivate a plot of plantation land and perhaps a nominal wage. The effect of abolition on this mixed labor system, paradoxically, was to lower standards of living and conditions for workers. In the first few years after abolition, when some 40,000 ex-slaves entered the labor market, wages in the sugar sector dropped to the level of the 1850s.[9] No associations representing cane workers existed, although a union for the relatively well-paid mill workers existed as early as 1890 (Eisenberg 1974, 185, 189). By the 1920s, mill workers organized strikes in Pernambuco and were subject to heavy repression by the police and mill owners through the 1930s (Lopes 1978, 4).

Those rural workers who did vote during this period tended to participate as part of the *voto do cabresto* (herd vote) organized by landowners. The landowners functioned as rural bosses and were known as *coronéis* (colonels) because of their membership in the state militia. The *coronel* provided a wide variety of services to rural clients in return for their political loyalty, which included voting for his candidate. The *coronel* was often described as "o indivíduo que paga as despesas" (the one who pays the bills) because, in addition to other forms of assistance, it was he who covered the costs of transportation, lodging, and food for rural workers on election day.[10] This system of political control through the patronage and alliances of landowners, each with his own coterie of rural workers, was known as *coronelismo* (Flynn 1978, 35–38; Nunes Leal 1949).

Confined within a system of political participation that allowed them only a dependent and thoroughly guided role, rural workers also had to contend with a racist ideology that was the legacy of slavery. In this ideology, politics was the exclusive domain of the white aristocracy. Politics required the refined manners of a man of leisure, the white suit of the plantation owner *(senhor de engenho)* or urban businessman, and the rhetorical and literary skills of a graduate of Recife's prestigious law school. In a region in which 75 percent of the population is black or mulatto, and only 25 percent white, the elitist implications of such an ideology are clear.[11]

The black and mulatto descendants of slaves who made up most of the work force in the cane fields thus lacked the requirements that would have allowed them to participate in politics on an equal footing with elites: white skin, wealth, and education.[12] In the dominant ideology, politics was seen as the vocation of *doutors*, university graduates; the emergence of a democratic counterideology based on the notion of equality of citizenship is relatively recent.[13]

Coronelismo formed the basis of the Old Republic, a regime marked by regionalism:[14] *coronéis* exchanged political support for the center, including the delivery of their herd votes, in return for the center's pledge of non-interference in their local areas. In this loose federation, all politicians were essentially state leaders, and the national leadership reflected the prevailing compromise between the states. The republican constitution of 1891, promulgated after the end of the monarchy in 1889, reflected a strong distrust of central control. For many politicians of the era, "the states were the reality, the Union . . . the fiction" (Flynn 1978, 32). The system was described as the "politics of the governors" (*política dos governadores*) (Hagopian 1990, 10) because state executives were dominant and federal controls weak. The two strongest states, Minas Gerais and São Paulo, alternated control over the presidency in a marriage of convenience between "coffee and milk" (*café com leite*, because São Paulo's main crop was coffee and Minas was a dairy state).[15] In Mainwaring's words, "State leaders and regional oligarchs worked against the creation of strong national parties, because such parties would have undercut their autonomy and power" (1988, 94). Congress was therefore also weak and regionally based, and only the bureaucracy—including the army—was truly national and integrative (ibid., 93). In such a system, local landowners, including Pernambuco's sugar mill and plantation owners, held unchecked sway in their domains. Rural workers had no access to countervailing power outside the region to which they could appeal.

Pernambuco's politics during the Old Republic therefore reflected, to a great extent, the dominant economic organization in the sugar zone, the plantation (Curtin 1990, 55–56). The plantation owners determined most of the conditions of workers' lives without any restraint from outside authorities.[16] For this reason, analysts of politics in Pernambuco refer to the "despotism of the mills" and the "republic of the mills" (Lopes 1978, 214; Perruci 1978).

The plantation owners had private militias and were responsible for law and order in their areas. They decided how many days the workers would work in the cane fields, how much and what type of land they were allowed to cultivate for their own use, even which members of the workers' extended family could live in the simple plantation dwellings. Many workers became permanently indebted to their *senhor* because of their debts at the plantation store. Landowners determined how violations of norms of work discipline would be punished, often dispensing rough justice—including death—on the spot, through their hired gunmen (*capangas* or *jagunços*). The owners' capacity to discipline and punish workers was almost limitless, as was their control over their employees' political behavior (Julião 1972). Their capacity to reward workers in general was limited, however, due to the decline of the northeast's economic and political position during the Old Republic. At the beginning of this regime, northeastern sugar producers had already lost their preeminence to São Paulo coffee producers, and they faced an increasingly difficult market position thereafter.[17] Development of the regional economy in the northeast was therefore sharply limited, and ambitious workers frequently migrated to the more dynamic and prosperous industries of the south and southeast. Improvements in sugar production and transportation technology begun in the late nineteenth century led eventually to the concentration of capital and milling capacity in the Pernambuco sugar zone. The Brazilian state took an active role in fostering the adoption of new sugar technology by providing cheap loans to mill owners for capital improvements and subsidizing the construction of railroads. In 1854 there were 532 sugar mills (engenhos) in Pernambuco, and in 1914, 2,756; by 1920 most of these had closed down, having been replaced by 54 much larger and more efficient mills (usinas). In 1965 there were 47 usinas, but only 35 in 1988 (Perruci 1978, 117; Taylor 1978, 68–70). These usinas grew about 40 percent of the cane used in sugar production on their own land.[18] This technology-driven concentration of capital also occurred in other sugar-growing areas throughout the world (Galloway 1989, 17).

In 1930, a crisis toppled the national political regime without changing the place of rural workers in Pernambuco's politics. An economic crash that sent coffee prices tumbling and a split between São Paulo and Minas Gerais over the presidential succession combined to precipitate a revolution. Getúlio Vargas assumed the presidency, where he remained for fifteen years, presiding over the construction of a new dictatorial regime, or new state (Estado Novo), between 1937 and 1945. While this new regime preserved some elements of the old regionalism, the mechanisms of central control were strengthened and the power of the São Paulo industrial elite consolidated.[19] The northeastern coronéis were incorporated into the national regime in a subordinate role, through the new Social Democratic Party or PSD (Partido Social Democrático) (Roxborough 1979, 105).

Under President Vargas, a political reorganization took place in the Pernambuco sugar zone, as it did throughout the country. In the new, highly regulated system, intimate links were established between the federal government and both mill owners (usineiros) and planters (fornecedores). But the role of cane workers in local politics remained essentially what it had been during the Old Republic. While the Estado Novo was officially dedicated to recognizing workers' interests and reconciling them with those of employers, in practice this did not occur in the countryside. A Ministry of Labor was created in 1930, and in 1931 it was authorized to organize workers into government-supervised unions, but almost all of the unions subsequently formed were in urban areas.[20] Similarly, rural workers did not have access to the system of courts established by the Ministry of Labor, nor was the minimum wage (established in 1943) applied to them.

In 1933 the federal government created the Institute of Sugar and Alcohol (IAA, Instituto do Açúcar e Álcool). The institute was established to revive and regulate the sugar industry, which had been badly hit by the world depression. It became a quasi-autonomous government agency, funded by taxes levied on producers. It set quotas by region, state, mill, and planter, regulating all aspects of production, down to the smallest plantation. The institute determined national allocations for export and domestic markets of sugar and alcohol, sometimes directly managing financially troubled mills and distilleries. It directly conducted the marketing of all sugar exports, depositing the profits earned by these sales into a special export fund, which was then reinvested in the sugar industry at the IAA's discretion (Nunberg 1986, 55). The IAA also shielded producers from world market prices. When international prices were low, it paid higher than the world market price; when prices were high, it paid lower than the going rate. The most powerful government organ entrusted with protecting rural workers' interests, the IAA was in reality geared to maintaining sugar production and employers' profits.

If the Pernambuco cane cutters had no rights to bargain in defense of their interests under the Estado Novo, neither could they reach out to politicians who might have been interested in representing them. The 1932 Electoral Code lowered the voting age from twenty-one to eighteen, guaranteed the secret ballot, and extended suffrage to women, but it still denied the vote to illiterates (Burns 1980, 404). And after Vargas's coup d'état in 1937, elections and political parties were banned, press censorship and the use of political police imposed, and the president's right to rule by decree established (Burns 1980, 409). This repression meant the denial to rural workers of any forum in which to present their grievances.

To some extent, rural workers benefited from the economic growth of the late 1930s and early 1940s. However, they did not benefit from the erosion of the national power of their patrons, the Pernambuco landowners. In 1930, Vargas decreed that the federal government would direct all local police forces, appoint all mayors, and supervise all municipal budgets (Burns 1980, 414). Similarly, state militias were absorbed by the regional army commands in 1937 (ibid., 409–10). But if the power of the center grew, the landowning elite remained cohesive and strong locally, resolving its differences within the IAA and remaining united in its determination to keep the workers compliant.

The Estado Novo, therefore, represented more continuity than change for rural labor in Pernambuco. Cane cutters were not recognized as a corporate body, while mill owners and cane planters were. Trade unions were not allowed in the sugar fields; politically, rural labor in Brazil was invisible. In a regime whose leader said that "individuals do not have rights, they have duties . . . [and] rights belong to the collective," this resulted in subordination and enforced political silence (Burns 1980, 410). Silence in turn perpetuated poverty.

It was only with the birth of the Second Republic (1945–1964), and the democratization of society that ensued, that rural labor in Pernambuco's *zona da mata* eventually began to win more recognition and influence. In 1945, during the disintegration of his dictatorship, Vargas appealed to Brazilian urban workers to participate in politics through his newly formed PTB (Partido Trabalhista Brasileiro, or Brazilian Labor Party). He also fashioned electoral legislation that enfranchised the working class and favored urban over rural voters (French 1988, 6). These laws maintained the literacy requirement for voting, which discriminated against rural areas and the *coronéis'* herd vote and made voting mandatory for virtually all literate Brazilians. Vargas thus enabled urban workers, for the first time, to participate in politics in an organized way. "The electoral marketplace in 1945 was totally transformed," writes French, "as participation increased from 10 percent of all adults in the 1930s to 33 percent in 1945, out of a total adult population that was about 50 percent literate" (1988, 7). In absolute terms, the national electorate increased from 1,466,700 in 1933 to 7,710,504 in 1946 (Cammack 1991, 35).

This expansion of urban working-class participation, in turn, eventually opened the way for alliances between rural and urban labor, such that rural labor could escape the yoke of the *coronéis*. This is what occurred in Pernambuco. After four hundred years, democratic rights were finally, slowly, and tenuously being gained by workers in the sugar zone.

In October 1945, Vargas was overthrown by a military coup, but the political alliance he had forged won many victories in the elections of 2 December of that year. Working-class activism in cities such as São Paulo and Rio de Janeiro became an important and increasingly powerful force on the political scene, as economic growth expanded the size of the working class throughout the Second Republic. In Pernambuco, urban trade unions formed a political coalition with middle-class and industrial interests to defeat a candidate favored by the rural oligarchy in the 1958 gubernatorial elections.

In the 1950s, during Pernambuco's first wave of rural labor mobilization, rural workers faced a landowning oligarchy with an immense amount of concentrated wealth and power. The distribution of landholding in Pernambuco's sugar zone was even more unequal than the average for Latin America, a region with perhaps the most unequal distribution of land in the world. About 1,500 landholders with properties of over 100 hectares controlled over 90 percent of all the land.[21] The vast majority of landowners had a marginal place in the rural hierarchy. Seventy-six percent of all properties—11,262 landholdings—had only 3 percent of the total available land. These holdings were all less than 10 hectares in size. Since the minimum amount of land required to feed a family of six—almost the average family size in the sugar zone—is fifteen hectares, it is clear that most of these holdings were not adequate for subsistence.[22]

Furthermore, the vast majority—about 85 percent of all rural families—had no land at all. While the total number of rural properties was 14,833, 200,000 workers cut cane each harvest (Taylor 1978, 96). Many of these were seasonal migrants from the neighboring *agreste* region. The sugar zone's oligarchical and exclusionary political system was thus rooted in a highly concentrated economic structure in which profits were derived primarily from land and the massive, seasonal exploitation of cheap labor.

The Peasant Leagues

Sugar production has three phases: growing and harvesting the cane, extracting juice from the cane (milling), and transforming the juice into sugar crystals (refining) (Galloway 1989, 16). As the artisanal and pastoral economy of the colonial period was replaced by the industrial park dominated by a few dozen immense mills that one finds today, modernization of the second and third phases was significant. Because of improvements in transportation—first the railroads, then highways—linking the mills and the cane fields, the mills got bigger, more efficient, and more capital-intensive. Innovation in growing and harvesting cane, however, came relatively late. These changes, initiated in the 1950s, created the conditions for the emergence of the modern rural labor movement in Pernambuco's cane fields.

In this period, steady growth in world commodity markets and the revolution in agricultural production, both features of the post–World War II world economy (Grigg 1992, 1–10), began to have an impact in the region. The output of the main agricultural commodity, sugar, was rising in response to increasing world demand. Furthermore, Pernambuco producers were squeezed by competition from more efficient, large-scale producers in the industrial southern state of São Paulo who were modernizing their production techniques. Although northeastern producers had attempted, through their control of the IAA, to limit Paulista expansion, this attempt failed, and by 1950 São Paulo had overtaken Pernambuco as Brazil's leading sugar-producing state.[23]

Pernambuco landowners at first reacted to these world market incentives and domestic pressures not by modernizing production, but by accumulating more land. They rid their properties of *moradores* (workers who resided on the sugar plantations and had access to small subsistence plots), planted more cane, and turned increasingly to wage laborers. As the sugar plantations expanded, other tenants, sharecroppers, and smallholders also lost access to land. Both peasants and rural workers were squeezed by commercial pressures in the sugar zone.

Their response to these pressures was to form new associations. As we have seen, there were no existing organizations claiming to represent them. While the Ministry of Labor had registered 1,262 unions for urban workers by 1960, only sixteen rural labor unions were registered in the whole of Brazil in that year (IBGE 1991, 425).

The first reaction to de-peasantization in Pernambuco occurred in the form of the Peasant Leagues, organizations that asserted and won recognition of the right of the rural poor to associate and organize. The Leagues represented peasants and rural workers who were negatively affected, in both material terms and in status, by the commercialization of agriculture in the 1950s.[24] They won national attention in 1959 when they successfully pressured the state government into expropriating an estate in Pernambuco, thus defending its tenants from expulsion. Pernambuco was a focal point of the Leagues' activities when Peasant Leagues mushroomed throughout the Brazilian northeast in the following years.

The Leagues' ideology was one of *agrarismo*, a diffuse, multiclass peasant orientation that focused on the redistribution of land-use rights and a critique of the *latifúndio*. Their impatient slogan was "Agrarian reform by law or by force." Some of their leaders, admirers of the Cuban revolution, established an armed wing, composed mostly of students, who were trained in rural guerrilla warfare (Page 1972; *Veja*, 30 March 1994, 42–43). The Peasant Leagues reflected what has been called the "politics of despair," periodic outbursts by northeastern peasants and rural workers marginalized by the development of capitalism in agriculture, which had manifested itself a generation earlier in the form of messianism and banditry (Forman 1975, 302–45; Pang 1989, 136–37). They also reflected the populism of the Second Republic, in which it was the norm for middle-class activists (priests, lawyers, students, politicians, journalists) to lead peasant organizations and to speak on behalf of the peasantry.

The brief but tumultuous existence of the Peasant Leagues has spawned a large literature. Most observers misinterpreted these organizations as constituting a purely peasant movement (da Fonseca 1962; Pearson 1967; Hewitt 1969; Morães 1970; Huizer 1972; Julião 1972; Page 1972; Forman 1975). This misunderstanding reflects the intellectual preoccupations of the time. The Cuban revolution of 1959 was conceived by many scholars, somewhat misleadingly, as a peasant revolution. Scholars of all political persuasions concentrated most of their attention on the peasantry, not the rural proletariat, as the only truly revolutionary class. The same can be said of the honorary president and spokesman of the Peasant Leagues, the lawyer and politician Francisco Julião (da Fonseca 1962, 37–40).

However, the history of the Leagues, at least in Pernambuco, shows that they were primarily proletarian, rather than peasant, in character. Whereas Julião had believed that peasants had greater independence from large landowners and would more effectively challenge the rural status quo, in fact, in the coastal sugar zone the most active Peasant Leagues were founded in towns where rural workers predominated. In the *agreste*, an interior region dominated by smallholders and tenant farmers, there were far fewer, and less active Leagues (Azevêdo 1982, 73; Price 1964, 42; Hewitt 1969, 374).

Unionization

While the Peasant Leagues got most of the attention, the rural trade union movement emerged in the late 1950s and early 1960s as an alternative, at times a competitor, to the Leagues. In 1957, the Brazilian Communist Party (PCB, Partido Comunista Brasileiro) formed a national union of peasants and rural workers in São Paulo, the ULTAB (União de Lavradores e Trabalhadores Agrícolas do Brasil). While a Peasant League representative attended the ULTAB's founding assembly and was one of its first officers, the Leagues did not affiliate with the ULTAB, nor did they accept the new organization's offer of two pages in its newspaper *Terra Livre* (Free land; Morães 1970, 480). The ULTAB promoted the Communist Party's line of an antifeudal, anti-imperialist "worker-peasant" alliance that would push first for a "bourgeois" revolution, and only later for socialism. It therefore advocated moderate agrarian reform with compensation to owners, and viewed the Peasant Leagues' maximalist demands for expropriation without compensation "by law or by force" as adventurist and reactionary. ULTAB leaders were instrumental in the later foundation of the state-affiliated CONTAG and formed the bulk of its early leadership.

The Catholic Church also entered the competition to represent the interests of rural labor in the late 1950s. Like the PCB, the Church criticized as unrealistic and dangerous the Peasant Leagues' uncompromising demands for giving land to the tiller. Unlike the PCB, clerics and activists within the Church discouraged proletarian militancy and instead promoted unions as instruments for uplifting peasants and harmonizing landlords' and workers' interests. In practice, their organizing was often seen by rural oligarchs as equivalent to that of the PCB; in the Pernambuco press, landlords complained about foreign, "Communist" priests with "bombs under their cassocks."

The early 1960s thus saw the Communist Party, the Church, and the federal government competing with one another to control the new rural trade unions. In 1961 Vice-president João Goulart assumed the presidency following the resignation of the incumbent president, Jânio Quadros. Goulart, a former minister of labor under President Getúlio Vargas, had been ousted from his post in 1954 due in part to the pressure of a land-lord association that feared he was planning the unionization of rural labor (Price 1964, 67). The new president saw rural labor as a potential base of support and authorized the federal government to encourage the foundation of rural unions. In Pernambuco a year later, Miguel Arraes, a populist-nationalist, was elected state governor and gave a decisive impetus to the rural union movement in Pernambuco. By 1963, union membership outnumbered that of the Leagues in the state.

Trade unions had advantages over the Peasant Leagues in the competition to represent rural labor. First, as institutions recognized by the Ministry of Labor, they were given exclusive representation rights to all rural workers, smallholders, and tenants in a given area, usually a *município* (equivalent to a county, although it can refer both to the principal town and the county itself). Farmers who owned their own land but did not employ wage workers could also be members of these unions. As quasi-official entities, the unions enjoyed protections that the Leagues did not. Second, unions had a much stronger financial base than the Leagues. The *imposto sindical*, administered by the Ministry of Labor, was a mandatory check-off that allowed the unions to receive the equivalent of one day's wages per year from all the workers in their jurisdiction.[25] The Leagues, on the other hand, relied solely on voluntary contributions.

The competition between the Leagues and the unions in the early 1960s was a formative experience for the leaders who later controlled the politically reawakened rural unions in the 1980s. In the early 1960s, leaders founded the first unions, made their first demands for workers' rights, helped elect a reformist governor, conducted their first strike, and were subject to violent repression and intervention at the time of the 1964 coup. They also saw the Peasant Leagues, which made radical demands for land redistribution and engaged in illegal acts and occupations, crushed by the coup.

These events were part of the memory of the majority of rural trade union leaders in the contemporary period. Of the leaders surveyed as part of this research, 82 percent had been ten years old or older at the time of the 1964 coup, and 34 percent were members of rural unions in that year.[26] The early history of the unions thus constitutes a period of political learning for the union leaders of the 1980s, a series of lessons that they learned directly, or secondhand from older unionists. Union leaders used the past to develop a strategy that met with some success in the 1980s.

Between 1961 and 1964, thirty-seven rural trade unions were founded in the sugar zone: six in 1961, four in 1962, eighteen in 1963, and nine in 1964.[27] The state rural workers' federation was founded in 1962, directed by leaders closely tied to the Catholic Church, and Pernambuco union leaders also participated in the foundation of the national confederation of rural workers, CONTAG, in 1963. More important than the founding of these incipient organizations, however, was the Pernambuco unions' successful organization of a major statewide strike in 1963. The 1963 strike, which brought a wage increase of 80 percent, proved the unions' effectiveness to rural workers. It was experienced as a defining moment of liberation, recognition of citizenship, and movement into the consumer market by workers, many of whom now purchased their first radios and bicycles. It was also, perhaps, a "moment of madness" (Zolberg 1972), in which the cane cutters' conception of what was politically possible was radically, and temporarily, expanded. It was certainly an event that workers still talked about with fondness and pride in the late 1980s.

The repertoire of collective action (Tilly 1986) of the rural movement at this time was eclectic, reflecting its affinity with the new social movements of contemporary social science literature. It included land occupations, marches, court cases, and strikes. Over forty local strikes occurred in the sugar zone in 1963 alone, as unions demanded the enforcement of the new Rural Labor Statute, which extended the rights and benefits of urban labor to the countryside in March 1963. These collective actions frequently met with violence on the part of landowners, who saw mere state recognition of the unions' right to organize as a threat to their livelihood and way of life and lamented the breakdown of the paternalistic social relations and worker deference that their own capitalist expansion had provoked. In 1963, the local press referred to a "crisis in the fields."

Pernambuco's rural labor movement was decentralized, with competition between various leadership groups which, in addition to the main three already mentioned, included Trotskyites and socialists. The Leagues did not have strong links with political parties, although politicians from various leftist parties supported them and Francisco Julião used the Leagues as an electoral base in his successful campaign for a seat in the Federal Chamber of Deputies, the lower house of Congress, in 1962.[28] The unions, on the other hand, were dominated by the PCB in the south of Pernambuco and by leaders with ties to the Catholic Church in the north. Their ideology, distinct from the *agrarismo* of the Leagues, could be described as one of *trabalhismo* (laborism), which accepted the existing distribution of land and pressured the state instead to grant rural workers the privileges and benefits that had been gained by urban labor.

Unlike peasants in parts of the Brazilian south, descendants of European immigrants who had a tradition of independent landownership, the rural workers of the northeastern sugar zone were descendants of slaves and a reconstituted peasantry that had always worked subsistence plots (*sítios*) at the discretion of a landowner. Unlike southern peasants, they had no tradition of a shared and common relationship with, and independent access to, the land. What united them was a common labor obligation to landlords. Their attitude toward land was thus less intense than that of uprooted smallholders in other parts of Brazil and of peasants who engaged in uprisings, such as that led by Zapata during the Mexican revolution of 1910–1920 and the Russian revolution of 1917. Although they experienced the loss of access to *sítios* as a hardship, it was one that could possibly be compensated for by secure access to wage employment. Like workers in Cuba's sugar sector after the 1959 revolution, they wanted a job, or some land, or both (Martínez-Alier 1977); since few of them had owned their own land, its retention was not necessarily essential. This explains Pernambuco rural laborers' early receptivity to the progressive trade unionism in the late populist period and why the Peasant Leagues were in decline even before the military coup of 1964.

The coup established a new order that used repression against popular organizations mobilized during the presidency of João Goulart. Demands for land reform, the kind of "agitation" that had prompted the coup leaders to act, were suppressed, and the Peasant Leagues were broken up—shattered, in the words of one observer, like "a fragile windowpane," their headquarters ransacked and members hunted down by the army, police, and landowners (*Jornal de Comércio*, 3 April 1964). In Pernambuco, the Communist Party was extirpated from the trade unions, which were left in the hands of the Church. The populist governor, Miguel Arraes, was deposed, imprisoned, and eventually sent into exile; his office was occupied by his vice-governor, who had supported the coup. The military regime that came to power denounced the populism not only of João Goulart, but of the whole series of governments that made up the postwar Second Republic, and embarked on a new project of authoritarian developmentalism that transformed the country.

Summary

Contemporary society in the Pernambuco sugar zone has emerged from a plantation economy based on slave labor in which for a long time the infrastructural power of the state was modest in comparison to the personal power of the landed oligarchy. Until the early 1960s, rural workers on the sugar plantations lacked democratic rights (to vote, assemble, organize, bargain collectively, and strike), even during most of the relatively democratic Second Republic (1945–1964).

However, after the mid-1950s, capitalist development in the sugar zone created the conditions for the emergence of an autonomous and militant labor movement by creating a landless working class living outside the plantations and the direct control of landlords. A strengthened central state, presided over by an ambivalent populist, then began to recognize and sponsor the unions founded by this movement, while trying to check the growth of the more independent and agrarian Peasant Leagues. The labor unions were briefly able to extend to the rural majority the democratic rights to assemble, organize, strike, and bargain collectively. Their strike of 1963 was a major challenge to the traditionally uncontested power of landowners.

These new democratic gains could not be consolidated. A large number of landowners vehemently opposed any recognition of trade unions and used violence against them. The existence of many small cane planters, for whom labor was a large percentage of total costs, increased the landlords' tendency to perceive the unions as an intolerable threat. The cold war and the prominence of the Communist Party within the unions also militated against a peaceful resolution of labor conflicts in the sugar zone. Both the Arraes government in Pernambuco and the Goulart government at the national level mobilized vulnerable and divided populist coalitions that alienated and frightened many in the middle and upper classes. The result was a military coup in 1964 that suddenly nullified many of the previous gains of the labor movement both in Pernambuco and the rest of Brazil. Rural labor paid a heavy price for the failure of the Second Republic.

II

Explaining the New Rural Labor Movement

~ 3 ~

Structural Change and Conservative Modernization

I n the 1964 coup, landlord and military actions combined to purge more than 300 leaders from the rural movement in Pernambuco's sugar zone. These men were either killed, jailed, removed from their union posts, or forced into hiding or exile. The Ministry of Labor representative in the state, Enoch Saraiva, was replaced by José David Gil Rodrigues, who vowed to get rid of "communist elements" in both the Ministry of Labor and the unions. FETAPE's president was removed from his post and jailed, although his companions remained active. Within months, Rodrigues had replaced the leaderships of all but four of the thirty-one unions in the sugar zone with *interventors*, politically vetted replacements (Lessa 1985, 80); nationally, this occurred in an estimated 90 percent of all rural unions (Ricci 1994, 8). A newspaper editorial in Recife's *Diário de Pernambuco*, 15 May 1964, reflected elite opinion when it declared that intervention was supposed to be "making the workers' unions a constructive force, an element of harmony, a factor of discipline and not a school for conflict between groups" (Lessa 1985, 78). It represented the "implantation of an authentic unionism, through a leadership dedicated only to union functions."[1]

The new system of labor relations forged under the military regime in Pernambuco was authoritarian. Meetings of rural workers were suppressed by the police. Collective bargaining was replaced by labor court decrees that adjusted wages without any input from labor unions. Strikes were not allowed in practice, and unions maintained a very low profile.

However, changes in both economic and institutional structures in the sugar zone under the military regime quietly and indirectly enhanced the unions' capacities for collective action. Without intending to, state managers under the military regime thus contributed to building up a new rural labor movement that reasserted its rights in the Pernambuco strike of October 1979. This chapter concentrates mainly on changes in production processes, class structure, and political institutions and how these combined to affect the union movement. The next chapter deals with the unions themselves and how they and the people within them were transformed by government programs. Both of these sets of changes were influenced by the developmental state's intervention in processes of economic development and popular representation.

Authoritarian Developmentalism

More so than its populist predecessor, the military regime of 1964–1985 based its legitimacy on its ability to achieve economic development. Its slogan of "security and development" was an updated version of the nineteenth-century Comtean phrase that is still embroidered on Brazil's national flag, "Order and progress." In the view of many regime leaders, development required security and the subordination of popular interests to a strong centralized state, whose monopoly of technical expertise and information gave it the right and the ability to control popular organizations and the process of capital accumulation. Reciprocally, security could best be achieved through development, because by expanding the forces of production and the goods and services available to the population, the basis for "subversive" grievances against the existing order would be eliminated. The imperatives of both security and development, in this view, required that only certain kinds of leaders of popular organizations would be tolerated in the new order.

The development strategy adopted after the coup involved a tighter integration of the Brazilian economy with world markets, stronger central control over the economy, the expansion of the state-owned sector, and the promotion of big capital, both domestic and transnational (much of which continued to be protected) at the expense of small business. Foreign direct investment increased markedly after the coup. Direct industrial investment from the principal source of capital at that time, the United States, climbed from about $60 million in 1963 to over $280 million in 1972 (Kaufman 1980, 193). As in other newly industrializing countries such as South Korea, state control over finance proved to be one of the keys to development (Woo 1991). In agriculture, the regime's provision of credit led to considerable investment in chemical fertilizer and pesticides, machinery and implements, and the consolidation of large estates. This boom of subsidized capital peaked in 1977 when credit represented 57 percent of the total value of agricultural production (Araújo 1983, 303).

As a result of the agricultural credit expansion, large producers modernized their holdings and land concentration increased.[2]

In the sugar sector, the populist policy of "balanced development" (*desenvolvimento equilibrado*) enacted by the IAA was reversed. This policy had tried to balance the interests of northeastern sugar producers against those of their São Paulo counterparts and the interests of sugar mill owners against those of plantation owners. After the 1964 coup, the military regime instituted a policy that clearly favored big capital (including the mill owners) and the Paulista producers (Ramos and Belik 1989, 204).

Under the military, São Paulo sugar producers thrived. They were already blessed with many advantages over their northeastern rivals: they were closer to the heart of Brazil's mass market and they had more access to capital, greater links with the farm equipment industry, flatter terrain that allowed for the easier introduction of machinery, and a better-organized labor market (Ramos and Belik 1989, 202). They also had more political power than their northeastern counterparts. While northeastern producers controlled the IAA, the São Paulo producers set up their own organization, COPERSUCAR, which became the thirtieth-largest firm in the country by 1976. COPERSUCAR eventually eclipsed the IAA in terms of its technical and administrative capacity. The Paulista producers had an average yield per hectare almost 50 percent higher than that of the Pernambuco growers and had higher-capacity mills.[3] In 1960 São Paulo produced 60 percent more than Pernambuco producers; in 1985, it produced over five times as much, with a total labor force of about the same size as Pernambuco's (Ramos and Belik 1989, 208–09; IBGE 1985).

Paulista production might well have spelled extinction for northeastern producers if the sugar sector had depended solely on market forces. But, as in other cases of late development, the Brazilian state attempted to manage the economy explicitly in order to control the process of national capital accumulation (Evans 1979). Barzelay refers to this system of state-managed markets as a "politicized market economy" (Barzelay 1986). According to him, Brazil seems to be distinctive not for the mere existence of political controls in and around its markets, but for the pervasiveness of those controls.

The military regime arrived at a division of labor within the sugar sector, reserving most of the domestic market for São Paulo and southern producers and allowing most northeastern production to be exported. The federal government subsidized sugar producers, especially those from the northeast, who were generally less efficient than their southern counterparts, and continued to regulate production through a highly detailed, centrally planned quota system. Partly due to state support, Brazilian sugar exports rose steadily, from 462,000 metric tons in 1955 to 3 million tons in 1985, 11 percent of the entire world market that year (Nunberg 1986, 58, 60–61).

This system worked well in the 1960s. Sugar prices increased gradually, and Brazil's exports to a growing world market increased, helped by the U.S. decision to stop importing Cuban sugar in 1961. In the early 1970s, after a decade of growth, the federal government created the National Program for the Improvement of Sugarcane, PLANALSUCAR (Programa Nacional de Melhoramento de Cana de Açúcar), in order to modernize sugar mills.[4] The state provided cheap credit to mill owners, who used the capital to buy new machinery that increased the speed and volume with which cane was transformed into sugar.

However, in the mid-1970s, after a boom in prices, the sugar market slumped, dropping in one year, between 1975 and 1976, from twenty to twelve cents per pound (International Sugar Organization 1975–1977). This led to a problem of oversupply both in world markets and in Brazil.[5] The state's response to this problem was the Proálcool program, which substituted alcohol made from sugarcane for gasoline. Begun in 1975 as a bailout to the sugar industry, and initiated primarily due to pressure from the Paulista producers, Proálcool developed into a full-blown energy policy that was further justified by the massive increase in oil prices in 1973. The alcohol program was part of a set of capital-intensive projects sponsored by the military regime. According to Schneider, the regime spent $10.5 billion on the alcohol program from 1975 to 1989, making it the most expensive federal government project in this period aside from the Itaipú dam, the largest dam in the world.[6]

Under Proálcool, the production of sugarcane for alcohol increased by 7.8 percent per capita annually in Brazil between 1977 and 1984, outstripping the comparable growth rate for food crops (−1.9 percent) and export crops (2.6 percent). Proálcool also buoyed sugar production in Pernambuco which, as table 3.1 shows, kept increasing through the 1980s, even though the international price of sugar was generally low.

By the mid-1980s, Brazil's automobile sector had adjusted in response to Proálcool; the majority of the country's new cars were designed to run on alcohol rather than gasoline.[7] A government decree set the price of alcohol below gasoline prices, to ensure domestic demand. Sugarcane production for alcohol in Pernambuco rose dramatically as a result, from 335,872 tons in 1979 to 8.5 million tons in 1987, or a twenty-five-fold increase.[8]

Proálcool propped up the vulnerable northeastern sugar sector, converting it from an export enclave to one intimately tied to the dynamic

Table 3.1 Sugarcane Production in Pernambuco, 1949–1989

Harvest Completed	Tons of Cane	Area Planted (hectares)	No. of Cane Plantations	World Market Price for Sugar (cents/lb.)
1949	4,977,864	174,542	7,514	—
1961	8,766,220	—	—	2.91
1966	7,579,943	—	—	1.86
1971	10,049,102	—	—	4.50
1976	12,750,072	—	—	11.51
1980	17,972,726	380,509	13,021	28.69
1986	21,472,259	—	—	6.04
1987	25,612,566	542,490	—	6.75
1988	22,557,277	445,452	—	—
1989	24,099,257	445,124	—	—

Sources: 1AA 1987; IBGE 1950a, 1980a, 1991; International Sugar Organization 1959–1987; "Safra Açúcareira 87/88 Pode Cair," *Nordeste Econômico,* September 1987.

Note: Dashes indicate data not available.

industrial economy of the south.[9] In effect, it shielded the northeastern producers from the deteriorating and volatile conditions of global markets, in which oversupply and declining prices were a recurrent problem, by giving them a captive, regulated domestic market with increasing demand. In economic terms, the program was a disaster; in 1985–1986, the cost of production of Brazilian alcohol ranged between $79 and $91 per barrel, far above the international price of oil during that period (Twomey and Helwege 1991, 43). But politically it was a success: the northeastern sugar producers remained loyal supporters of the military regime, and of the conservative civilian government of José Sarney that succeeded it.

As a result of Proálcool, the Pernambuco sugar zone underwent a period of major capital investment, changes in production processes, improvements in labor productivity, and tremendous increases in the marketed output of sugarcane, as table 3.1 shows. Overall, production almost doubled between 1976 and 1989.

This picture contradicts the stereotype of the northeast as a stagnant agricultural backwater. Clearly, the northeastern producers were still less efficient than producers in the south and were subsidized heavily.[10] However, in this period, the northeastern sugar sector experienced modernization at a rate comparable to that in the south (see tables 3.2 and 3.3). As a result, the economy expanded opportunities for higher incomes on the part of small landowners, as well as the number of permanent jobs for

Table 3.2 Economic Development in Agriculture in São Paulo, 1959 and 1985

Category	1959	1985	% Change
Trucks	19,344	37,442	93.6
Tractors	27,176	159,625	487.0
Wages as % of total costs	41.1	18.3	⁻55.5
Investment in capital goods (vehicles, machines, implements) as % of total investment	24.8	23.1	⁻6.9
Permanent workers	419,733	410,466	⁻2.2
Temporary workers	292,827	240,433	⁻17.9

Source: IBGE, 1960, 1985.

Table 3.3 Economic Development in Agriculture in Pernambuco, 1959 and 1985

Category	1959	1985	% Change
Trucks	627	3,445	449.0
Tractors	1,002	4,821	381.0
Wages as % of total costs	58.3	34.8	⁻40.3
Investment in capital goods (vehicles, machines, implements) as % of total investment	16.1	14.0	⁻13.0
Permanent workers	97,945	129,973	32.7
Temporary workers	334,886	292,827	⁻12.6

Source: IBGE, 1960, 1985.

field workers, even as it displaced thousands of peasants from the land and lowered per capita employment.

The expansion of sugar output also benefited some rural workers. Between 1960 and 1980, the number of permanent workers in the sugar zone increased from 74,590 to 108,379. At the same time, the number of temporary workers declined from 91,637 to 58,859. Permanent workers' share of total employment thus rose from 45 to 65 percent. However, the labor force at its seasonal, September peak in the 1980s was probably roughly the same—250,000—as it had been in the 1950s. The tremendous expansion of sugar output had not increased overall employment because the use of machinery and herbicides had lowered labor requirements on the plantations (Cabral 1986, 172–73).

This meant that the ratio of labor to land declined. Between 1960 and 1980 alone, the ratio dropped from .422 to .316.[11] Modernization had made sugar production less labor-intensive. As labor declined as a proportion of total costs, landowners became more willing, if they were pushed, to concede to the wage demands of trade unions. And state subsidies and guaranteed prices gave them the means to make such concessions.

Modernization was therefore a mixed blessing for labor. For those who had jobs, the opportunity for permanent positions, as well as for real wage gains, increased in the 1970s.[12] Modernization also did not polarize the class structure. It created instead a large number of new intermediate technical and supervisory positions, such as those for agronomists, economists, chemists, truck drivers, and machine operators. For workers in general, however, the failure of the sugar industry to create new jobs was disastrous, because sugar was overwhelmingly the most important sector in the state's economy, and the state population doubled from about 3 to 6 million between 1960 and 1980.

The result was massive emigration from the sugar zone, whose population remained constant at about 1 million between 1960 and 1980, despite high birth rates. Workers, especially young males, went in search of employment to cities such as Rio and São Paulo, frontiers such as Matto Grosso, and most typically, to nearby Recife, whose population rose from 524,682 to 2,265,493 in this period (IBGE 1950b, 1980b). In Hirschman's terminology, "exit"—emigration—was an alternative to the exercise of "voice"—staying where one was and struggling for political change in the sugar zone (Hirschman 1970). Among the rural majority, the rural trade unions represented the clearest opportunity to exercise "voice."

Among other things, the unions expressed the grievances of many former peasants who had lost access to land in the transformation of the region. Modernization promoted sugarcane production at the expense of subsistence agriculture. There is a clear trade-off between an agrarian system based on very small, family-tilled, subsistence plots and a system of large estates producing a marketable surplus of sugar for export. Brazilian regimes, both civilian and military, have consistently promoted the latter at the expense of the former. The labor movement represented those who had enjoyed the use of subsistence plots in times past. While it was rhetorically wedded to the notion that all workers had a right to subsistence plots, by the 1980s it was operating within an agrarian system in which such a demand was no longer realizable within the existing distribution of property rights.[13] This is because there was simply not enough land in the sugar zone for every worker to have a subsistence plot *and*, at the same time, to maintain overall levels of sugar production.

Thus, FETAPE formally insisted that every permanent sugar worker should be entitled to two hectares of plantation land for growing subsistence crops. It successfully inserted this provision into the collective contract, knowing that it would be virtually impossible to enforce. In this way the union federation made a rhetorical concession to the "peasant" yearnings of its members. Meanwhile, it concentrated almost all its efforts on the arduous, carefully planned strike that took place almost every year in the 1980s prior to the negotiation of the new contract. In its practice, if not in its rhetoric, the union federation recognized the "end of the peasantry" as a fait accompli.

The decline of subsistence agriculture reduced the space within which workers outside the market could survive and drove up the price of food for those buying it on the market. While highly favorable to sugar, state policies in Pernambuco allowed the production of basic food crops consumed by the poor—rice, beans, manioc, corn, and the like—to decline.[14] Seventy percent of Pernambuco's food supply was imported, because the best lands were devoted to sugar.

On the other side of the labor-employer divide, the most significant effect of the alcohol program's gargantuan consumption of sugar was to expand opportunities for small cane planters. There was a tremendous growth in the number of cane-growing landowners. There were about 3,000 in 1964, but almost 10,000 in 1988, according to membership figures from the Cane Planters' Association, APCP (Associação dos Plantadores de Cana de Pernambuco). This increase reflects the ability of some workers to obtain small amounts of land and become independent suppliers to the mills. Looking more specifically at properties with more than 10 but fewer than 100 hectares, there were 2,378 of these in 1960, but 5,386 in 1985. In addition, the concentration of land at the top was reduced: while 152 super-estates accounted for 22.5 percent of all land in 1960, by 1985 just 83 such properties held only 16.3 percent of the land. What statistics on landholding show is that the tremendous expansion of sugar production, though chiefly benefiting the large mills, allowed numerous small landowners to engage in sugarcane cultivation and to make money by meeting the mills' increased demand for cane. (For the basic pattern of landholding in the sugar zone, see table 3.4.)[15]

The political upshot of these economic changes was to attenuate radicalism on both sides of the labor-landowner divide. Declining propor-

Table 3.4 Class Structure in the Pernambuco Sugar Zone, 1988

Class Fraction	No. of Properties or People
Mill owners	35 mills, 7 distilleries
Large cane planters (100–1,000 hectares)	1,500 properties
Small cane planters (10–100 hectares)	5,000 properties
Smallholders	21,000 properties
Mill workers (including technical and administrative personnel)	20,000 at harvest time
Field workers	250,000 at harvest time
Resident on plantations	25,000
Legal workers living in towns	100,000
Illegal workers living in towns	75,000
Migrant illegal workers from interior	50,000

Sources: For mill and distillery figures, IAA 1988; landholding data, IBGE 1985; mill workers from 1970, Lopes 1978, 2–3; field workers, *Diário de Pernambuco*, various dates, 1988, and interviews with FETAPE officials, 1988.

Note: Figures are approximate.

tional labor costs and the expansion of permanent and skilled jobs lessened the labor movement's threat to Pernambuco's landowners. Many newly secure employees, who might otherwise have turned against the economic status quo, saw themselves as its beneficiaries. At the same time, the expanded opportunities for small landowners meant that some workers were upwardly mobile, joining the ranks of the sugar producers. These changes served as a brake on demands for land redistribution during the revival of democratic politics in the 1980s. The result was a labor movement in which the interests represented were more monochromatically working-class than they had been in the diffuse, multiclass, and more spontaneous movement of the early 1960s.

Due to these changes, the 1979 strike in the Pernambuco sugar zone established a regular pattern of tripartite bargaining between labor, two employers' representatives, and the state. However, the account of agricultural modernization and structural change given here should not lead to the conclusion that the resulting system involved smooth bargaining and a Western European–style social democratic consensus. Labor was not involved in negotiations over anything apart from wages and working conditions.[16] Agreements were not easy: from 1979 to 1988, there was a strike almost every year, nine times out of eleven, at harvest time, before employers would come to an agreement.

Furthermore, agricultural modernization had occurred in the context of an agrarian economy incapable of absorbing surplus labor; thus, tens of thousands of people were marginalized. Seasonal unemployment remained a serious problem (over half the labor force was laid off after the harvest), and levels of poverty were extreme. An oversupply of workers made labor's position a vulnerable one. One study found that 30 percent of the sugarcane work force consisted of children and adolescents from seven to seventeen years old (U.S. Department of State 1994, 20). A government report stated that the labor market in Pernambuco had a "low level of remuneration and chronic unemployment" (Governo do Estado de Pernambuco 1987a, 31). In 1980, 42 percent of the economically active population (347,771 people) worked in agriculture. Eighty-seven percent of these received a salary equal to or less than one minimum wage (less than the equivalent of $100 per month at that time). An estimated one-half of the labor force in the cane fields were *clandestinos*, illegal workers who did not enjoy the benefits (social security, paid holidays, and the like) of documented employment. Furthermore, large influxes of migrant laborers from the neighboring *agreste* region made union organizing difficult (see table 3.4). Labor's ability to push for the extension of democratic rights was hampered by these economic conditions.

In addition, employers in the sugar zone often favored *clandestinos* over legal workers. By hiring "off the books," employers could avoid making payments for social security and other benefits to workers. Illegal workers could earn higher wages than legal workers in the short run; hired via labor contractors (*gatos* or *empreiteiros*), the *clandestinos* were often allowed to cut cane on the best land, where the terrain was flat and densely grown with high-quality cane. In contrast, unionized, legal workers were assigned to cut cane on hilly terrain where cane was sparser. According to one report, "While unionized workers sweat on these steep hillsides, the illegal workers earn double or triple wages cutting on smooth terrain."[17]

Liberalization

We have seen how local changes in production processes and class structure—induced, in large measure, by state policies in the sugar sector—altered the capacity of the rural labor movement to mobilize the labor force. A more highly proletarianized work force was available for mobilization around wage issues, and landowners, whose production methods had been modernized and for whom labor costs were now lower as a proportion of total costs, were better able to absorb wage increases associated with collective bargaining. It would be misleading, however, to suggest that these dynamics are the whole of the story of the 1979 strike and its aftermath. The timing of the political reemergence of rural labor in Brazil also has to do with the change of regime then taking place at the national level and the rural movement's relationship to those changes.

The announcement of *distenção* (decompression) by the military regime in 1974 was followed by a fifteen-year regime transition that involved a complex array of elites and popular organizations. Certain features of this transition deserve mention. First, while the military regime was initially repressive in the sugar zone and elsewhere, in relative terms it did not use large amounts of repression in subduing civil society. The number of political dissidents killed in Brazil by the security forces was much lower than the thousands reported killed and disappeared in Argentina and Chile in the 1970s. Per capita levels of incarceration were not as high as in Uruguay. Of these four authoritarian regimes, Brazil's is seen by almost all observers as having employed the least overt repression against popular organizations and leftist groups.

Related to this is the fact that the Brazilian military regime maintained elections at the local, state assembly, and congressional level throughout its rule. While elections for president and governors were indirect, these other arenas were open to controlled, two-party competition. Thus, to a greater extent than in other regime changes, the Brazilian transition took place through elections rather than dramatic external events (such as in the Greek and Argentine transitions in 1974 and 1983, respectively). Third, the gradual and incremental nature of the Brazilian transition to democracy meant that the line between regimes was not clearly drawn. A high degree of continuity, of both personnel and institutions, marked the change of regime.

These characteristics—a selectively repressive regime, elections as the chief means of opposition, and an extremely slow and gradual liberalization that preserved most institutional forms of state power—combined to create a distinctive type of democratic transition in Brazil. The Brazilian military, unlike its Argentine counterpart, did not withdraw from the commanding heights of the political regime after a disastrous defeat in war, but instead tried to engineer a "slow, gradual, and sure" retreat from power. It was not entirely successful in doing this. The transition involved a constant struggle between the architects of the military's "opening project" and the popular organizations all with their own agendas—that used their political opportunities to create an "opening process."[18] These popular organizations included the National Bar Association, OAB (Organização dos Advogados do Brasil), business pressure groups, the Catholic Church, trade unions, neighborhood associations, environmental groups, associations of women and blacks, organizations of the landless, and many others.

The zig-zag course of the transition developed because of the tension between elite attempts to design a smooth, preemptive, and restricted process of regime change and these grass-roots efforts to accelerate the extension of democratic rights and win symbolic or material benefits for their members. Sometimes, the mass mobilization organized by the popular organizations overcame formal barriers to participation erected by the military regime and forced revisions in the transition plan and concessions to those below. At other times, military planners foresaw potential challenges to their prerogatives and successfully manipulated the rules of the political game in order to thwart the demands of the popular organizations. Throughout, the transition involved subtle calculations and anticipated reactions on the part of both elites and popular-sector groups, in which the official limits of political behavior were in doubt and thus constantly being tested by grass-roots movements anxious to make up for years of inactivity. Such a dynamic was clearly a part of the political reactivation of the trade unions in Pernambuco's sugar zone, as in many other parts of Brazil.

A key point at the beginning of the transition was November 1974, when congressional elections were held. The only two parties in these elections were those created by the military government in 1965: the pro-regime National Renovatory Alliance, or ARENA (Aliança Renovadora Nacional) and the semiopposition Brazilian Democratic Movement or MDB (Movimento Democrático Brasileiro). In these elections, the MDB made substantial and surprising gains, indicating widespread disaffection with the military government. The MDB gained 78 seats in the lower house of Congress, 13 in the Senate, and outright control of the state legislatures in São Paulo, Rio Grande do Sul, Rio de Janeiro, Paraná, Acre, and Amazônas.[19] Its campaign had denounced the trend toward more unequal distribution of income, the human rights violations of the military government, and the growing foreign presence in the Brazilian economy (Skidmore 1988, 173). Such a platform won the allegiance of many of the grass-roots organizations with an interest in the democratization of society. In Pernambuco, MDB candidate Marcos Freire won a seat in the Senate, and in almost all the *municípios* of the sugar zone, the MDB won between 15 and 35 percent of the vote (Reis 1976, 107).

Within CONTAG, *distenção* began somewhat earlier than in the society at large. In 1964, the military government had intervened in CONTAG and substituted its leaders with *interventors*. However, in 1968, the replacement president was himself replaced when José Francisco, a union leader from the sugarcane zone of Pernambuco, was elected. Just as leaders from São Bernardo came to dominate the Brazilian metalworkers' confederation, leaders from Pernambuco came to dominate CONTAG, and José Francisco remained in the CONTAG presidency until 1989.

As in the larger polity, a considerable degree of continuity and moderation marked the CONTAG election. José Francisco, while seen as a more activist president than his predecessor, José Rotta, had been trained by the American Institute for Free Labor Development (AIFLD), an arm of the AFL-CIO and an advocate of U.S.-style "business unionism."[20] Furthermore, only four of the nine members of the CONTAG directorate from 1965 to 1968 were completely replaced by the election. Three of the nine remained in the directorate from 1968 to 1971, and two were on the list of *suplentes*, substitutes for the directorate (CONTAG 1993b, 44). Therefore, the change within CONTAG was gradual and incremental. Its more activist orientation was shown when it organized its second national congress in Brasília (ibid., 17), a much livelier affair than the first congress, which took place in São Paulo in 1966.

State power was used in this period to control rural labor unions. At the beginning of the 1970s, the FETAPE president was barred from running again within the federation by the government. CONTAG leaders were interrogated by the federal police and the political police, the DOPS (Departamento de Ordem Política e Social), as suspected subversives. The CONTAG paper, *O Trabalhador Rural*, was censored, and some union courses were suspended. As late as 1977, CONTAG elections were interfered with by the minister of labor under pressure from the National Security Council (Conselho de Segurança Nacional) (*O Trabalhador Rural*, November 1985). And in 1980 the president of CONTAG, José Francisco, was prosecuted by the government, along with other union leaders, including the metalworkers' leader Luís Inácio da Silva ("Lula"), for participating in a rally denouncing the assassination of rural union leader Wilson Pinheiro in the state of Acre. While the charges were later dropped, the federal government prosecuted José Francisco and the other leaders under the National Security Law, for "violently inciting struggle between the classes and collective disobedience to the laws of the country" (CONTAG 1993b, 20). This kind of harassment of the labor movement by the security forces continued after the democratic transition. In 1995, journalists discovered that the Secretariat of Strategic Affairs, SAE (Secretaria de Assuntos Estratégicos), Brazil's principal intelligence institution and the successor of the SNI (Serviço Nacional de Informaçoes), established by the military regime, had bugged CONTAG headquarters (*Veja*, 6 September 1995).

In April 1977, a package of constitutional amendments was passed by the government with the aim of protecting ARENA's electoral advantages and avoiding in 1978 a repeat of the 1974 elections. The amendments decreed that in 1978, state governors and one-third of the federal senators would be selected indirectly by state electoral colleges, which included mayors, the majority of whom belonged to ARENA. These governors and senators were so elected and nicknamed "bionic" politicians by the press and public. Candidates' access to radio and television time was also strictly limited (Skidmore 1988, 191). In Pernambuco, these rules enabled the governorship to be maintained by ARENA and its candidate Marco Maciel, a supporter of the 1964 coup and former assistant to the first governor after the coup, Paulo Guerra. Maciel later became vice-president of the national government of Fernando Henrique Cardoso, elected in 1994.

Union activity in São Paulo began to accelerate in 1978. Metalworkers in São Bernardo do Campo staged a sit-down strike in May 1978, protesting the fact that since 1973 the government's official statistics had understated inflation and thus deprived them of their correct wage increases (Skidmore 1988, 205). The strike spread to 90 firms in the São Paulo area, with about half a million workers eventually on strike. This successful strike in the auto industry sparked great interest and served as a signal to the rest of the Brazilian labor movement. It showed that the military government could be forced to accept a strike and allow direct negotiations between employers' and workers' representatives. The metalworkers had also been led by advocates of the "new unionism" (*novo sindicalismo*) such as Lula, who denounced corporatist union structures and urged the ouster of the traditional labor bosses (*pelegos*).[21]

The process of liberalization, involving the pressure of various groups and movements in civil society, eventually wrought changes that widened the scope of participation within Pernambuco politics. Within the new political structure, which allowed multiparty competition and relatively open elections, the cane cutters' unions were able to win back democratic rights and gain a more prominent role in the making of state decisions that affected them.

Liberalization was accelerated in 1979 by the military government of General Figueiredo, when it announced a policy of *abertura* (opening). Economic pressures were a factor in the reform. A rise in both the price of oil and interest rates on Brazil's large debt slowed the economy substantially and forced the government to seek new bases of support. The government declared a general amnesty for all those imprisoned or exiled for political crimes since 1961 (Skidmore 1988, 217–18). The amnesty bill passed Congress in August 1979 and allowed figures such as former governor Miguel Arraes and former Peasant Leagues President Francisco Julião to return to Pernambuco. The two political parties were reformed, the MDB became the PMDB (Partido do Movimento Democrático Brasileiro), and most ARENA politicans in the northeast moved into the newly founded PDS (Partido Democrático Social). Many other new parties were created at the same time.

Within this liberal context, CONTAG held its third congress in Brasília in May 1979, attended by over 1,000 delegates. Adopting a more oppositional political posture than previously, CONTAG publicly expressed support for agrarian reform, union autonomy, land occupations, and strikes (CONTAG 1993b, 20–21). Within the congress, trade union leaders also discussed and planned a general strike in the Pernambuco cane fields.

The strike, between 2 and 8 October 1979, was successful. It surprised the landowners and resulted in the reinstatement of the Rural Accord signed in 1963 and ignored after the 1964 military coup. The accord reestablished the right of the unions to bargain collectively, and replaced the previous top-down system installed by the military, in which labor courts imposed wage increases on a silenced work force (*Jornal de Comércio*, 9 October 1979; Sigaud 1980).

The strike was seen as a victory for rural unions and their supporters. The latter included the Church's Pastoral Land Commission, formed in 1975, one of the few organs that could safely express opposition ideas during the repressive 1970s (Pandolfi 1988, 115). More important, the unions received encouragement and support from several local members of the PMDB, whose size in the state was growing. A PMDB member of the state assembly, for example, hailed the unions' "truly extraordinary gains, in comparison with the situation of the rural worker only two years before, when he couldn't even think of going on strike . . . [because] they would all have been imprisoned as subversives, as Communists."[22]

Meanwhile, employers in the state's sugar sector began to grow disillusioned with the ruling PDS. One landowner complained that "when the state lives through a climate of tension which could get out of control... the PDS politicians sleep in a splendid cradle, waiting for the outcome of events." He criticized the PMDB for agitating in favor of the strike, but said that "at least they do something," unlike their PDS counterparts, who "only during election campaigns...awake from the lethargy in which they live" (*Diário de Pernambuco*, 30 September 1980). Such comments prefigured the decline of the PDS and the transformation of the PMDB in the mid-

1980s into Pernambuco's ruling party, with significant backing from landowners ready to switch electoral horses when it suited them.

Another important step in the tenuous process of regime transition was the 1982 elections, the first direct elections for governor since 1965. The Workers' Party (PT, Partido dos Trabalhadores), founded in São Paulo in 1980 and relying on significant support from industrial workers, competed in the elections for the first time. In Pernambuco, the PMDB narrowly missed winning against the PDS candidate for governor, Roberto Magalhães. For the first time since 1962, literate rural workers in the sugar zone could vote for competing gubernatorial candidates.

As the economy deteriorated, public support for the military regime waned, and by 1983 a strong campaign for direct presidential elections had built up. Huge rallies of millions of people, organized by opposition parties, took place in southern and southeastern cities. The rural northeast, including Pernambuco's sugar zone, where the PDS was still entrenched, remained relatively uninvolved in what was called the *dirétas-já* (direct elections now) campaign. Although the campaign failed to reach its objective when Congress rejected a direct elections amendment in April 1984, the campaign demonstrated the strength of groups in civil society and helped make Tancredo Neves's indirect electoral college victory in January 1985 a highly popular one. Neves's civilian running mate, José Sarney, took office in April 1985 after Neves died, and a new civilian regime was born.[23]

In Pernambuco, civilian rule saw the return of Miguel Arraes to the governorship and the rise of the PMDB to a position of dominance in state elections in November 1986. Arraes was the first opponent of the 1964 coup to win the governorship in Pernambuco since the transition began. FETAPE saw Arraes's election as a democratic advance and participated actively in his campaign. The governor's party was a mixed bag, however, typifying the continuity of the Brazilian transition. For example, seventeen of twenty-three PMDB deputies in the state legislature in 1988 were former ARENA members. Arraes won the governorship again in elections in 1994, after serving in Congress for four years after the end of his first gubernatorial term.

The consolidation of the civilian regime was enhanced by the presidential elections of 1989 and 1994. In 1989, the goal of the *dirétas-já* campaign was finally realized, and the first direct election for president in twenty-nine years was held. In the second round, two ideologically distinct candidates, Fernando Collor de Mello and Lula, engaged in a highly charged contest. While Lula carried the day in Pernambuco, winning in all but two of the sugar zone's *municípios*, Collor de Mello was the clear national winner overall, with 35 million votes to Lula's 31 million.[24] In

1994, Fernando Henrique Cardoso and his three-party electoral alliance defeated Lula's coalition and other challengers in the first round, obtaining 54 percent of the vote to Lula's 27 percent.[25] This was the largest election ever staged in the country, including races for state governor, state assembly, and national Congress, as well as for president. The electorate was also the largest ever—about 95 million people—and included all adults sixteen years old and older. These elections represented an extension of democratic rights within Brazil.

Internal splits among elites and agencies within the military regime were ultimately crucial in enabling these democratic presidential elections to take place. They allowed grass-roots opposition groups, especially labor unions, to push for the democratization of society, beginning in 1974 and especially from 1979 on. While the military regime's liberalization project envisioned a marginal role for labor, unions were often able to push the regime beyond the limits it had set for them.

Summary

Agricultural modernization, involving an increase in the capital-intensiveness of production and a decline of the relative importance of land and labor as costs, occurred in northeast Brazil and not just in Brazil's dynamic heartland of the south. The Proálcool program accelerated modernization in the northeast's sugar sector, transforming it from what had essentially been an export enclave to an integral part of the nation's expanding industrial economy. Agricultural modernization led to the "end of the peasantry," a diminution of that class of cultivators to whom the Peasant Leagues had appealed: tenants and sharecroppers with insecure access to land. At the same time, it led to the consolidation of the class that is the mainstay of CONTAG, small farmers and rural workers.

Brazil's slow and gradual regime transition created the political conditions in which a revitalized labor movement forced the state to expand democratic rights in the sugar zone. The achievements and character of the rural union movement owe much to agricultural modernization. First, sugar production had become less reliant on cheap labor than before; landowners were now more willing to allow workers the freedom to bargain, strike, and assemble. Second, the unions were less willing than before to mobilize their members around the old Peasant League demand for land redistribution, preferring instead to focus on the more pragmatic and realizable goal of wage increases. This is because modernization had changed the pattern of interests in the sugar zone. Liberalization allowed that new pattern of interests to be politically expressed.

4

The Regulation
of Conflict

tructural factors in the economy of the Pernambuco sugar zone—the decline of the peasantry, a rise in permanent employment, a decrease in the labor-to-land ratio—made it more likely both that a working-class (rather than a peasant) trade union movement would emerge and that it would be grudgingly acknowledged and bargained with by landowners in the 1980s. Political liberalization gave the trade unions the opening that they needed to expand their activity from that of quietly representing individuals in the labor courts to publicly, and rather noisily, representing them as a class in meetings, marches, and strikes. However, structural change does not explain everything about the rural labor movement in Pernambuco. While structural change affected the interests and opportunities of individuals in the sugar zone, it did not in itself lead directly either to the organization of people with common interests or to their mobilization (Tilly 1978, 52). We must also explore how trade unionists perceived and acted upon that change.[1]

An important factor in analyzing trade union behavior is how union resources were used by leaders to represent their members and to forge class consciousness. This chapter argues that institutional change within the unions increased union resources, led to a new conception of rights in the countryside, and helped leaders to shape a collective identity that mixed elements of an older, "peasant" consciousness with newer, working-class sensibilities. The first part shows the institutional change wrought by the welfare programs begun in the 1970s. The second section discusses how the unions, whose resources were expanded by the welfare programs, used those resources to engage in a cultural struggle to promote class consciousness in the sugar zone. And the final part analyzes how the unions, partly because of the success of their cultural struggle, were able to mobilize workers and to help create a new labor system in Pernambuco's sugar zone in a pattern similar to others that have taken place all over rural Brazil.

Institutional Change

Military rule in Brazil exhibited a higher degree of continuity with the prior populist regime than did its counterparts in Uruguay, Argentina, and Chile. It might even be said that it engaged in a kind of populism of its own. While most of its populist practices were reserved for the middle class, such as in its expansion and subsidy of federal universities and in underwriting low-cost housing programs (Melo 1993), some were directed, albeit within a highly controlled structure, to organized labor.

One of the most significant of these was the creation, in the early 1970s, of a fund to finance health, dental, and retirement programs that union leaderships could choose to administer.[2] This was the Fund for the Assistance of the Rural Worker, FUNRURAL (Fundo de Assistência ao Trabalhador Rural); two-thirds of the money to finance it came from a tax on urban firms, while the remaining third came from a tax on rural produce. Under the programs that it financed, health and dental services were provided free of charge to paid-up union members. Eventually, retirement benefits were added to the package for those workers of retirement age with legal work documents. Unlike patronage programs controlled by unions in the populist period, these resources were not centralized but instead distributed at the local level (Erickson 1977, 8–10, 62–63).

These programs were modest compared to the standards of European welfare states. In addition, government funding for the medical program was often late, adding to the already substantial burdens imposed on the unions administering it. Similarly, the rural social security program reached a small number of people because relatively few rural workers survived until the retirement age of sixty-five. The pension, 50 percent of the minimum wage for workers and 30 percent of the minimum wage for surviving spouses, was probably below subsistence level.

However, in the context of rural Brazil, the programs were major innovations. They allowed for labor mobility within Brazil, because workers could transfer their right to benefits from one rural area to another. FUNRURAL thus facilitated agricultural modernization and weakened clientelistic dependence on landlords. The new social benefits that it provided were also universal, unlike the more corporate and fragmented provision of welfare benefits for urban workers. For the rural poor, previously unable to obtain any kind of health or retirement services, these programs made the union attractive. By 1980, over half of the Brazilian government's rural medical services were being managed by trade unions (Maybury-Lewis 1994, 40).

Union leaders found themselves with a new drawing card. The programs boosted the resources available to them, providing existing unions with a powerful magnet to attract members and encouraging the establishment of new unions in counties that did not yet have them. As a result, the foundation of rural unions increased dramatically in the 1970s. While the number of all unions in Brazil roughly doubled in the 1964–1980 period, agricultural unions increased almost tenfold from 266 at the end of 1963 to 2,144 in 1980. By 1987 the agricultural workers' confederation, CONTAG, was the largest confederation in the Brazilian labor structure.[3] The number of rural unions in the Pernambuco sugar zone increased from 32 in 1964 (Price 1964) to 46 in 1988.[4]

Thus, despite initial repression, rural labor made extraordinary organizational gains under the military regime. It might seem surprising that the military regime encouraged such a massive rate of rural unionization, in effect completing the project envisaged by the populist Goulart administration before the coup. Explanations for this outcome are complex, but four factors are important to consider. First, the military leaders in charge of the regime had some knowledge of, and some genuine desire to diminish, rural poverty. They therefore sought to carry out policies, according to then Minister of Labor Jarbas Passarinho, that the populist politicians had promised but not delivered, as long as it was clear that these were favors bestowed from above and not something that the rural population itself achieved through "agitation."[5]

Second, the regime was aware that the agricultural modernization promoted by its policies marginalized a large percentage of the rural population and wanted to ensure that this population did not become a threat to political order. The rural welfare scheme, along with Amazonian colonization, was one solution here, a kind of benign anti-insurgency campaign. The free reign given by the regime to the American Institute for Free Labor Development, which built union centers in the Pernambuco sugar zone and trained union leaders throughout Brazil during this period, was another part of this strategy. Third, the government had the finances to fund the program. Prosperous after the high-growth years of the "Brazilian miracle," the government could afford to create this new social entitlement without cutting any of its other projects. Finally, the regime's leaders seemed to have calculated that the welfare programs would keep rural unions politically quiescent and easily controlled. This assumption was also made by critics of the programs within the labor movement itself, who lamented the "welfarism" (*assistencialismo*) of unions at this time and saw them as willing partners in the military regime's scheme to deliberately bureaucratize and deradicalize the labor movement.

In its fourth calculation, the military regime can now be seen to have been mistaken. The welfare programs were a double-edged sword. In the hands of *pelegos*, they might have been used for nothing more than *assistencialismo*, but they could also be used by activists to build up CONTAG and attract and mobilize new members. In impoverished rural areas, this was especially true. As it turned out, the welfare programs, far from leading to a thoroughly controlled and noncombative type of rural unionism, led to a resurgence of militancy in some places, symbolized by the Pernambuco sugar workers' 1979 strike. Other researchers have discovered similar examples in which popular movements "navigate within the system and turn attempts at control into material to use in fortifying their autonomy" (Starn, in Escobar and Alvarez 1992, 105). How this occurred deserves some analysis.

In purely material terms, the welfare programs provided the unions with a financial base that had previously been lacking. Rural unions are much less able than their urban counterparts to raise funds through voluntary union contributions, due to the poverty and dispersion of their members. Whereas 64 percent of urban unions collected voluntary dues from 80 to 100 percent of their members in 1988, only 6 percent of rural unions managed to do the same.[6] The welfare programs, by inserting dental and medical services into the unions (legal services already existed), attracted members and raised the level of finances available through voluntary contributions. This money was used to host training for union leaders at the state federation and confederation level, as well as the CONTAG congresses that brought thousands of rural unionists to Brasília every five years. Combined with rising levels of education in the rural areas, this produced a better-educated, and at least potentially, more combative labor leadership. The new resources were also used in the cultural struggles described in the next section.

The "populist" aspect of the military regime's rural welfare programs was not lost on union leaders in the Pernambuco sugar zone, most of whom entered the labor movement during military rule. These leaders tended to see the military regime as capable of concessions as well as repression, carrots as well as sticks. Trade union leaders played a key role in channeling the exploited workers' anger and action in a reformist direction. In mobilizing the rural poor in strikes for higher wages, in helping them use the labor courts for individual grievances, and by providing them with state-funded social services, they offered an alternative to the risky and seemingly utopian siren calls of agrarian radicals interested in gaining access to land. In the 1980s, the effect of their mediation in the Pernambuco sugar zone was that those among the rural poor who did attempt to seize land were few and marginalized.

The welfare programs also led to a process whereby the social right to welfare services engendered a discovery of (and demand for) the economic, civil, and political rights that had been suspended in practice by the military regime. Labor leaders, in explaining the basis of legal workers' new rights to medical and dental services, were led to the right to strike, the right to the minimum wage, and other rights enunciated by Brazil's legal codes.

The Unions' Cultural Struggle

In the Pernambuco sugar zone, much of what unions do is to help individual workers defend their interests in the labor courts (see chapter 5). They do so within a context of a universal discourse of rights codified in the legal statutes of the Brazilian state. However, unions also engage in actions outside the realm of individual rights and assert the collective identity and nonuniversal, specific rights of rural workers and peasants. In marches, assemblies, rallies, and meetings, they provide a forum for the expression of rural workers' political grievances, their sense of themselves, and their hopes for the future. Union leaders engage in a cultural struggle that is part of their effort to mobilize their members.[7] If the strike represents the key moment in their war of maneuver, this daily cultural struggle is part of the union leaders' war of position.[8]

While the peasantry has been marginalized in the Pernambuco sugar zone and most workers had no access to land by 1980, they are still part of a "peasantariat" that shares characteristics of both peasants and workers.[9] Peasantarians have a "psychological ambiguity" in which they see "'peasanthood' or 'workerhood' as states of mind" that can be changed and readopted as the social circumstances demand (Cohen 1991, 74). Peasantarians are not necessarily more or less radical than full proletarians. They are equally able to define their interests in terms of access to land or increases in wages. No specific set of conditions predetermines the kind of identity that is chosen, although some conditions are clearly more conducive to the emergence of one type of identity than another. And clearly both identities can exist within different people side by side, or within the mind of one person.

A peasantariat tends to arise in areas such as the Pernambuco sugar zone where wage employment is neither universal nor permanent for most workers. Seasonal and temporary work, migration, informal (and illegal) work, occasional ownership of small plots of land, and kinship ties with other smallholders characterize the peasantariat.

Individuals within the ranks of the peasantariat have to decide whether their primary political activities reflect a peasant identity—fighting to reclaim lost access to land—or a proletarian one—struggling to improve their condition within the system of wage labor. They are also torn between two kinds of survival strategies. The first is to cultivate a vertical relationship of dependence upon and loyalty to a large landowner; this is the traditional patron-client relationship in the sugar zone. Such a strategy implies an individual pact with the landlord. The second strategy involves the cultivation of horizontal ties to other rural workers, the forging of solidary relationships that can be used in struggles against the landlord. These strategies are not necessarily mutually exclusive, but do involve various kinds of trade-offs and tensions. In Pernambuco, a crucial institution in determining to what extent people engage in these different political activities and survival strategies is the rural trade union.

On a cultural level, the rural labor leader became a sort of secular priest or preacher: many leaders acquired their positions through association with the Catholic Church. The fact that the unions they controlled were among the few institutions in rural areas, along with the Church, that directed resources to the rural poor and spoke in their name, gave the unions tremendous influence over their members. Freed from the burden of daily work in the fields, able to travel to other parts of Brazil, generally more politically knowledgeable and well connected than their members, trade union leaders could shape the ideological outlook of the workers in their areas. Because they decided who was a legal rural worker, and thus who was eligible for the union's free medical services, the leaders were important figures in their communities.

Trade unions in the sugar zone became far more bureaucratized than the incipient unions that provoked the "crisis in the fields" in 1963. As recipients of part of a mandatory tax on all legal workers in the area, as administrators of a state-funded health program, as providers of legal services, and as part of a union system that extended upward to the national level, unions gained material and ideological resources in short supply among the rural poor. By the 1980s, trade union leaders had control of an enormous amount of institutional, symbolic, and juridical power. They were not the "outside organizers" often mentioned in the literature on peasants, but locally based workers and smallholders who had been full-time cultivators themselves. They were socially mobile, gifted members of the class they claimed to lead. This gave their discourse an aura of credibility, as well as status and prestige.

Language is particularly important for popular social movements that cannot count on the power of wealth, tradition, or military force (Bowles and Gintis 1986, 155). Trade union leaders used language in an attempt to make an agglomeration of workers into a cohesive body. To achieve class action, a leader needs "a compelling discourse that . . . [is] capable of making sense of and defining a common interest and identity" that transcends "the diverging and particularistic aspects of workers' individual lives" (French 1992, 26). In particular, trade union leaders tried to encourage workers not to engage in strategies of survival and social mobility that depended on individualistic, vertical relationships with landlords. Instead, they urged the forging of horizontal linkages between workers and a united front against the landlords. In their everyday interactions with their members, union leaders thus tried to force a recognition of class on the workers and peasants who, in most instances, were likely to see their problems in individual or at most kin-group terms (ibid., 28).

The rural trade union leaders' power to influence attitudes was exercised through the use of words in a variety of settings. In individual consultations, in meetings of groups of workers at union headquarters, in visits to the fields to talk with rural workers and smallholders, in assemblies to which the entire union membership was invited, and in rallies open to the general public, unionists honed their speaking skills and helped to shape local perceptions of politics.

The prevalence of vertical, patron-client relationships with landlords in Pernambuco's rural culture can be seen in the local *literatura de cordel*. This popular literary form consists of cheaply printed pamphlets (*folhetos*), sold in local markets, that tell stories in verse (Borges et al. 1986). These verses are modeled on popular songs played by musicians in the region. Many of the stories involve peasants and their relationships with landlords. In one such story, an honest peasant is entrusted with looking after a landowner's prize bull. The landowner makes a bet with his friends that the loyal peasant will not lie. He then tempts the peasant by sending his daughter to seduce him. The daughter goes to the peasant and says that she will sleep with him if he kills the prize bull. Eventually, the peasant gives in, kills the bull, and sleeps with the daughter. When the landowner confronts him, he confesses the truth. The delighted landowner wins the bet with his friends and rewards the honest peasant by giving him his daughter's hand in marriage.

This fantasy points to the rewards of personal loyalty to and honesty with the patron. It extols a vertical relationship between the rural poor and the landowner. In another story, physical courage vis-à-vis the landlord is exalted. A simple peasant boy falls in love with a landowner's daughter. He asks the landowner for permission to marry the daughter but is refused. The landlord, angered by the presumption of the peasant boy, sends gunmen to kill him. The peasant boy kills all the gunmen, a truce is called, and the landlord capitulates, offering his daughter's hand in marriage. Again, the story is a fantasy compared to the reality of life in the sugar zone. And again, the path to upward mobility is shown to be a vertical relationship with the landlord—in this case a violent one, in which the peasant's bravery and cunning defeats the landlord's superior wealth and power.

Against these cultural influences, the union offers a different strategy to the rural poor. Like the story of the honest peasant, the unions encourage personal loyalty and honesty, but to *companheiros*, fellow rural workers, rather than to the landlord. Like the story of the brave peasant boy, the unions try to instill physical courage in their members, not for engaging in individual battles with the landowner, but for confronting collectively, and nonviolently, the landlords' threats and pressures.

The language used by union leaders in this cultural battle varies. Some leaders appeal to their common status as wage laborers, the untrustworthiness of the landowning employers *(patrões)*, and the need for worker solidarity and collective action. Others use the language of *agrarismo*, reminiscent of that of the Peasant Leagues, stressing members' fellowship in a broader category of "little people" in the countryside who must work the land themselves, as opposed to the large landowners who avoid physical labor.[10]

In addition to speeches, leaders print verses similar to the *folhetos* to attract, mobilize, and influence members. For example, FETAPE distributed verses that were sung at union assemblies. These verses emphasized the common identity and interests of workers vis-à-vis landlords, as in the following lyrics, from a union song entitled "I Am a Cultivator": "I am bought for one hundred grams of smile / I am worried by a grain of treason / I run from him who has a smooth face / My face is full of wrinkles." Here, the identity of the rural workers as those with wrinkled faces, due to prolonged work in the sun, is contrasted with those with smooth faces, including landlords and politicians. Other songs emphasize the injustice of large landowners, as in the "Our Rights Will Come":

> Just because you have much land and many
> Cattle, you deny the worker,
> This poor nobody. But watch out . . . one
> Day in the cemetery
> Our flesh will mingle.

The grave will be your home
The worm your companion
Life will disappear
There, there is no use for money.
I want to hear your defense,
Where will be your wealth
Which bought the whole world?[11]

Verses such as these are part and parcel of the unions' mobilization of rural workers in the sugar zone. One FETAPE official, whose nickname is Beija Flor (Hummingbird), became well known for writing them in the 1980s. He wrote a poem commemorating the 1979 strike (reprinted in Sigaud 1980) and sometimes sang his verses, to musical accompaniment, at union rallies.

Another example of the unions' use of popular culture to express a common identity occurred in Recife on 11 November 1987. On that day, FETAPE transported thousands of workers from the countryside to protest the federal government's proposal to abolish the national land reform agency INCRA (Instituto Nacional de Colonização e Reforma Agrária), and the apparent abandonment of land reform that this action represented. About 5,000 rural workers joined disgruntled INCRA employees and left-party activists on a march through Recife's main streets. The marchers wound from FETAPE headquarters to stop in front of the state legislature, the governor's palace, and finally the main city square. A band with a loud and insistent drummer played music and kept time as people walked and danced through the streets. Several workers carried bananas on their heads; another sported a large melon. High-powered loudspeakers were used by the marchers to draw attention to themselves and to inform the public of their complaints. In the square, the old Peasant League slogan, "Reforma agrária na lei ou na marra" (Agrarian reform through law or by force) was used many times in the speeches given by union leaders and party representatives. Slogans such as these justify the use of the word *movement* to describe the trade unions and their supporters, because they share a collective memory of past struggles, gains and losses, enemies and friends.

At the rally held after the march, anger was directed at the federal government, and particularly at President José Sarney, who was labeled a supporter of the anti–land reform landlords' organization, the Democratic Rural Union, UDR (União Democrático Ruralista). Near the end of the day, two marchers clambered atop a truck and enacted a pantomime about President Sarney to the delighted crowd. One man shaved the mustache of the other, symbolically "shaving Sarney's moustache." The pantomime symbolized the marchers' lack of faith in the president's promise of land reform. The ritual was boisterous comedy, but it imparted a serious political message: the rural movement had broken with the president and his administration.

Other examples of the unions' use of popular culture can be seen in the annual strike. In cultural terms, the strike in the sugar zone serves a function similar to that of Carnival in the wider society. It is a time when ordinary social relations are turned upside down, when conventional hierarchies of deference and status can be violated, when subalterns can ridicule authority figures and act out fantasies of defiance and freedom. In the sugar zone, the strike is a time when workers can challenge foremen in the fields, when union officials have access to most plantations, and when the imperative to work is temporarily done away with. For example, on one plantation during the strike, I saw a worker take away the staff of a foreman and angrily cut it into pieces with his *foice*—an act for which he probably would have been punished, at least fired, in normal times. Like Carnival, the strike is a temporary inversion of social reality, and when it ends, the social hierarchy remains essentially unchanged. The challenge that it offers to the landlords' dominance is fleeting and illusory, but the catharsis that it offers may not be.

The unions' cultural struggle was not without ambiguity. While the "end of the peasantry" was well advanced materially, it had not been accomplished culturally. In the songs FETAPE used to try to create a common identity, the identity most usually invoked is the old *agrarista* image of the Peasant Leagues, rather than a worker identity predicated on a common experience as wage laborers, and reflective of contemporary realities in the sugar zone. Union songs abound with references to peasant, rather than worker identities—"us" is invariably a cultivator, a poor person, a person with calloused hands. Among over two dozen union songs collected in the sugar zone, only one—"I Am Going to Stay on This Side," very similar to the U.S. labor song "Which Side Are You On?"—clearly projected a working-class identity.

The reason for the durability of a peasant identity in the sugar zone, despite widespread de-peasantization and the formation of an almost exclusively working-class movement, can be ascribed to a number of factors. First, there is a disjuncture between economic and cultural production. Popular songs remain popular, despite their declining relevance to contemporary economic realities. Second, while FETAPE is primarily a workers' movement, it is subordinated to the confederation CONTAG, dominated by small landowners. Finally, small landowners and rural workers who would like to become small landowners do form part of the community, and the membership base, within which FETAPE leaders work. A peasant identity therefore provides them with a more inclusive category and allows them to concentrate their confrontational tactics during the strike on large landowners employing relatively large numbers of workers.

Using popular culture, union leaders in the Pernambuco sugar zone were able to transform a bureaucratic system for the distribution of patronage into a genuine social movement. The organizational and cultural resources at their disposal, in addition to the material power represented by workers' control of their labor power, help explain how they staged nine major strikes in eleven years between 1979 and 1989.

The New Labor System

The political impact of the first of those strikes was encapsulated in the colorless words of Marco Maciel, governor of Pernambuco in 1979. He affirmed that his government's position in the conflict was neutral and that "the demands that the workers make will naturally be the object of negotiations between employers and employees, which is the responsibility of the Labor Delegate" (DRT, Delegacia Regional do Trabalho). He said that "an adjustment of interests" could and should "avoid the paralysis of our state's agroindustry" (*Jornal de Comércio*, 3 October 1979). "Ajustment of interests" connotes the other world of federation officials, far from the cultural struggle that went on at the base of the union movement. In this world, technical language, economic statistics, and bargaining skills were used to produce a contract that regulated work conditions for a twelve-month period.

The bargaining process in the sugar zone of the 1980s was laborious, incremental, technocratic, routinized, and adapted to the resolution of positive-sum conflicts over wages. It involved a large number of state institutions that linked the negotiations to the national center. The principal actor among these was the Ministry of Labor, which mediated the talks, but also present as observers were representatives of the IAA, the Pernambuco governor's office, and the Pernambuco state secretariat for labor and social action. In addition, the labor courts, with an appeals process that reached to the Supreme Labor Court in Brasília, served as a back-up to adjudicate parts of the collective contract that could not be agreed upon by the various parties involved. These parties were, on the employers' side, the associations of mill owners and cane planters. On the labor side, local unions and the state federation were represented, although in practice the national confederation coordinated the negotiations for labor. As this summary suggests, the annual bargaining was tightly integrated into national political institutions that used highly formal and legalistic procedures.

The sugar zone's bargaining process represented a significant extension of the democratic right to binding consultation over state policies to a previously excluded sector of the citizenry. (Since refined sugar, cane, and alcohol prices are set by the state, and since the industry is highly regulated, wage levels set forth in the annual collective contracts are essentially state policies.) This right existed briefly during the first Arraes governorship in 1963–1964, but was annulled by the military coup and denied by the subsequent regime. The difference between the first two Arraes administrations reflects the degree of democratization that took place in the sugar zone. The first administration engendered severe landlord opposition merely for recognizing the unions' right to negotiate, and was aborted by a coalition of military and landlord interests. In the second administration (1986–1990), Arraes served out his entire mandate, included the unions in annual decisions regarding the sugar sector, and even listed a former FETAPE lawyer as his secretary of labor.

The unions certainly had strong grievances by the end of the 1970s. While the sugar industry had been modernized, with large federal subsidies going to mill owners to buy new equipment, the salaries of cane cutters remained low. Annual wage increases were decreed by the government and formally real wages increased, but the landowners' response was to manipulate the piece-rate system, increasing the amount of work necessary to earn the new wage. The result was hardship for many workers in the sugar zone.

In the months before the 1979 strike, for example, the salary of a cane worker was 54.80 cruzeiros per day or 1,643 cruzeiros per month. Based on an average family of six people, this amounted to 273 cruzeiros per person per month. Yet at that time a kilogram of *charque* (salted beef, common in the area), cost 120 cruzeiros, a kilo of beans was 20 cruzeiros, coffee was 144 cruzeiros per kilo, milk 8.70, and bread 1.20. Given these prices, it would seem that even rural workers lucky enough to work all year long in the cane fields had families going hungry (*Diário de Pernambuco*, 3 October 1979).

The perception that living standards of rural workers had declined in the 1960s and 1970s with the decline in subsistence agriculture and the growth of the market was widespread in the sugar zone. One union leader put it this way: "In that time [1963], you earned little money and ate a lot; now you earn a lot of money and eat little" (Field notes 1988). Furthermore, inflation spun out of control in the 1980s, averaging 419 percent per year in that decade. In 1987, annual inflation was 389 percent; in 1988, 984 percent, in 1989, 1,765 percent.[12] Amid the uncertainty generated by such inflation, even the wages of an earlier era seemed more generous; in 1988, FETAPE's president José Rodrigues said:

> Before the coup, at that time you worked one day and could buy one kilo of charque with the salary and there was still money left over . . . [whereas] in 1978 and until 1979, until we had our campaign, the worker was getting a daily wage that was only enough to buy one-half of a kilo [of *charque*].[13]

This sense of decline was echoed throughout the sugar zone. When the fifty trade union leaders surveyed for this book were asked whether the standard of living for rural workers in the sugar zone in 1988 was higher, lower, or equal to the standard of living under Governor Arraes in 1963, only eight of them said that the 1988 standard of living was higher than that of 1963. One said that it was equal, and forty-one that it was lower than that which had existed twenty-five years before.

The employers' response to this reality was in most cases not to deny it, but to claim instead that it was the government's, not their, responsibility. Cane planter Paulo Roberto Falcão spoke for many of his colleagues when he said, "We are tired of assuming the social burden in the countryside. If the worker has a right to a better salary, as we also understand, then the government should give us the means to increase this salary, paying a fair price for our product, rather than determining the rate for a ton of sugarcane on a political basis" (*Diário de Pernambuco*, 5 October 1979). The workers' misery was thus a political football passed back and forth between representatives of the employers and the government. When political conditions became more favorable in the late 1970s, the union movement was able to mobilize workers and democratize the local collective bargaining system.

However, the right to consultation within that system was still highly concentrated within the union movement itself. While thousands of workers participated in the strikes, the annual negotiations themselves did not allow for a great deal of participation at the grass-roots level. These were always handled by the state federation, FETAPE, with little direct participation by its member unions.[14] The FETAPE directors, on the one hand, were elected indirectly by the union presidents in the state. But the union presidents' role in the strike negotiations was merely consultative. The annual contract was drawn up in discussions between employers' representatives and FETAPE directors, lawyers, and economists; the union presidents approved and signed it. The organization of the unions on the plantations was also weak; many plantations did not have union representatives (*delegados*).

FETAPE seemed to calculate, probably correctly, that the centralization of wage negotiations ensured a unified front and the best possible collective contract. However, the price for such centralization was that local unions were unable to negotiate directly with local employers for a contract; this was a central demand of the "new unionism" that arose in São Paulo in the 1980s. Thus, particularly well-organized workers could not gain higher wages for themselves, but instead had to abide by the statewide agreements made by FETAPE.

Furthermore, negotiations were always supervised by the federal Ministry of Labor. If the talks failed to produce agreement, the case went automatically to the labor court (TRT, Tribunal Regional do Trabalho), where a compromise ruling (usually more favorable to employers than employees) was made. Except in 1979 and 1990, such rulings were made every year in the sugar zone in the 1979–1990 period (Teixeira et al. 1991, 39).

In reality, employers had little incentive to make concessions to FETAPE when they knew that if they were intransigent, their case would get a favorable ruling from the TRT. The TRT remained a key institution in the sugar zone during the 1980s, with the power to declare strikes illegal and remove particular union demands from the collective contract. All of this is in direct contrast to the gains of the metalworkers' unions in the ABC region of São Paulo during the same period. There the unions won the right to bargain directly with employers, without the involvement of the labor court (Humphrey 1982). In addition, they won large wage increases in a dynamic, high-technology industry in which the average wage is four times the minimum wage.

Unlike the widely publicized metalworkers' strike in São Bernardo do Campo in March 1979, the Pernambuco sugar workers' strike was legal and did not provoke the Ministry of Labor to intervene in the unions. In fact, a Ministry of Labor official said during the strike, "It is a shame when . . . the majority of strike demands are copies of clauses of the Consolidated Labor Laws [the 1943 legislation that regulates labor-management conflict in Brazil], and the biggest victim of this is the workers," and he pledged that the ministry would enforce the labor laws more strictly in the sugar zone (*Jornal de Comércio*, 9 October 1979). The evidence suggests, however, that the ministry's enforcement procedures did not improve after these statements were made.

The October 1979 sugar workers' strike also did not involve the rise of new union leaders or the creation of parallel workplace organizations, as occurred in São Bernardo do Campo and the rest of the ABC region of São Paulo during the March strikes. A major strike leader in Pernambuco, for example, was Agápito Francisco dos Santos, who had been selected as an *interventor* of the São Lourenço da Mata union in 1964 by the military regime and who had retained the presidency ever since. The sugar workers' strike was fought for the recognition of previously established but long unused legal rights, whereas the São Paulo metalworkers' action served to challenge the corporatist legal structure.[15]

Thus, while the sugar workers were part of the 1979 strike wave between January and October, in which there were more than 400 strikes, they did not challenge the regime in the way that the São Paulo unions did (Skidmore 1988, 214). During Brazil's democratic transition, the metalworkers of São Paulo's ABC region became emblematic of the entire Brazilian labor movement, but this disguised the reality that democratic rights had been extended differentially within Brazil and that some unions had greater rights to consultation than others. Thus, when a congressman from the PMDB, Carlos Bezerra, called the Pernambuco sugar zone "the ABC of the countryside" in 1980, the comparison was only partly accurate.[16] The ABC unions had won the right to collectively bargain as early as the 1940s, whereas it was not until 1979 that this right was respected in the sugar zone. In terms of freedom from arbitrary state action and consultation over state policies, the ABC unions had won significantly greater rights than had their Pernambuco counterparts. The latter also had a far more advanced agenda in the 1980s (the "new unionism," delinking from the state, the founding of a new political party) than that of the Pernambuco rural unions, which were still wedded to the "old unionism" of state tutelage and temporary alliances with populist leaders.

Brazil's labor structure, discussed in more detail in chapter 5, constrained the unions in the sugar zone in at least one other important respect. As well as not permitting decentralized bargaining at the plant or plantation level, it did not allow sectoral bargaining—that is, on behalf of all workers in the sugar sector nationwide. Bargaining was limited to the state level. This meant that the Pernambuco rural unions could not bargain alongside their counterparts in São Paulo, whose wages were about 30 percent higher.[17] Similarly, the unions' suggestion in 1993 that the state negotiations be unified for all the northeastern states was rejected by employers.[18] Divide and rule was evidently the preferred strategy of employers in the sugar industry. In contrast, sectoral bargaining did exist in the automobile sector, although this was greatly facilitated by the fact that the auto industry at that time existed in only one state, São Paulo (Martin 1994).

Despite being limited to state-level negotiations, FETAPE achieved substantial gains, at least on paper, for its members in the 1979–1989 period. The collective contract was expanded from twenty-three to fifty-seven clauses; the forty-hour week was won; and wages, which were increased annually, were pegged 10 percent above the minimum wage. But most of these clauses of the contract were never enforced. Seasonal unemployment and illegal hiring remained a condition of about half of the work force, and the minimum wage declined in real terms during the 1980s.[19]

Many other neglected provisions can be found in the collective contract. Added after the crucial clauses governing salaries and piece rates, these clauses were FETAPE victories. But local unions were left with the task of trying to make the benefits real, usually a hopeless task. For example, according to the following clauses of the 1987 collective contract, employers were supposed to provide for their workers' cutting implements (12), adequate housing (18), drinking water (27), safe transport to work (28), safety equipment for the application of pesticides (30), schools for their children (36), and transportation in case of accidents or sickness (39). Although one or two of these clauses might have been honored by some of the large employers, in general they had little to do with the reality of working and living conditions in the sugar zone in that year.

Workers did gain the right to influence state decisions that affected them in Pernambuco. FETAPE organized nine strikes in the eleven years of the 1979–1989 period. However, these stoppages rarely affected the production of the sugar mills in the area. This is because the mills were able to stockpile cane and procure supplies from the many plantations which continued to cut cane during the strike. Furthermore, the cane cutters' unions were unable to ally with the mill workers and get them to go on strike at the same time, as they did in 1963. The mill workers' contract was renegotiated in May, five months before that of the cane cutters, hindering efforts at cooperation. Moreover, the mill workers did not have union headquarters in every town of the sugar zone, as did the cane cutters. Instead, they had only one central headquarters in Recife, hindering efforts at organization (Lopes 1978).

Price increases for cane, sugar, and alcohol were invariably decreed by the federal government after the renewal of the workers' contract in October. There is considerable evidence that the mill and plantation owners in Pernambuco favored the annual cane cutters' strike because it created a climate of social unrest which they could then exploit in lobbying the government for price increases. The media helped this campaign by consistently exaggerating the level of participation in the strike and playing up the violent incidents that occurred.[20] The employers certainly did not make strong efforts over the years to prevent the annual strike, which they could have done by offering preemptive concessions or arranging a long-term contract. The president of the Palmares workers' union in 1982 said, "The workers don't want a strike . . . the majority of union leaders agree, the paralysis only interests the employers, who will use the movement to gain price increases for their products" (*Diário de Pernambuco*, 22 September 1982).

While it would be a caricature to portray the strikes in the sugar zone as an elaborate ballet choreographed solely by the employers, an element of exploitation existed in these acts of ostensible worker defiance and strength. The strike in the sugar zone became predictable, sadly necessary for the workers, and an indication of weakness as well as strength.[21] The fact that employers benefited from the strike, that it was organized from the top down by the state federation, and that it was a virtual requirement in order for the workers to receive meaningful pay increases all point to this conclusion. The workers paid the cost, in terms of forgone wages, of the employers' publicity campaign. They were pawns of a system that benefited the employers more than it benefited them. Because of steeply rising inflation in the 1980s, the federation had to spend an enormous amount of organizational and financial resources just to tread water.[22] Under these circumstances, the political significance of the strike declined, "transforming itself into an exclusively economistic movement," in the words of one commentator (*Diário de Pernambuco*, 6 October 1989).

All of this is a far cry from the picture presented by an academic advisor to FETAPE, Lygia Sigaud (1986). Her analysis of the Pernambuco strikes captures the outlook of union militants but glosses over considerable problems within the union movement. One of these is class differentiation. Of the union leaders surveyed for this book, 24 percent were members of the small landholder class, distinct from the proletarians who made up the majority of the membership.[23] Nationally, small landowners were even more prominent in the rural workers' movement—57.8 percent of all CONTAG presidents in 1988 were in this category.[24] This signifies the possibility of considerable differences of interest between members and leaders, in the sense that many presidents might have come from better-off segments of the peasantry than most of their members. There was also a tendency for union leaders to use their positions as springboards for local political offices, the acquisition of which further distanced them from the class they set out to represent. Another difficulty for unions was lack of participation. Sigaud's 1986 article mentions individual voting in elections to approve or disapprove of the strike, but in a 1988 strike vote in Nazaré da Mata that I witnessed, the strike was approved by a perfunctory and listless raising of hands.

Sigaud's article conveys the sense of a unified mass taking control during the sugar strikes, but this is far from the case. Obstacles to cohesive collective action, discussed in later chapters, were simply too great. Outside of well-organized communities such as São Lourenço da Mata (where organization was facilitated by the small number of employers and proximity to Recife) and Paudalho, adherence to the strike was spotty. In Goiana, for example, few workers participated in the strikes of the 1979–1986 period, until a new and more militant union directorate was elected in 1987. Several other communities, especially the smaller ones in outlying areas, shared a similar history.

Finally, resentment of FETAPE existed among some local unions. Some leaders felt that while the federation promoted the strike from Recife, it did not support them in their strenuous (and often dangerous) efforts to shut down the plantations. FETAPE was also criticized for not doing enough to ensure the enforcement of the collective contract after it had been signed. Despite regime transition in the 1979–1989 period, therefore, the local political system had not been fully democratized in the sugar zone. In its narrowness and incrementalism, the collective bargaining apparatus was best able to represent only one category of worker in the sugar zone—the permanently employed wage worker. It was less responsive to the grievances of other categories of workers—illegals (many of whom were migrants, women, and children), temporary workers without job stability (whose seasonal unemployment meant that for much of the year, they did not benefit from wage increases negotiated by the unions), and subsistence peasant producers. There was no shortage of workers' problems in the sugar zone, but there was a shortage of institutional mechanisms to resolve them. While they allowed for some degree of participation, the institutions of bargaining in the sugar zone dealt intensively with a narrow range of those problems rather than encapsulating comprehensive and enduring solutions to a broad range of them.

Democratic consultative institutions remained in the sugar zone despite severe economic difficulties in the 1980s. However, much of the unions' new freedom was spent in a losing battle to halt the erosion of members' wages, which were pegged to the declining official minimum wage. In the latter half of the 1980s, the unions got much less of what they asked for than earlier in the decade, as is shown in table 4.1. The most dramatic slide in the real minimum wage and increase in inflation occurred after 1986, when a national civilian regime was in power. This eroded the advantages of civilian rule in the eyes of many rural union leaders.

Nevertheless, it is undeniable that significant democratic change occurred in the sugar zone in the 1980s. The rural workers' unions did succeed in winning back rights to binding political consultation—both at the ballot box, and more crucially, at the bargaining table—that they had lost in 1964. Whereas labor mobilization had provoked violent landlord support for the military coup in 1964, the same phenomenon was institutionalized within state structures that recognized a place for organized labor in the 1980s. Landlords no longer regarded unions as intrinsically subversive. They bargained with union officials who were treated by government mediators, at least formally, as their equals. And they respected the results of democratic elections. These changes were no small achievement in rural Pernambuco.

Summary

The emergence of a vigorous, politically active, working-class rural unionism in Brazil and Pernambuco was not the ineluctable outcome of automatic processes. The structural context in which this new rural unionism was born was created, in large measure, by increasing state

Table 4.1 Labor Conflicts in the Pernambuco Sugar Zone, 1979–1989

Year	Strike?	Duration	No. of Unions Involved in Strike	Wage Demand (%)	Wage Increase (%)
1979	yes	8 days	2 on strike 26 supporting	100	52
1980	yes	6 days	2 for entire strike 41 for 2 days	92	61
1981	no	—	—	57	55
1982	yes	3 days	45	n.a.	n.a.
1983	yes	3 days	45	62	62
1984	yes	10 days	6 for entire strike 38 for 5 days	71	66
1985	no	—	—	116	100
1986	yes	12 days	45	35	15
1987	yes	8 days	45	200	100
1988	yes	10 days	45	73	35
1989	yes	8 days	45	229	84

Sources: Diário de Pernambuco, Jornal de Comércio, various years.

capacity and government policies. Chapter 3 showed how changes in class structure and political institutions produced by government interventions provided opportunities for union organization. This chapter showed how leaders seized those opportunities to build a movement, drawing on new resources provided by welfare programs to engage in a cultural struggle that mobilized members, and then using successful mobilization to force concessions at the bargaining table. Institutional change is thus the other half of the puzzle in understanding how Pernambuco's rural labor movement reemerged in the 1980s.

Rural unions were promoted by successive Brazilian governments—first as an alternative to the Peasant Leagues, then as a bulwark against other potential forms of rural radicalism. Under the military regime, the welfare programs were intended to keep unions quiet, docile, and oriented to individual representation. Like many of the military regime's policies, however, the sorcery doubled back upon the sorcerers themselves (Fleischer, in Soares and D'Araujo 1994, 154). The military unwittingly gave unions the means to develop a class-conscious and militant unionism devoted to representation on a collective basis and using mass mobilization as a pressure tactic. While in the 1980s it was clear that the radical agitation for land of the Peasant Leagues was dead, at least in the northeast, the new rural unionism was a more successful vehicle for the extension of democratic rights than the Leagues had been.

There are thus two main reasons why the rural labor movement in Pernambuco—and much of the rest of Brazil—looked different from its precursor of the early 1960s. First, because the interests it represented had changed, the number of peasants decreased, the number of permanent jobs grew, and wages rose. Most of those peasants who adapted to modernization had found some niche, no matter how tenuous, in the capitalist economy. At the same time, the institutions available to express popular interests were transformed. The implantation of welfare programs into the unions had raised the costs of entry into the "market" of rural labor representation, deterring competitors to the unions. The welfare programs also empowered a new category of professional union leaders, connected to the state, with a high degree of influence over their members, but with little interest in challenging the existing distribution of property rights. These leaders saw their main responsibility as representing rural workers, in a way analogous to their counterparts in urban unions. They helped to create a new consciousness that broke free, at least to some extent, of the clientelism, verticalism, and orientation to land of an older, peasant identity.

The rural labor movement's readoption of public collective action and reemergence as a political actor in the 1980s is not the end of our story, however. It remains to be seen why, once collective action was again possible, the movement made use of that opportunity in the way it did. Furthermore, the *impact* of the trade unions on politics remains to be explored. The next four chapters take up three of the most important issues concerning the unions' political involvement and impact. Chapter 5 looks at the internal organization of the unions and how this favored the leaders' engagement in welfare and wage work at the expense of land issues. Chapter 6 analyzes the problem of violence in the sugar zone and the state's unwillingness to curb illegal landlord power. Chapter 7 deals with the leaderships' relationships with Brazil's political parties and politicians. And chapter 8 examines the politics surrounding CONTAG's principal political demand: agrarian reform.

III

The Unions in the
New Republic

~ 5 ~

Sons of Cane
Leadership Dilemmas Within the Unions

At dawn on 2 October 1979, groups of men formed pickets outside sugar plantations in São Lourenço da Mata, in the state of Pernambuco, northeast Brazil. As members of the local trade union, the men had voted to go on strike and were there to make sure that the plantations remained barred to workers. Many of the men were nervous. Rural strikes had been effectively prohibited by Brazil's military regime for fifteen years. Recently the regime had been liberalizing, but no one was sure whether or not this strike would be violently repressed.

The first day passed successfully for the strikers. Most workers stayed home. Trucks filled with strikebreakers were turned back from the plantation gates. Neither the army nor the military police were sent out to attack the picket lines; the military police were in force mostly to prevent violence. For seven more days the strikers kept up their vigil in São Lourenço and the neighboring county of Paudalho, until news came from the state capital, Recife: the union federation that represented them had reached an agreement with landowners. Plantation workers' salaries throughout the state's sugar zone were to be increased by 52 percent. The unions' right to strike and collectively bargain had been accepted by both the landowners' representatives and government officials.[1]

As shown in chapters 3 and 4, changes in the class structure of the sugar zone and the state's welfare programs increased the resources of the unions under the military regime and transformed the unions' capacity for collective action. The 1979 political opening gave the unions an opportunity to apply this capacity. What remains to be explained is *how* the unions chose to use their collective power in the 1980s, and what political impact those decisions had.

This chapter deals primarily with the internal organization of the unions themselves. Externally, the unions' strategy consisted of three interrelated elements: wage campaigns, electoral coalitions, and mobilization for agrarian reform. Internally, union leaders had to balance their responsibility to defend worker rights with their obligations to administer welfare programs. While the welfare programs enhanced the unions' ability to mobilize workers in wage campaigns, too much welfarism threatened to engulf the unions and incapacitate them as defenders of labor rights. Furthermore, the tensions of balancing workerism and welfarism pushed land issues off the agenda of most union leaders. Paradoxically, a rural labor movement officially committed to land reform paid almost no attention to land issues in its daily activities.

The land issue was not ignored by unions because the peasantry had by now entirely disappeared. Despite widespread de-peasantization and the commercialization of smallholdings, many small cultivators producing for subsistence with family labor continued to exist. Furthermore, many rural workers continued to identify themselves as peasants or *camponeses* (from *campo*, field or countryside). While only a minority had access to a subsistence plot, many wanted such access, especially as inflation accelerated in the 1980s and made food purchases increasingly difficult. The land question was therefore not subordinated to the wage and welfare issues in the sugar zone merely because people's "objective" interests had changed, and peasant demands were no longer salient. Rather, the dominant institutions of representation—the unions—had a bias against land demands in favor of wage and welfare demands. The fact that the unions administered welfare programs raised the cost of entry for potentially competitive organizations, essentially allowing the unions to enjoy a monopoly in representing the interests of the rural poor.

This chapter first argues against a prevalent conception in the analysis of Brazilian trade unionism—that union behavior can be explained purely in terms of the corporatist labor structure—to analyze the performance of the Pernambuco unions as an interaction between the union structure and the decisions of individual leaders. It attempts to shift the focus of analysis from broad macrostructural constraints to that of the micromotives of local officials operating within the structure. The second and third parts of the chapter argue that the union leaders' relative lack of militancy on the land question stems to a great extent from the internal structure of the union: within the union bureaucracy, leaders had large incentives to provide health and other benefits to members and to represent them as workers, but they faced few incentives to get involved in struggles for land. Such struggles are usually confrontational and sometimes violent and, unlike wage negotiations, cannot result in gains for all members, only for selected groups. Union organization thus militated against decisive action on land issues. Because of the poverty of the Pernambuco sugar zone, few outside resources were available to leaders seeking to overcome these institutional barriers and to pressure employers and state officials for local land redistribution.

Rethinking Brazilian Unionism

Brazil's labor relations system, basically constructed in the 1930s, has five main components that affect union performance (Keck, in Stepan 1989, 253). The first three of these were explained in chapter 1: the *contribuição sindical*, the obligatory contribution which the Ministry of Labor extracts from all documented workers and channels to the unions;[2] the monopoly of representation for a category of workers in a given area—*unicidade*; and a union hierarchy presided over by the Ministry of Labor that gives important controls to the state federations. The fourth feature is the unions' obligation, imposed by the state, to provide members with legal services and their option to offer medical and dental assistance. Finally, a system of labor courts means that binding, obligatory adjudication of labor disputes by a court is a more common form of dispute resolution than collective bargaining.

Academic analyses of this union structure and the unions within it vary considerably. One strand of thinking prevalent during Brazil's Second Republic defends the structure as well suited to Brazilian society, a valuable shock absorber for interclass tension. In this view, Brazilian society suffers from a lack of cohesion. The collective psychology of the people is marked by low levels of cooperation and solidarity with others (Morães Filho 1952, 311). Compared to Anglo-Saxons, Brazilians are just not good at voluntarily associating with one another. The Brazilian tends to be individualistic and egoistic.[3] The Brazilian attitude toward society is what Edward Banfield, in describing southern Italy, described as "amoral familism"—everything for those within the extended family, nothing for those outside it (1951).

In such a culture, it is better for the state to impose association, because harmonious association would not occur of its own accord. Therefore, the state construction of the union system during the Estado Novo was beneficial; the union monopoly was necessary to build social solidarity (Morães Filho 1952, 319).

In this approach, the corporatist union structure is a well-functioning machine to resolve labor disputes in an incremental, peaceful manner, forcing both sides to compromise.[4] It fits the Brazilian character, which is also marked by an aversion to direct conflict and a tendency to seek compromise.[5] The few, sporadic acts of trade union militancy that take place are the result not of pressure from the base (because the base is usually pacific and conciliatory) but from a professional leadership group that has a vested interest in agitation. This group uses conflict to secure its own position within the union movement. Such an interpretation of unions was not just that of conservative intellectuals. It was common, for example, among mill owners and planters in Pernambuco's sugar zone.

A second approach to Brazil's union structure reaches opposite conclusions. Emerging from the failure of the Second Republic and repudiating its populist legacy, this perspective sees class conflict and voluntary worker association as very much a part of Brazilian life. The bureaucratic unionism licensed by the Estado Novo was constructed precisely to curb the more autonomous and militant working class demands (Cohen 1989). Free trade unions, unions without the "straitjacket" of corporatist controls, would be more confrontational than existing unions because they would more directly represent the working class, which is by no means conciliatory and pacific. However, state manipulation and repression created a system that rewards *pelego* trade union leaders.

For authors with this view, the *contribuição sindical* is a prime example of everything that is wrong with Brazilian unionism. Free unions should rely on the voluntary contributions of their members. Within such a framework, leaders are forced to be responsive to the grassroots in order to keep members contributing. In Brazilian unions, however, all workers are automatically taxed by the Ministry of Labor, which then transfers most of this money to the local union. Leaders thus have no incentive to respond to members, and are heavily reliant on the state. The *contribuição sindical* destroys union representativeness and autonomy, creating a dependent, bureaucratic network of unions geared more to the provision of social services than the protection of the rank and file.[6] In the words of one analyst, the *contribuição sindical* is the result of cooptation of unions by the state in which the unions "maintain themselves through the shameless exploitation of the salaried masses."[7]

The latter perspective gained currency in Brazil during the liberalization of the military regime beginning in the late 1970s. The metalworkers' strikes in the ABC region of São Paulo in 1978, 1979, and 1980 unleashed the new unionism that criticized the state's corporatist controls over unions and demanded changes in labor law, including the abolition of the *contribuição sindical*, the Ministry of Labor's right to intervene in unions, and (among some activists) the union monopoly system. The new unionism also emphasized greater contact between leaders and the rank and file, less attention to social assistance, and demanded direct collective bargaining for small groups of workers rather than statewide adjudications by a labor court (Keck in Stepan 1989, 260). The assumption of the new unionism was that grass-roots demands were not effectively represented by the corporatist system. Far from "agitating" for their own benefit in the name of a contented work force, most union leaders were complacent, unresponsive to members, and noncombative. Many were corrupt, receiving money from employers or taking it from the state. Only by increasing workers' ability to organize and represent themselves spontaneously, independently, and locally could the many workplace problems be addressed (Costa 1986; Rodrigues 1987; Troyano 1978). In the Pernambuco sugar zone, such an interpretation of the union movement can readily be found among left-wing, nonunion party activists such as those in the Workers' Party.

Both the defenders of the "old unionism" and the advocates of the new unionism tend toward functionalism because they derive trade union characteristics from the union's perceived function (Elster, in Roemer 1986, 202). The first approach sees the real function of unions as facilitating social harmony. The union structure is designed to enable unions to do this, basically reflecting the docile, conciliatory national character. However, the structure can be exploited by opportunistic labor leaders for their own political ends.

The advocates of new unionism see the real function of unions as that of representing rank-and-file workers in their inevitable conflict with capitalists. The union structure smothers "authentic" expressions of class conflict, subverting and repressing them under the weight of corporatist institutions, laws, and coopted *pelego* leaders.[8] When the labor law is changed, and unions are restored to their true function, workers' demands will finally be aired in society, and working-class militancy and power will increase.

What both approaches ignore is that remarkable differences in trade union militancy, both in time and space, have existed in Brazil within the same union structure. The structure has existed since the 1930s, despite changes of regime at the national level. In the populist republic of 1945–1964, for example, unions were more independent, politically active, and confrontational than they were in the preceding Estado Novo and subsequent military periods. In the late 1970s, the ABC metalworkers' unions were able to defy the military regime and win important concessions despite the fact that the union structure remained unchanged.[9]

The way the national political regime applies labor law, the way it attempts to use the union structure, is thus a crucial variable in explaining union behavior. It has received considerable attention; many analysts have examined how the post-1964 military regime, for example, used existing labor law to purge unions of leftist leaders and create a new "apolitical" unionism.

However, another crucial variable has been largely ignored: how trade union leaders decide to respond to the union structure, the system of incentives and sanctions that the structure presents, and the goals, values, and experiences that go into the decisions leaders make. The basic component of the Brazilian trade union system—the local union—is generally a "black box" in most analyses. The system is said to have characteristics that automatically produce certain kinds of behavior. Why and how union leaders behave as they do—why for example, they should want to be more or less militant—is not investigated. It is invariably assumed that this is obvious, but it is not.

The structure of the union system puts limits on the actions of both members and leaders. Such an approach helps to explain why the performance of local unions differs both *within* the *zona da mata*, and *between* unions as a group in the *zona da mata* and unions in other parts of Brazil. Some unions do very little to foster participation in the strike or to ensure enforcement of the collective contract and concentrate primarily on providing health services on an individual basis.[10] Meanwhile, others have high rates of strike participation and strong workplace organizations that challenge abuses of the collective contract, and they take on employers in the labor courts. These unions operate within the same union structure, suggesting that structure itself cannot explain all differences in union behavior. It is rather the interaction between structure—the network of incentives and disincentives embedded in the unions as institutions—and individual leaders' choices that explains union performance.

Constraints on the Sugar Unions

How much unions could actually help to solve workers' problems depended mainly on union resources, the strength of local plantation organization, and the ability of the leadership, but certain external factors a priori made union performance more or less difficult. These were size, location, the number of local employers, and the percentage of members with access to land. Each of these factors will be discussed in turn.

Size was an inescapable limiting factor in union organization in the sugar zone. Small unions seemed to lack the "critical mass" for really effective action. Their financial base was small, leading to all sorts of problems. A small union might not be able to afford a car for its directors, for example, or to afford its own building.[11] Size could also affect the ability of a union to secure legal and health services. Union lawyers in the sugar zone received commissions for every case they won in labor court. They therefore tended to avoid small unions where the caseload was likely to be light.

The correlation between union size and strength in the sugar zone was not perfect, but there was a close fit. The union in São Lourenço da Mata, where adherence to the strike was probably higher than anywhere else in the 1980s, had the sixth-largest membership. But the leading unions—the ones that participated most actively in the strike and furnished the officials of FETAPE—all had more than the average of 4,214 members. Conversely, the weakest unions all had below-average membership. As will be discussed more fully in chapter 7, small unions were less effective vote banks for local politicians and thus more likely to be passed over when successful politicians found themselves in positions to hand out patronage.

In addition to size, locality also affected the ability of unions to effectively represent their members' interests. The weakest unions in the sugar zone were not only small, they were far away from Recife on the edge of the sugar zone. They received less help from FETAPE than the unions closer to Recife. They were less able to attract the interest of outside supporters—journalists, party representatives, Church activists—who were based in Recife. Their leaders had to spend more time and effort traveling to Recife to meet with fellow union leaders and federation officials, and were more likely to miss such meetings due to the relatively high costs they had to incur to attend them.

Neighboring the sugar zone is the intermediate *agreste* region, and unions on the border of these two regions faced special problems. Residents of the *agreste* were primarily small property owners rather than rural wage workers. Their dues could not automatically be funnelled to the union because they were not paid by an employer. Many smallholders in the *agreste* did not make the voluntary contributions that the union asked for. Unions in the border regions between the *agreste* and the sugar zone thus had financial problems that unions in the latter region did not experience.

The number of employers is also an important factor in assessing union strength. In São Lourenço da Mata, for example, two large *usinas* employed most of the union members. In nearby Nazaré da Mata, on the other hand, workers were scattered out on over 85 small plantations. It is not surprising that adherence to the strike in São Lourenço was higher than in Nazaré. The São Lourenço union leaders had a concentrated work force that was relatively easy to mobilize. The Nazaré leaders, on the other hand, could not visit all the workplaces in their area during the strike, even if they had wanted to. They had to select a few key locations and hope that strikebreakers did not continue working on those plantations that the leaders were unable to visit. Strikebreaking inevitably took place.

Once the strike was over, the São Lourenço union had an easier time securing the enforcement of the collective contract. It had two main employers, rather than over eighty-five, with whom to negotiate.[12] Those employers were also large firms with relatively fat profit margins. Paying the new, higher wage was not such a problem for them. Small planters, on the other hand, had more difficulty meeting increased labor costs and were more likely to fight the union on that issue.[13] Perversely, the areas in which employers were most likely to cheat on the collective contract, paying piece rates below the legal minimum, were exactly those areas made up of numerous small plantations where union efforts to monitor the situation were most difficult.

The percentage of members with access to land is the final, and quite important, consideration when considering union strength. Here we are speaking primarily of rural workers who had small subsistence plots on the plantations, not about independent, small landowners such as those in the *agreste*. As Lygia Sigaud points out, workers with access to land could provide a store of food to the union that improved the union's ability to weather a strike (1986, 319–43). Union dues could not officially be used as strike funds, so food contributions were especially important in this context. Workers with subsistence plots also worked in the community, unlike the illegals who lived in town but often worked outside the *município*. The plantation workers were thus more rooted in the community than the illegals, and often more committed to a successful strike.

One factor affected unions equally, and that concerns finances. In the sugar zone, finances were quite centralized. Unions relied on three sources of funds: the *contribuição sindical* collected by the Ministry of Labor, the *imposto social* (social tax) collected by each local union from members, and the *taxa assistencial* or welfare fee, a yearly payment made by employers to the unions. The *imposto social* was a voluntary contribution and, considering the low wages in the sugar zone, did not amount to much. The *imposto sindical* and the *taxa assistencial* went to a large degree to the state federation. Fifteen percent of the *imposto sindical* was allocated to the federation, while a little more than half was given to the local union (Mericle 1974, 113). But half of the *taxa assistencial* went to the federation. In *municí-*

pios without a union, 100 percent of the *taxa* was taken by the federation. FETAPE was thus far richer than any single union in the sugar zone.[14] Its centralized negotiating during collective bargaining was matched by its large share of total union finances.

Unions in the sugar zone faced certain common problems that they solved with varying degrees of success. The external factors listed here—union size, union location, number of employers, and number of workers with access to land—shaped the extent of union success, but they did not determine them. There was scope for collective action to create unions that were responsive to the members, vigilant in defense of workers' rights, and combative in the face of employers' abuses.

Inside the Unions

Members

Internal union organization was quite simple. The paid officers usually consisted of a president and his (and in rare cases, her) slate of officers, elected together: a secretary, a treasurer, and sometimes a vice-president, serving for a three-year term. Lending support to these three or four officials was a union directorate of several more unpaid officers. The union office, depending on its resources, might have had some office staff. A lawyer to handle workers' cases in the labor courts, a doctor, and a dentist usually visited the office several days a week. Beyond this skeletal bureaucracy, outside the union headquarters, lay the heart of the union: the *delegados* on the plantations, the active members who attended meetings and paid their voluntary social dues, and the mass of workers who were nominally members but rarely, perhaps never, active participants in union affairs.

Estimates of the number of active members in the unions vary. Union leaders reported that approximately 38 percent of their members paid the voluntary union dues, and about 24 percent of the members voted in union elections. While the voting figure reported by the officials is typical of Brazilian unionism, the dues-paying figure is not. The Pernambuco sugar unions reported a lower level of dues paying than their urban counterparts—in 1990, 64 percent of all urban unions counted on 80 percent or more of their members to pay voluntary dues. On the other hand, the sugar unions were far above the average among rural unions, 45 percent of which got 19 percent of their members or fewer to pay dues in the same year (IBGE 1991, 426).

However, there was a marked tendency for union leaders to exaggerate the level of dues paying and voting in their unions. In table 5.1, oral answers to the survey questions about dues paying and voting are compared with official data obtained from the Ministry of Labor. Some of the discrepancies can be attributed to memory lapse on the part of leaders who were unaccustomed to keeping detailed written records. But in most cases the official data reveals a lower level of participation, and sometimes a much lower level, than that reported in the interviews.

Most rural trade union leaders seemed to feel the need to inflate both dues-paying and voting figures when talking with outsiders. The official figures reveal that the Pernambuco rural unions were not above average in raising voluntary dues, despite their above-average record of militancy and strikes. The inflation of figures by officials was partly due to the unions' understandable practice of projecting the strongest possible image to the outside world, in order to further their goals, and to discuss problems and weaknesses only internally and in private. But it may also indicate a certain amount of union sensitivity to the charge, often leveled by members of the general public, that their unions were not as representative and participatory as they might have been.

In addition, only 58 percent of the leaders surveyed said that they had faced opposition in their last union election.[15] Thus, while trade union leaders often preferred democratic competition to authoritarianism in the wider society, they did not always experience it within their own ranks. Within their own organizations, the need for unity in the face of landlord hostility was often valued more highly than democracy. In Mansbridge's

Table 5.1 Comparison Between Official and Survey Data on Union Dues Paying and Voting in the Pernambuco Sugar Zone, 1988

	Dues Payers		Voters in Last Election	
	Survey	Official Data	Survey	Official Data
Cabo	1,000	76	552	570
Ipojuca	3,000	2,684	n.a.	n.a.
Escada	2,800	1,381	758	1,855
Igarassu	3,321	2,240	1,869	1,257
Goiana	1,800	852	1,492	575
Moreno	3,000	n.a.	1,364	1,445
Carpina	1,500	1,012	1,030	697
Barreiros	1,500	1,943	1,760	1,793
Limoeiro	2,100	1,181	2,100	890
Nazaré	3,500	1,833	1,388	1,388
Paudalho	850	841	1,200	814
Ribeirão	2,000	1,017	1,180	1,303

Source: Union Division Archive, Regional Labor Delegation, Ministry of Labor, Recife, 1988.

terms, "adversarial democracy" was not always practiced or valued within the unions.[16]

Union leaders usually sought to build up a loyal base of activists, both to ensure their reelection and to mobilize in campaigns planned by the federation. These active members formed the base of any local union. No matter how committed, energetic, and courageous the local union's leaders were, to a large extent their achievements were determined by the consciousness and courage of the workers they represented. Union leaders sometimes despaired at the difficulties they faced in trying to organize their membership. The cane cutters in the sugar zone were workers for whom bare survival was a struggle.[17] Chronic malnutrition was widespread. For many workers, the brutal conditions of everyday life posed large barriers to union participation.

Even if they have the time and the energy, workers may not act to defend their interests due to risks of loss or a low probability of success (Mericle 1974, 317). For many workers in Pernambuco, resistance to the landlords took the relatively safe form of circumvention rather than overt defiance.[18] The many tricks (*jeitos*) workers devised to fool the foremen (*cabos*) illustrate this point. Asked to weed a cane field, for example, a worker might clear the ground very well where the ground was visible from the road but be much less careful farther into the field where the foreman was less likely to go.

A strong union in the sugar zone was above all a union with an extensive, active, and communicating network of union representatives on the plantations. The *delegados* were the eyes, ears, and legs of the union; in the words of one official, they were the transmission belt between the union and the base, passing along information about any irregularity practiced by the employer. To be effective they needed the cooperation and protection of a *grupo de apoio*, a support group of four or five workers who could prevent the *delegado* from being pressured and threatened by plantation management.

However, getting workers to accept the job of *delegado* was often difficult for union leaders. Workers with less than ten years' experience at the workplace did not have job stability, and could lose their jobs once they became *delegados*.[19] As is explained more fully in the next chapter, landlords also engaged in violence against *delegados* who threatened their prerogatives.

There were thus powerful disincentives to participate actively in the union. But there were carrots as well as sticks. As one union leader put it, "The landowner isolates the *delegado* and offers him benefits so as to '*apelegar*' him (i.e., turn him into a *pelego*). The landowner is like a bat who sucks the blood of the cow, beating its wings so the cow doesn't notice. The cow thinks the fanning is nice; only later does it hurt."[20]

Sometimes the benefits offered included positions as foremen and guards on the plantation, made to the most astute and demanding workers as a way of defusing possible labor conflicts. More often, the potential union activist was intimidated or induced to help the employer rather than the union by refusing the *delegado* job. One union leader said that this was the principal problem faced by the union. The workers "don't want to take the job of *delegado*—they don't want to 'mistreat' the employer, they don't want to be regarded badly." This is because "the worker doesn't have confidence in himself or in the union to defend his rights."[21] Survey results confirmed these findings. The conditions for organizing at the plantation level were very difficult. A vast majority of leaders, 82 percent, said that their most active union members were often fired. A further 74 percent reported that their most active members were denounced to police by employers.

The members' extreme poverty presented another problem to union organizers. Poverty led many workers, for example, to avoid the union altogether and accept the role of an illegal, a worker paid under the table on a casual basis. However, poverty actually facilitated collective action when it came to the annual strike. This was because the daily wage was so small that workers found it a small sacrifice to forgo it and participate in the strike.

For skilled workers, such as those in the São Paulo auto industry in the late 1970s, a strike was a much more serious matter (Humphrey 1982, 160–67). The wages that they had to forgo were relatively high, and if they lost their jobs, the chances of finding one equally well paid were low. For the sugar workers in Pernambuco, such considerations were less important. If the union provided them with a free meal during the days of the strike, as many did, then the loss of the wage was relatively minor. Many could expect to be laid off in the dead season anyway, so job security was less of a consideration. Extreme deprivation led some workers who were sympathetic to the strike to continue working, a predicament understood by striking workers and rarely punished severely.[22] The members' poverty also made short strikes relatively easy to initiate but long strikes unsustainable. During a two-week strike that I observed in October 1988 in Nazaré da Mata, the drop-off in adherence and participation was noticeable during the second week.

The union members' harsh conditions of existence meant that they often saw the union, not as a defender of their rights as workers, but as a provider of drugs, medical services, and other palliatives. The union leaders recognized that medical assistance was the single most important specific reason why people joined the union, and medically related demands formed the second most common type of demand behind salary problems. In my survey I asked union leaders why people joined the union, and 67 percent of them said "to obtain medical and dental services," the largest group after those who chose the vague terms "to defend their rights" (80 percent), and a far higher number than the 41 percent who mentioned agrarian reform. Similarly, while 94 percent of leaders cited work problems (concerning wages, the regulation of piece rates, holiday pay, and so on) as the most frequent demand brought to them by union members, 50 percent mentioned medical or dental assistance and only 30 percent referred to land issues.[23] While some union officials begrudged this reality, they acknowledged it nonetheless. One leader admitted that "the majority [of members join] only for medical assistance" and that only "20 percent of the workers had a consciousness of the mission of the union."[24]

Leaders: The Welfare Function

Leaders were crucial to the revitalization of the rural trade union movement in the Pernambuco sugar zone. The base needed to be organized if it was to accomplish anything, and the leaders were supposed to do that. They had access to the outside world and its resources not enjoyed by ordinary union members. How leaders used those resources was critical in determining whether workers felt isolated and weak or part of a genuine movement that represented their interests.

Trade union leaders in the sugar zone were torn between their two most important roles—that of workplace organizer and representative, and that of social welfare provider. The central dilemma for leadership was how much time and resources to devote to each of these two functions.[25]

The average age of the leaders surveyed in the *mata* was forty-five. With the exception of four who were born in neighboring states, all were born in the sugar zone itself, and twenty-one in the county where they lived at the time of the survey. They had little formal education—an average of three years, and had spent a long time in the union directorate, an average of eighteen years. They thus had few alternative paths of upward social mobility outside the union movement.

These leaders were rural workers who had the talent and good fortune to rise to the comparative privilege of a union position. They no longer had to wake up at dawn like most cane cutters. They were spared the hard, back-breaking physical labor of the fields, and instead worked at desks in comfortable offices. When they wanted to go somewhere, they could take the union car rather than walk as the workers did. They could afford to eat in town in good restaurants frequented by labor court judges and local politicians. They were treated as notables by local people. Their salaries were generally higher than those of rural workers, and their jobs, should they ever have had to return to them, were secure.[26] Furthermore, the leaders, save those who aspired to an office with the state federation or in local politics, were unlikely to rise to a higher position than that of union leader. At the same time, they faced the constant prospect of losing their privileges and returning to the status of field worker at the next union election. Under these conditions, they had strong incentives to cultivate a base of support and use all the means at their disposal to win the next union election.

To do that, union leaders used the benefits they controlled to cultivate a personal following within the union, much as local politicians built up machines on the basis of patronage. Union resources could be given to members as a personal favor of the union president, creating feelings of obligation to and dependence on the president. The desire to secure support within the union often led union presidents to amplify their role as social welfare provider and neglect the duty of protecting the worker rights of the membership as a whole. Land issues usually placed a distant third on the leaders' list of priorities, because land conflicts were so difficult to win and were likely to benefit few people.

For these reasons, there was a gap between the leaders' perceptions of the correct goals of the union and their performance. Most leaders did not consider the provision of social services such as medical and dental care to be the main task of the union. Only 50 percent of those leaders surveyed mentioned the provision of social assistance when responding to the question, "What is the function of the union?" On the other hand, and despite the fact that they spent almost no time on the issue, 90 percent responded to the question with reference to the struggle for land reform. This and the fight to increase workers' salaries (82 percent of respondents) were ranked higher than social assistance as functions of the union.

Social assistance was often seen as a burden and a diversion from the union's true purpose. The majority of union leaders surveyed (54 percent) listed the number one union problem as the duty of providing social assistance to their members. Coming close behind were the problems of landlords' lack of respect for the collective contract (48 percent), lack of money (40 percent), a shortage of land for workers (22 percent), landlord violence against union members and workers in general (22 percent), and a low level of consciousness among the workers (22 percent). It is revealing that, despite the severity of the other problems mentioned, the social welfare programs emerged as the principal union problem in the survey. Nevertheless, all but two sets of leaders in the sugar zone were unwilling to free themselves of the "burden" of providing health services. The reason for this apparent contradiction is that the medical and dental services were a strong drawing card for the leaders, a way of bringing in workers and securing a base of support for themselves within the union.

Unwilling to free themselves of the welfare programs, leaders often saw those programs as taking away from their ability to organize the membership. One union president cited an incident in which the union's only car was going to be used to take the leaders to a meeting on a plantation. But a gravely ill woman came to the headquarters needing a ride to the hospital, and the president felt obliged to take her there and miss the meeting. In the words of another leader, "The union is spending a lot of time and resources to give medical assistance to its members. It can't function like a union" (Field notes 1988).

This social assistance burden was exacerbated by the fact that FUN-RURAL money was often delayed, forcing the union to spend its own resources on the health programs in the short term. One leader called the FUNRURAL program a "white elephant" that ate all the resources of the union. Another felt that the medical program created expectations in the rural community that the union could solve all the people's health and welfare problems. This was an unrealistic expectation, since so many of those problems were caused by low salaries, unemployment, and poor working conditions. The union offered palliatives—medicine, examinations, advice—rather than real solutions. In the words of one frustrated leader: "People seek out the union with their problems—health, work, et cetera. The union doesn't have the ability to solve them. The union deals with all the problems of the rural workers; . . . it can enter the labor court system, but with other problems it is unable to help" (Field notes 1988). Many union leaders pointed out that providing social assistance was the duty of the government. This duty was evaded by the military government and placed on the shoulders of the unions. One trade union leader said, "Social assistance is the duty of the government. It's written in law . . . . Unfortunately, this law is not enforced." Running a government program created a bureaucratic mentality in some union leaders. One said, "We are employees of the government" because the unions provide social assistance. Another said, "Without it [the government] we wouldn't be anything. The government has power. We need it" (Field notes 1988).

The prevalence of such a mentality was indicated in my survey, which revealed that forty of the fifty union leaders who were asked, "What is the function of the union?" responded that it was to help the government, while only eight felt that it was to struggle against the government. The FUNRURAL program did much to foster this sense of duty to and dependence on the government. It fostered a relationship that the leaders could not bring themselves to break. It provided them with tangible benefits to distribute that could bolster their positions, but it also made them dependent on the state.

Some leaders blamed local employers for their overinvolvement in the health problems of the labor force. Clause 39 of the 1987 collective contract in the sugar zone stated that it was the employer's responsibility to transport sick, injured, and pregnant employees to the hospital. Nevertheless, many employers shirked this responsibility, referring the workers to the union. Many workers, for their part, mistrusted the employers and preferred to ask the union for help. The result was a burden for the union.

One union official claimed that the doctor at the local sugar mill deliberately created problems for the union by sending sick and injured workers—whom he could have treated himself—to the union. This official believed that the doctor was trying to undermine the union's organizing efforts by loading it down with sick and needy people. Responding to people's immediate health care needs, it was unable to monitor violations of the collective contract and create the conditions for long-term improvements in the workers' health.

Two unions in the zona da mata eventually felt that the health burden was too great. In the words of the Paudalho union president, "The Paudalho workers decided that it was better to close the medical service than close the union." In 1984 they, along with the nearby union of São Lourenço da Mata, decided to contract out the medical and dental services. Both unions signed an agreement with FUNRURAL that allowed union members to receive services at local hospitals.

The two unions that did this were considered to be two of the most combative unions in the mata. In the path-breaking 1979 strike, it was the São Lourenço and Paudalho unions that actually stopped work, while the other unions threatened to join them if negotiations were not held. Since then, the strike efforts of these two unions have been considered exemplary by the federation. When asked why other unions had not also contracted out of the FUNRURAL program, the president of the Paudalho union suggested, "Perhaps they don't have a base organization that is well developed."[27] The implication of this remark was that if a union were really doing what it should, organizing the members in the workplace, then it would dispense with social welfare services.

A different perspective was given by union leaders outside of São

Lourenço and Paudalho. At the Jaboatão union, the vice-president reported that his members wanted the social services. They felt that services that were contracted out were usually worse than those done within the union. He claimed that many workers had come to him from São Lourenço asking to join the Jaboatão union, saying that the medical and dental services available in São Lourenço were inadaquate.

Leaders: The Workplace Function

Aside from those in São Lourenço and Paudalho, leaders in the sugar zone did not feel free to neglect the social welfare function. If they were unable to provide medical and dental services for their members, they risked alienating the membership and failing to get people to come to union headquarters. Social services were seen as the individual responsibility of each union directorate. They were not only a service offered by the state but an indispensable tool with which the union leadership could cultivate and maintain a loyal following.

The leaders' duties as workplace representatives, on the other hand, allowed them more discretion. Perhaps most important, negotiation of the annual collective contract, the document that determined the pay scale for the cane cutters, was not the responsibility of the individual union. Although the individual union presidents signed the document, negotiations were handled by the president of FETAPE and a small group of federation and confederation officials, lawyers, and economists. Union presidents played only a minor role in these negotiations. They met at FETAPE headquarters and had some input into the formulation of FETAPE positions, but the negotiations themselves were highly centralized, elite affairs. The contract was ratified by votes in the unions, but these votes always endorsed the FETAPE position.

There was thus some distance between the union directorates and the process of determining the collective contract. Some union leaders even seemed to be unfamiliar with the document. While conducting the survey in late November 1988, I encountered several unions that did not yet have copies of the collective contract, signed two months before.[28] This is in stark contrast to the unions in São Paulo's ABC region studied by Humphrey, which in the late 1970s demanded and eventually won the right for each workplace to bargain directly with employers. Thus Ford now negotiated with its workers, Volkswagen with its, and so on. In the Pernambuco sugar zone, the employers' representatives dealt with a federation representing all the 250,000 who cut cane on the 10,000 properties in the zone.

Inevitably, the document could not reflect the conditions of work on all of those properties. Although the collective contract had very detailed pay scales for several different conditions—cutting burnt and unburnt cane, on soft and hard ground, weeding on hills and on flat ground, and so on—these descriptions were open to varied interpretations. The contract was therefore a very rough set of guidelines as to what constituted a legal labor arrangement in the sugar zone. Whether or not the legal clauses linking pay to work performed became actual practice on the plantations was very much up to the local unions.

It is in this regard that union leaders could fall prey to *peleguismo*, the failure to defend workers' interests in order to curry favor with employers, the government, or both. Union leaders in the sugar zone spoke of two kinds of *peleguismo*: *peleguismo accommodado* (accommodated) and *peleguismo comprado* (bought). The first referred to an official too lazy or frightened to visit workers in the fields and learn about their problems. He was instead content to stay at headquarters, dispensing welfare services to those who appeared. The second was a leader who took money from an employer in return for noninterference in the employer's labor relations. This could mean dissuading workers from filing a claim against the employer in the labor court, avoiding visits with the employer's workers, and generally refusing to defend the workers' interests against the employer.

From the workers' point of view, the effects of *peleguismo accommodado* and *peleguismo comprado* were the same. In both cases, they could not count on the leadership to voice their demands to the employer. They were on the plantation alone, reliant only on their own resources. But for other leaders, the second kind of *peleguismo* was worse than the first. The *pelego accommodado* was not a good union leader because of inaction or timidity. With encouragement he could become better. The *pelego comprado*, on the other hand, had betrayed the class to which he belonged. He had joined "the other side," the side of the landowner, and his redemption would be difficult.

The accusation of *peleguismo* was bandied about in the sugar zone. Union leaders called other leaders *pelegos*. But proof of payoffs and deliberate avoidance of duties is, not surprisingly, hard to come by. Each union directorate had a band of loyalists who were prepared to say that the leaders were working hard for the good of all. When union elections produced new leaders, which they occasionally did, the old guard was often condemned by the new directorate as *pelegos*. *Peleguismo* was thus a reproach and a suspicion, but it was never an established fact in the sugar zone. Like beauty, it was in the eye of the beholder.

One large incentive for inactivity when it came to workplace problems was due to the structure of union finances. Most union financing came from the dues automatically checked off by the Ministry of Labor and employers. Very little was gathered through voluntary union dues. Therefore, leaders tended to become complacent about their memberships. They did not have to work hard to gain their financial support. There was also little supervision of the use of union funds by the Ministry of Labor, even though required by law. Some leaders were able to buy cars and homes illegally with union money.

In the area of finances, there was the additional problem of unions that did not send FETAPE its 50 percent share of the *taxa assistencial*. This was usually done by remote unions whose leaders had no hopes or ambitions of becoming FETAPE officials. They saw no benefit in or reason for sending the money to the federation. One union president, for example, complained that FETAPE officials only came to his area briefly during the strike. They visited a few plantations, incited the workers to strike, and then left him to face the threats of the landowner and the apathy of the workers. He said that he would prefer that his union organized the strike campaign on its own.

Another disincentive came from the structure of bargaining in the sugar zone. Because the contract was statewide, leaders' incentive to organize an effective strike in their local areas was not as high as it would have been if local contracts had been the norm. Workers in Itambé, most of whom continued to work during the 1988 strike, were governed by the same new pay scale as those in São Lourenço, where adherence to the strike was high. Other than prestige and a desire to rise to the level of a federation official, therefore, there was little motivation for local leaders to perform well during the strike. The wage increase won was the same across the board, where the strike was massive and where no one participated.[29]

This weak strike performance—and the lack of penalties for union leaders with such performance—was revealed in the survey when respondents were asked about the level of participation in the last strike. While most officials were anxious to stress the high rate of strike adherence (in many cases exaggerating the figures), four leaders said that it had only been 15 to 35 percent, two said that "almost no one" had stopped work, and three said simply that the strike had been "weak."

Salaries, while low, were legally required to be paid to the workers, and making sure that they were was a key function of the union. Ninety percent of the union leaders surveyed stated that at least part of the collective contract was not being respected by local employers; of these, 24 percent said that not even the pay scale (the most basic part of the collective contract) was being enforced. As one leader put it, "There is a war between the *patrão* and the union . . . if the [collective contract] were respected, it would be different, we would all live in peace" (Field notes 1988). And yet 40 percent of the leaders reported that they did not have frequent contact with employers or their representatives about these violations of a legally binding agreement.

For half of this 40 percent, the lack of frequent contact was due to the employers' refusal to deal with the union. This can only be described as union powerlessness in the face of employer intransigence. Furthermore, the lack of frequent contact, in the leaders' eyes, was not due to the fact that workers did not have problems on the plantations or that, if there were problems, these could be solved without their intervention. They *did* recognize the need for union intervention in defense of the workers. As one leader put it, the workers needed the union to give them courage to stick up for their rights. But there was a disjunction between what the union leaders felt they *should* do and what they actually did.

Despite the extreme seriousness of violations of the contract on the plantations, only seven of fifty leaders said that they spent more than half their time away from union headquarters. At headquarters, leaders were likely to spend a lot of time dealing with individual complaints—medical problems, workers who wanted to file claims against employers, and so on. The plantation, however, was where they could contact large numbers of workers and see that the contract was being enforced. This was simply not a priority for many leaders. Such oversight was tiring and could be dangerous, because landlords were wont to threaten or confront leaders who spent too much time "indoctrinating" "their" workers. (In theory, union officials were supposed to have unfettered access to the plantations to talk to their members. In practice, many plantations turned union leaders away at gunpoint, forcing the leaders to ask Ministry of Labor officials to accompany them.) Leaders might also blame the workers themselves for a low level of consciousness and/or timidity, feeling that it was not their responsibility to speak up for them. If they were deliberately underpaid and they said nothing, what could a union leader do?[30]

Such an attitude was evinced by a union president making the rounds in the northern sugar zone. On one plantation, he encountered a group of workers cutting 300 *cubos* of cane for one daily wage, when the collective contract stated that the maximum to be cut for a daily wage was 125 *cubos*.[31] (A *cubo* is a unit of measurement of about six feet by six feet.) There were three young boys in the group who looked as if they were only nine or ten—that is, below the legal minimum work age of fourteen. Although these workers complained to the president, his response was that they should all, or at least two or three of them, come to the union meeting on Sunday. He said that he couldn't do much unless they united and complained together. (There was no *delegado* on the plantation.) This is an example of a union leader unwilling to take up the case of workers in direct negotiations with the employer. Instead he left the workers to resolve the problem themselves, or hinted that he could provide some help only if they participated in a union function.

Unlike the ABC metalworkers' movement described by John Humphrey, the Pernambuco sugar unions did not generate a reform movement during the liberalization period. This is partly because rural unions had a fundamentally different relationship to the military regime from that of urban unions. Although repressed at the time of the coup, rural unions expanded and received new benefits under authoritarian rule. For their part, urban unions saw their previous freedoms denied without any new addition of benefits. Therefore, in the ABC region of São Paulo, a new unionism sprang up that challenged old *pelego* leaders, brought new grassroots leaders to the fore, and urged the abolition of the old corporatist controls on the unions.

The majority of sugar union leaders (54 percent) felt that Brazilian labor law should be "profoundly reformed" (although a surprisingly large number—42 percent—felt that it did not need to be changed or needed to be changed only slightly). However, when presented with a concrete example of reform, they were almost universally opposed to it.

The proposal to introduce union pluralism grew out of São Paulo's new unionism. Some activists felt that the old monopolistic system allowed many unions to be dominated by *pelegos*. They felt that giving workers the option of starting a new union in the same area as an old one would increase the leadership's responsiveness to the base. This stance was based in part on clause 87 of the International Labor Organization's 1948 declaration of workers' rights. One interpretation of clause 87 is that the state monopoly system enshrined in Brazilian labor law violated the workers' right to choose the form of their representation. A close reading of clause 87 indicates that having one union per category does not in itself violate this right, but does if it is imposed by the state rather than springing from the workers' free choice.[32]

The vast majority of union leaders in the *mata*—92 percent—disagreed with the pluralist interpretation of clause 87. They believed that the proposal for union pluralism was "divisive," something that would weaken the movement. In the polarized sugar zone, they felt that such a system would be used to create unions that landlords could control. The proposal also directly threatened their positions as union leaders by allowing organizational challenges to their leadership. It is thus understandable that they opposed the measure. But it gives an insight into one of the bases of their power—corporatist labor legislation.

Another factor that diminished leaders' workplace activity in the sugar zone was the nature of authority relations in the unions. Some union directorates were collegial, with all officials taking decisions together. However, a common pattern was for the president to regard his power as a personal prerogative, and to treat his co-directors as subordinates. One union president, for example, declared at a union meeting that he was the driver of the car—the union—but he needed all the pieces that make the car run in order to do his job properly. The metaphor was revealing. The rest of the directorate, the union members, and functionaries were compared to inanimate objects, while only the president was given human status. Such conceptions of authority were not universal, but where they did exist, internal union hierarchies tended to be more sharply drawn.

Leadership Dilemmas

The leaders' social welfare and workplace functions differed markedly. The welfare function enabled the leader to provide services that members wanted and asked for: medical and dental treatment, transportation, recreational and social events, legal help in individual claims against employers. It enabled the leader to be seen to respond to the immediate "felt needs" of his constituents, and build personal, clientelistic ties of obligation and dependence between leaders and members.

The welfare function, with the possible exception of legal services, was also by and large "safe" for the union leader. It fell within the legally defined duties of the union. It usually did not challenge the landlord. Indeed, it often indirectly helped the landlord, by performing services that otherwise might have been expected of him—that might even have been his legal obligation.[33]

The workplace function, on the other hand, challenged the leader to raise the consciousness of his members, to encourage them to resist employer exploitation, and to make demands that they otherwise would not. It was an effort to reshape members' preferences, to turn them away from palliatives toward long-term, collective goals: building workplace solidarity, a political platform, an awareness of workers' rights.

This was a more dangerous course for leaders. It was likely to meet the resistance of landowners who felt that their power and prerogatives were threatened. Leaders also ran the risk of getting too far ahead of their members, expecting them to engage in collective action that they were not ready to undertake. This function could not be provided, as an alternative, by the landlord; instead, it was a challenge to him.

Summary

Changes in class structure and institutional resources transformed union interests and capacities during the military regime. The opening up of that regime during the democratic transition gave the unions an opportunity to engage once again in public political activity in 1979. How union leaders channeled their power in subsequent years is a complex topic. A functional approach to Brazilian trade unions—focusing almost exclusively on the presumed inherent qualities of the labor relations system— obscures wide regional, sectoral, and temporal differences in the behavior of actual unions. Certain features of the Brazilian labor system such as the obligatory union tax, the union monopoly of representation, the practice of statewide negotiation, and the use of labor courts rather than workplace collective bargaining do seem to have encouraged leadership passivity at the local level, but the activity and leadership style of local union leaders varied enormously.

Sources of variation among the leadership included the size of the union, its proximity to Recife, the number of employers it faced, and the number of its members with access to land. On the other hand, all the unions shared a common tendency to focus primarily on wage and welfare rather than land issues, even when agrarian reform was the official goal of the national rural labor movement. This was due to certain institutional features of the local union structure, such as the power of the federation over the local union and the latter's emphasis on wages, the need for union leaders to win periodic elections, and the small number of members likely to benefit from land redistribution as opposed to wage increases. Past experience also influenced behavior. The mobilization for land of the early 1960s had been violently repressed by landlords, and most leaders had lived through this period. Landlords still wielded substantial coercive power, and union officials therefore strove to avoid further repression by making "reasonable," incremental demands in positive-sum conflicts over wages rather than provoking zero-sum standoffs over land.

In this setting, in which the concentrated power of the landed oligarchy could only be effectively challenged by an equally concentrated power on the part of labor, it is understandable that the Pernambuco sugar zone did not evolve toward decentralized collective bargaining, as did parts of industrial São Paulo. The state union federation maintained control over wage negotiations and the state labor courts remained central to the resolution of labor conflict. The union leaders in the *zona da mata* thus were generally unsympathetic to many of the demands of the new unionism, opposing such reforms as the abolition of the mandatory tax and the union monopoly, because they felt that these demands reflected a very different environment from the one they knew.

The ability of union leaders to negotiate on behalf of their members, to organize workers in collective action, and to ensure the enforcement of contractual benefits all depended in good measure on this external environment, and not just the internal characteristics of the union system. One aspect of the external environment—landowners' use of violence against the union movement—is therefore the topic of the following chapter.

∼ 6 ∼

Sugar with the Taste of Blood
Landlord Violence

A t the end of 1988, the president of the rural workers' union of Xapuri, in Acre state, was gunned down outside his home. The death of Chico Mendes became a cause célèbre, because Mendes had fought for the defense of the Amazon rain forest as well as the interests of his members, rubber tappers whose livelihoods were squeezed by the advance of cattle ranchers and their deforestation of large tracts of land. Because of the international attention that the Mendes case generated, something extremely unusual in the Brazilian countryside occurred: the murder of a rural labor leader was investigated, and two men were charged with, tried for, and convicted of the crime.[1]

The Mendes case is the exception that proves the rule about rural violence in Brazil. In cases that do not garner international attention, murders of rural union leaders and members are rarely investigated or punished. One study listed 1,730 killings of peasants, trade union leaders, lawyers, priests, and religious people in the countryside between 1964 and 1992. Just thirty of these cases resulted in a trial and in only eighteen of them was there a conviction (Sutton 1994, 24).

Landlord violence is a major problem facing rural trade unionists in contemporary Brazil. The question of violence is linked to the failure of state institutions to protect rural workers and enforce the law in the countryside. Despite the fact that it is heavily involved in the organization of large-scale agricultural production, the Brazilian state has a weak presence in the countryside. The first section of this chapter looks at the state's weak enforcement of labor law, while the second examines rural labor leaders' alienation from the state, engendered in part by this weak enforcement. The third section examines the nature of rural violence, while the fourth compares the structure of landholding in Pernambuco and São Paulo, suggesting that the prevalence of small landowners with narrow profit margins in the former exacerbated the problem of violence there. Rural violence was thus more severe in Pernambuco and the rest of the northeast partly because of the lower degree of agricultural modernization and the consequent weight of small, labor-intensive plantations in that region.

Labor Law

Labor law has never been consistently respected in the Brazilian countryside. Although Brazil's first labor law concerned rural workers, it was not enforced.[2] Later, the consolidated labor laws (1943) were not effectively applied to rural workers. This is partly because most rural laborers at that time were not full proletarians but had some kind of dependent relationship with a landowner, exchanging labor or part of a crop, for example, for land use rights. In addition, rural labor was not well enough organized to demand the legal protection of its rights; vertical patron-client ties were stronger than horizontal class ties. Even in 1963 with the passage of the Rural Workers Statute, enforcement of labor law was patchy and exceptional. Finally, large landlords were part of dominant political coalitions throughout Brazil, strong enough to suppress efforts by state bureaucrats to enforce labor law.

In the 1980s, the most significant violation of labor legislation concerned the illegal hiring of seasonal employees, called *bóias-frias* (literally, cold lunches) in the south, and *clandestinos* in the northeast and north. In my survey of fifty trade union leaders in the Pernambuco sugar zone, forty-four said that illegal workers were "a problem for the union," principally because they did not contribute financially to the union. Despite the fact that illegality was seen as a problem, only ten of the union leaders surveyed said, in a subsequent open-ended question, that they had contacted the local Ministry of Labor office or another government office about it. Two of these said that the Labor Ministry had been effective in reducing illegal hiring, while two said that ministry officials had repeatedly failed to appear as promised in their area. What these responses show is the low expectation on the part of union leaders that the state would enforce labor law, an expectation reinforced by poor state performance in monitoring reported violations. The majority of leaders surveyed, thirty-three of fifty, said that they were trying to solve the illegality problem solely with their own organizing efforts: talking with workers, making agreements with local owners, coordinating with nearby unions, and so on.

Another violation of labor law in the sugar zone was the employment of minors under the legal age of fourteen, a practice widespread during strikes. The accident rate for these young employees was higher than that for older, more experienced cane cutters, the most common accident being a self-inflicted cut on the hand or leg with a *foice* (FUNDACENTRO 1987, 1). The application of pesticides was another area where frequent violations of labor law occurred—workers were not supplied with the required protective clothing and were consequently exposed to chemical poisons.

In the Pernambuco sugar zone, unions struggled most for the enforcement, not of labor law in general, but of the statewide collective contract. The contract detailed the piece rates at which cane cutters should be paid. It also contained numerous provisions relating to working conditions (in 1988 the contract had fifty-four separate clauses). Forty-seven of the leaders interviewed cited violations of the collective contract as one of the most common complaints that their members brought to the union (especially in the area of piece rates). Furthermore, in an open-ended question about the union's principal problems, twenty-four of the fifty respondents cited the owners' lack of respect for the collective contract. Similarly, only three of the officials said that all the provisions of the collective contract were being enforced at the time of the interview.

Another problem for the union officials was the slowness of the labor courts, where disputes between employers and employees over such matters as severance pay were adjudicated. Many leaders said that the courts were too slow, taking up to five to six years to resolve a case. Others questioned the impartiality of the labor court judges, saying that they were in the same social class and often had frequent social contacts with landlords. This was implied by one leader when he said of the judges, "The river always runs to the sea."

While forty-one of the respondents felt that Brazilian labor law should be changed (the majority of these saying that it operated against workers), it seems that the simple enforcement of existing labor law would have created a revolution in social relations in the sugar zone.

Alienation from the State

The fact that the state was weak in rural areas had consequences for the attitudes and behavior of rural trade union leaders. Put simply, it engendered a sense of alienation toward the state and a belief that positive social changes would come about only through the efforts of rural workers themselves. While benefits from the state would naturally be

welcome, they were not always expected, and the request by state officials for commitment to any particular state program was viewed with suspicion. Because the state was marginal to many aspects of the day-to-day
struggle of the union leaders, the democratic transition at the national
level—involving as it did the modification of institutional arrangements
and personnel of the state, such as occurred in 1985—was seen as less
important than it might otherwise have been.

This view stems from the nature of work relations in the sugar zone.
The cane workers were originally bound to plantation owners in a kind of
quasi-feudal system of paternalistic relations, bonds of peonage that went
far beyond the sphere of work and extended to family relations (*com-
padrice*, or godfatherism), and ceremonies of birth, death, and harvest.
While most workers became full proletarians in the 1960s, a capitalist
mentality toward work—contractual, monetary, short-term, impersonal—
had not fully permeated the region even in the 1980s, not least because a
significant portion of the work force still lived on the plantation under
the landlords' supervision.

The landlords' abandonment of traditional obligations created a sense
of injustice amongst those abandoned. The landlords, most of whom now
lived in the city by the 1980s, saw the de-peasantization of the labor force
as inevitable, necessary, and progressive. For them, it was part of the capitalist modernization of the plantation, a process from which they had
benefited. Workers, on the other hand, saw their expulsion from the plantations as neither necessary nor progressive. They were not consulted in
the decision to change the relations of production; they experienced the
decision as something done to, not for, them. Their nostalgia for a golden
age when they were on the plantation, growing their own food within a
small, pastoral, and essentially nonmonetary community, contrasted
sharply with their frequent criticism of life in the towns, with its stress,
confusion, and demands for cash. Although some among the younger generation preferred the town, a surprising number shared their elders' belief
that times had been better on the land.[3]

Because the workers felt a sense of loss due to the destruction of
patron-client ties, their image of the landlord was ambiguous. The landlord was criticized as a wealthy man who, despite his wealth, was willing
to trample on any worker's right in pursuit of his own gain, a "fox among
the chickens" whom only a guard dog (the union) could restrain.[4] But this
criticism was based on an image of an ideal landlord who personally protected and rewarded his workers. Such an image was implied in comments
about the landlord such as, "His heart is in his wallet," "He doesn't treat
the worker with compassion," and "He chews up the worker and throws

away his skin as he would an orange." What the landlord could and should be, the concept of the ideal employer, was held up as a rebuke to the real landlord for his perceived harshness and insensitivity.

This dualistic image of the landlord was analogous to the workers' image of the state.[5] The union leaders surveyed made frequent comments that the state should help them, reflecting an assumption that it was a neutral agency capable of acting on their behalf. This contradicted a radical skepticism also frequently expressed, that it only protected "sharks" (capitalists, landlords), exploited the poor, was led by corrupt and dishonest politicians, and would not help them. This latter view led many leaders to declare that the situation would change only if workers did something for themselves. It also manifested itself in an "us vs. them" mentality, and a belief that the state would become benevolent only when some of "us" (rural workers) were elected to office. In the 1988 municipal elections in Pernambuco the rural movement acted upon this belief when a record number of union officials ran for local political offices.[6]

It is significant that many union songs sung in the *zona da mata* in the 1980s criticized the landowner, but none made mention of the state. The police, for example, did not appear as characters in these songs. The song lyrics sought consolation from the landlord's exploitation not in state intervention, but in a mystical nullification of worldly inequalities through death and God's judgment. This is a traditional consolation of the weak. The lyrics, as in the song "Our Rights Will Come," looked forward to the time when death obliterated the inequality between landlord and worker. The song lyrics ended with an appeal not to any earthly power, but to God. They appealed to Him to look at the universe he had made, "full of perverse hearts which deny human rights."[7] The song showed the perceived lack of salience of the state in the lives of rural workers.

Trade union officials' criticism of the state and the social order over which it presided could be sweeping. One secretary, for example, said, "In this country, justice is money."[8] In this view, the legitimate rights of the poor were denied and the rich and powerful were able to act on every whim, no matter how unlawful or immoral, with impunity. Such a social order was upside down, radically unjust, because "he who has a right does not have a right, and he who does not have a right has a right," as one worker said.[9] Such a vision approaches the millenarian's picture of the world before the second coming of Christ, a world of unconstrained evil in which the weak are set upon by the powerful and the depraved, sustained only by a faith that the social order will eventually be turned right side up and "the meek shall inherit the earth." Although potentially a basis for political action, this attitude can easily become a justification for a resigned, otherworldly passivity in the face of oppression. It was not surprising, therefore, that evangelical Protestantism has found many converts amongst the rural poor in Brazil. In Pernambuco, the Protestant population (traditional and Pentecostal) quadrupled between 1950 and 1980.[10]

Rural unionists' anger toward the state, like their anger toward the landlord, stemmed from the state's perceived inability to consider and protect workers' interest, and it took a personal form. In expressing disgust for President Sarney (1985–1990), unionists implied that because he was a large landowner, he would be unlikely to sympathize with the rural poor. Theirs was not a liberal conception of the state, in which the latter's role was merely to enforce certain rules of the game—although, as has been argued, they decried the fact that rules were unenforced. Similarly, their view of citizenship went beyond that implied by a representative model of democracy, in which their right as citizens was essentially that of choosing between competing elites.[11] Instead, they saw the necessity of state officials listening to their demands, then intervening on their behalf, granting them material benefits. The unionists experienced alienation because this so rarely happened. The survey results reflect these attitudes. Of thirty-four respondents who were asked, "Is it important to consider the consequences for the government when making demands?" sixteen said no and four more said "only the state government." In the words of one respondent, "For us the struggle is to think of our members, and not the government." Similarly, when asked what recent political changes had given them the most hope, six of thirty-nine said "nothing," and ten described something to do with increased union organization. Of the latter group, typical responses were "The force of the union itself is our hope"; "Who betters the situation of the worker is the worker and the union"; and "We don't work with the union waiting for party political benefits."

When asked about what their union was doing to fulfill its duties, most officials responded by mentioning activities related to the union's own internal organization, such as holding meetings (56 percent), strengthening the system of union delegates on plantations (36 percent), ensuring the enforcement of the collective contract (36 percent), providing legal help (24 percent), and orienting workers about rights (18 percent). These activities were more frequently mentioned than activities that required officials to make demands on the state: raise salaries (18 percent), fight for agrarian reform (6 percent), and denounce violence against workers (2 percent).[12]

Furthermore, 77 percent of the respondents said no when asked, "Was the political change marked by the inauguration of President Sarney important and positive for the unions here?" This was significant, because Sarney's inauguration in 1985 was seen by most political observers as the formal end of the military regime that came to power in the 1964 coup. Similarly, 96 percent of the trade union leaders surveyed in 1988 did not believe that the Sarney government had the will to carry out a land reform, despite the announcement of official government plans for large-scale land redistribution in 1985.

The responses of those surveyed revealed ambivalence about the democratic transition. Asked if the situation of their union had improved after direct elections for governor were reintroduced in 1982 (after seventeen years of military-appointed governors), an equal number (46 percent) said no and yes. Similarly, when asked, "How do you see the military regime in comparison to the current civilian regime?" 41 percent of the labor leaders saw no difference between military and civilian rule at the federal level, while only 54 percent did.[13] Such findings suggest that union leaders reacted to political subordination by turning inward, judging political change on the basis of local conditions rather than in terms of national politics. Asked about what political change had given them most hope in the years prior to 1988, only four of thirty-nine respondents mentioned the indirect election of Tancredo Neves in 1985 (a landmark in Brazil's official history—the first election of a civilian president since 1960). Of far greater importance to them were the union's own activities (fifteen of thirty-nine).

It is plausible that the Brazilian state's failure to extend democratic rights to the rural poor was related to these attitudes. In the areas of labor law and rural violence, the state was conspicuous by its absence, inaction, or favoritism toward large landlords. Partly as a consequence, rural union leaders had a bifurcated view of the state in which the reality of repression and neglect prevailed over hopes deriving from an ideal state. This view resulted in a defensive political strategy. The leaders mobilized members to defend themselves against possible losses, as they had done in the strikes at the peak of each year's cane harvest. But they were far less likely to mobilize in response to possible gains.[14]

The Problem of Violence

Despite the fact that the annual wage negotiations in the sugar zone were highly routinized after the 1979 strike, labor-capital relations in general were highly conflictual and often violent. Of the union leaders surveyed in Pernambuco's sugar zone, 76 percent (thirty-eight out of fifty) said there was some type of violence against rural workers in their area.

In addition, thirty-two of the thirty-eight said that owners did not respect the collective contract, and responded with violence when workers pressed for their rights. This violence is best explained by combining structural and institutional analysis, in much the same way that the emergence and character of the rural labor movement in the 1980s was explained in chapters 3 and 4.

Violence against rural workers and peasants escalated in Brazil as the democratic transition proceeded in the 1980s. A number of reports have documented this violence, which was typically carried out by landlords' hired gunmen against workers with whom the landlord had a labor or land dispute (Amnesty International 1988; U.S. Department of State 1988). Most killings arose from land disputes. The state of Pará, which has a frontier in the Amazon jungle, reported the highest number of murders of rural workers and peasants (U.S. Department of State 1994, 5). Amnesty International in 1988 stated that despite "notorious, widespread and persistent" killings, "the Brazilian Government has failed at every level to take effective measures to stop them." The human rights group was concerned about "allegations that full and impartial investigations by the competent authorities into such killings are not being carried out" and that, consequently, "those responsible for killings, threats, and other brutal acts of intimidation against the rural poor enjoy de facto immunity from prosecution, which encourages further killings and violence" (U.S. Department of State 1988, 471).

Responsibility for this state of affairs rested with the three main law enforcement agencies in Brazil: the civil, military, and federal police. The response of the civil police (responsible for investigations of crimes) to killings of rural workers, many of them commissioned by members of politically powerful local elites, was often to do nothing. However, the federal government did not send federal police to intervene; officials explained that this was against the constitution and that "the restoration of democracy could best be achieved by trying to strengthen local institutions" (Amnesty International 1988, 67). The police were also themselves responsible for many killings. In the state of Alagoas, in the northeast, police were suspected in 80 percent of the 600 murders that occurred in 1992 (U.S. Department of State 1993, 5).

The judiciary also failed to restrain the escalation of violence. It was dependent, both financially and administratively, on the state government, and judges were susceptible to political pressure. A common explanation for the failure of judicial authorities to investigate assassinations of rural workers was lack of resources and staff (Amnesty International 1988, 10).

Whereas violence in the populist period of the early 1960s in Pernambuco's sugar zone had erupted over both land and labor issues, in the 1980s labor issues predominated almost exclusively. Of twenty-four murders of rural workers between the years 1985 and 1991 for which I could obtain information, only two involved disputes over land, whereas six involved disputes over wages, four involved other types of conflicts between rural workers and employers, and nine involved union activities (three cases were for reasons unknown). Of thirteen beatings or woundings between 1987 and 1989, four involved the expulsion of resident workers from plantations, but the other nine involved confrontations during strikes (five) or employer-employee conflicts unrelated to residence (four). Of thirteen threats in 1987–1988, nine concerned conflicts in strikes and four concerned wage disputes. Rural violence in the Pernambuco sugar zone thus reflected the predominance of the wage relation and the relative absence of peasant conflicts over land, which characterize much rural violence elsewhere in Brazil.[15]

An example of the endemic violence in the Pernambuco sugar zone occurred on 2 September 1985. On that day, the president of the rural workers' union in Aliança was shotgunned to death in his own home. The chief suspect in the killing was José Bento de Santana, the former union president, believed to be acting in concert with local landowners. José Evanduir Pereira da Silva was a vigorous twenty-nine-year-old who had assumed the presidency of his union only four months before. In union elections in May, the workers had finally shaken off the fifteen-year grip of president José Bento de Santana; Santana had been dubbed by local unionists a *pelego*.

Pereira da Silva embodied the members' hopes for a more aggressive defense of their interests and for the democratization of local society. He had declared that he and his *companheiros* would organize strongly for the upcoming strike in the cane fields, scheduled for the end of the month. But the union leader never lived to lead the strike in Aliança. Instead, the traditional pattern of violence in the sugar zone, which benefits those who own the land, emerged to claim another victim and to crush hopes for change. In losing Pereira da Silva, the rural workers had lost a leader and a chance to attain the promises offered by the political elite at the end of military rule. On 3 September, 5,000 of them said goodbye at his funeral (*Jornal de Comércio*, 4 September 1985; *Diário de Pernambuco*, 4–6 September 1985; Movimento dos Trabalhadores Rurais Sem Terra 1987, 422–23; Field notes 1988).

This kind of violence generated a climate of fear in the sugar zone. Despite the fact that the collective contract prohibited plantation foremen and supervisors from carrying arms without special authorization (clause 5 in the 1988 contract), cane cutters were accustomed to working under the eyes of armed foremen who, in the words of one of them, considered walking unarmed to be "a sentence of death" (*Jornal do Brasil*, 9 September 1984). In such a setting, workers who demanded rights or participated in union activities risked being threatened, harassed, beaten, and ultimately killed.

To an open-ended question about rural violence, fifteen of fifty officials mentioned that a worker or workers in their area had been killed in recent years in conflicts with landlords. At one union, the president said that his predecessor had been gunned down in 1985, while another union's lawyer had been murdered in 1982 and their current lawyer was being threatened. Almost everyone in the sugar zone unions was aware of such incidents.

Forty-eight percent of the trade union leaders surveyed said that they knew a member of their union who had lost his job for union activity, while the same percentage knew a member who had been jailed for the same reason. The potential costs of union activity, therefore, were constantly presented to workers, dampening the zeal of all but the stout-hearted. As one leader said, "I don't want to end up on the side of the road with flies in my mouth." For others, the violence provoked a greater determination to resist. "If they kill one of us," said a young union secretary, "we only get stronger" (Field notes 1988).

The state was seen by the rural poor as weak, because it could not protect against violence. Just as weak state enforcement affected union strategy in the area of labor law, it also affected union action on violence. Having little faith in the state's ability to address their concerns, union leaders spent relatively little energy in exerting direct pressure upon it. The following case illustrates this point.

Several days before a labor court hearing against his former employer, on 4 April 1988, rural worker José Batista da Silva was abducted from a Recife market by civil policemen. The officers, who had an arrest warrant, said that they were taking the worker to his former employer for questioning. Batista was not seen again. Hearing about the case, leaders of Batista's rural union in Cabo decided to take action.

Significantly, the action was not a legal one. Instead, the union decided to use public space to bring attention to its plight. It planned a march to protest what it considered to be another act of violence on the part of landowners, this time in conjunction with the police. The march was scheduled to end in front of the police station in Cabo.

However, in a meeting with the trade unionists, the state secretary of public security indicated that if the march passed in front of the police station, he would not be responsible for anything that happened.[16] The workers thus decided to change their route. On 15 May, supported by various organizations, the march took place, avoiding the heavily guarded police station.

The Cabo case reveals the union leaders' lack of faith in the legal system and the state. Although the abduction of their colleague was blatantly illegal, the union's main response was to try to convince the public of the rightness of its position, rather than seek official redress. While the state governor appointed a special delegate to investigate the kidnapping, this was done at the request of the employer and his association, the Pernambuco Union of Cane Planters (Sindicato dos Cultivadores de Cana de Pernambuco). In addition, after union officials denounced the landlord as responsible for the kidnapping, they, along with the worker's wife and brother, were sued for calumny and defamation by the landlord.[17]

Violence against rural workers and peasants increased considerably as political liberalization continued in the 1980s. According to one set of figures, 58 workers and peasants were killed in the country in 1982, 96 in 1983, and 123 in 1984. However, in 1985, the year that a civilian regime ostensibly committed to land redistribution was installed, the number of killings soared to 222 and remained at over 200 for the next two years. For the period 1982–1987 as a whole, the total exceeded 899, of which 36 occurred in Pernambuco.[18]

This upsurge in violence occurred because the transition to democracy, and the proposed agrarian reform plan that accompanied it, created a climate in which it seemed that the demands of the landless might be met. Landlords, facing direct action on the part of workers and peasants, feared the loss of their property and privileges. Employing private gunmen and retaining their traditional influence over the local police, they answered the workers with violent confrontation.

This account is at variance with others. Some argue that the increase in rural violence occurred at this time because with the transition landlords lost control over the police and the legal structure. Unable to use the police for repression, the landlords turned to private gunmen, who were more violent in their methods (CEPIS 1985, 6). This argument might be true in some areas, but is a misleading general explanation. In my research in Pernambuco, some trade unionists said that the police in their area had become more neutral after the election of Miguel Arraes in 1986. But many said that the behavior of the police did not change, and police violence against workers still occurred.

Another argument is that the increase in rural violence preceded the agrarian reform plan, which was intended to diminish the number of killings. While it is true that rural violence had been increasing before the official announcement of the reform in 1985, government consideration of reform had been going on for years before this date. Furthermore, there is no evidence that supporters of the plan, either in government or civil society, saw its chief merit as its ability to stem the tide of violence.

Whatever the reason, the death toll from landlord violence increased under the civilian regime. Violence was a major impediment to the practical extension of democratic rights formally won by the trade union movement. This violence was much more severe in the north and northeast of the country than in the south. It is important to understand the basis of this regional difference.

Landholding and Violence

The severity of the problem of rural violence in Pernambuco is linked to the way in which agricultural modernization affected the structure of landholding. Northeastern cane planters had considerable influence within the IAA, whose regulations prohibited northeastern mill owners from growing all the sugarcane they needed on their own land.[19] The vertical integration of sugar production, a natural outcome of the modernization process, was thus checked in the northeast. (In Pernambuco, mill owners grew about half the cane in the state; the rest was produced by planters.)

Consequently, the gains from the huge expansion of sugar production in Pernambuco, though going chiefly to the large mills, also accrued to numerous small and medium-sized landowners. As noted in chapter 3, the structure of landholding, rather than becoming more concentrated, became more diffuse between 1960 and 1985 (see tables 6.1 and 6.2). While more egalitarian at the level of landownership, this development had antidemocratic consequences in the area of labor relations. Small and medium-sized planters, for whom labor costs were a high proportion of total costs, had a large role in production. They frequently responded to union demands for higher wages with violence. They constituted a class of landlords engaged in labor-intensive production who felt threatened by workers' assertion of their rights to change jobs, associate, organize, strike, and engage in political activity.

The peculiarity of Pernambuco's landholding structure is revealed when compared to that of São Paulo (see table 6.3). Unlike their northeastern counterparts, São Paulo producers were not hampered by IAA regulations limiting their expansion. Large plantations of over 1,000 hectares

Table 6.1 Distribution of Landholding in the Pernambuco Sugar Zone, 1960

Area in Hectares	No. of Properties	% of Total	Area	% of Total
Less than 10	20,993	83.1	54,031	5.4
10–less than 100	2,378	9.4	61,729	6.1
100–less than 1,000	1,736	6.9	666,357	66.0
Over 1,000	152	0.6	227,427	22.5
Undeclared	1	0.0	—	—
Total	25,260	100.0	1,009,544	100.0

Source: IBGE, 1960.

Table 6.2 Distribution of Landholding in the Pernambuco Sugar Zone, 1985

Area in Hectares	No. of Properties	% of Total	Area	% of Total
Less than 10	20,660	74.8	46,359	5.5
10–less than 100	5,386	19.5	128,523	15.2
100–less than 1,000	1,494	5.4	530,756	63.0
Over 1,000	83	0.3	137,534	16.3
Total	27,623	100.0	843,172	100.0

Source: IBGE, 1985.

produced almost half the sugarcane in the state, in a landholding system that was far more top-heavy than Pernambuco's. The vertical integration of production went much farther, and small cane planters supplying the mills became a marginal factor in most parts of the state.

A detailed look at data from one region in São Paulo provides a rough and revealing comparison with Pernambuco. In Capivarí, a sugar-producing region of São Paulo, the share of properties under 50 hectares in landholding declined from 27 percent to 13 percent between 1960 and 1980 (Maybury-Lewis 1994, 82). The share of properties under 100 hectares in landholding in the Pernambuco sugar zone, on the other hand, increased from 11.5 percent to 20.7 percent between 1960 and 1985, as is shown in tables 6.1 and 6.2. At the other end of the social pyramid, in Capivarí, the share of land held by properties of over 500 hectares increased from 33 to 49 percent between 1960 and 1980 (ibid., 82), whereas in the Pernambuco sugar zone the share of land held by properties over 1,000 hectares dropped from 22.5 percent to 16.3 percent between 1960 and 1985.

Table 6.3 Distribution of Landholding in the São Paulo Sugar Sector, 1985

Area in Hectares	No. of Properties	% of Total	Area	% of Total
Less than 10	1,899	12.1	5,874	0.4
10–less than 100	8,492	54.1	190,380	11.2
100–less than 1,000	4,666	29.7	771,593	45.5
Over 1,000	632	4.0	727,146	42.9
Total	15,689	100.0	1,694,993	100.0

Source: IBGE 1985.

The degree of land concentration was therefore much higher in São Paulo than in Pernambuco. It was said that by the 1980s, five closely related families controlled over half of all São Paulo's sugar output. While oligopolistic in terms of ownership, this production system was more benign in terms of negotiations with labor and compensation to workers. Because of higher capital-intensiveness, labor costs were a much lower percentage of the total than in Pernambuco. Productivity was higher, wages were about one-third higher than in Pernambuco, and labor unions were handled with more equanimity by employers. Incidents of landlord violence against workers and union officials were far less frequent in São Paulo than in Pernambuco. In a summary of killings of rural trade union leaders, CONTAG found that between 1964 and 1993 more leaders from Pernambuco—26 out of 135—were killed than in any other state.[20] During the entire period, only one leader in São Paulo was listed as having been killed, in 1975.[21]

The lesson of this comparison of landholding and production structures in the two different states is that modernization of agriculture does not produce uniform results. State intervention influences how modernization affects social movements in the countryside. Thus, as Paige argued, increasing capital investment and technological improvements paved the way for the emergence of a militant but reformist labor movement in Pernambuco's sugarcane fields (1975, 49–51). However, contrary to Paige's account, that process was neither ineluctable nor purely market-driven. In São Paulo, where the state did not inhibit the expansion of industrial capital in agriculture, modernization went even further than in Pernambuco, leading to a greater degree of compromise between capital and labor and the relative absence of labor-intensive small and medium-sized landholdings owned by employers prepared to react violently to union organization.

An implication of the argument offered here is that explanations of Latin American violence that refer in general terms to "history" or "political culture" are inadequate (Rosenberg 1991, 17–19). In this case, the relative peace in São Paulo's countryside cannot easily be ascribed to the existence of a more pacific or civic culture in São Paulo and a more pathological one in Pernambuco. Indeed, many workers in the fields of São Paulo were northeasterners—people with the same culture as the workers in Pernambuco. Similarly, in the 1950s and early 1960s, São Paulo planters did not hesitate to use violence to repress rural labor organizations (Welch 1990). While cultural practices may be intertwined with violence in causally significant ways, the evidence on production and landholding in this comparison leads us to the form of the local political economy, and in particular the relative significance of labor costs in production and the degree of smallholding, as plausible sources of variation. São Paulo's more capital-intensive, vertically integrated, and concentrated production resulted in a relatively small number of employers being more amenable to the peaceful resolution of labor conflicts than their counterparts in Pernambuco. In this instance, local political economy seems better able to account for differences in the level of violence in each state than references to violent political cultures among certain individuals, groups, or regions.

Summary

Landlord violence against rural workers and union leaders occurred in Brazil because the rural poor used the opening provided by the democratic transition to make long-repressed demands for land and better wages. This prompted a landowner backlash. Landlord violence flourished because the state did not punish it; instead, state police forces often collaborated in its commission. The Brazilian state, especially in the northeast, where the political weight of landlords was greatest, did not enforce the rule of law or protect the weak from the predations of the strong. This was a major barrier to the extension of democratic rights in the country. In addition, the lack of strong enforcement of law in the countryside engendered a strong skepticism about the state among rural trade union leaders. In their political activities, they often did not appeal to state officials because they expected no support from them. When it came to political change, they relied on the strength of their membership base rather than on state institutions.

The nature of agricultural modernization influenced the pattern of violence in the Brazilian countryside. In São Paulo's sugar sector, where vertical integration proceeded quite far, and small, labor-intensive plantations were marginalized, the rate of rural violence was low. In Pernambuco's sugar fields, where a large mass of small, labor-intensive plantations still existed, violence was a much more serious problem. Many landlords resisted even seemingly mild union challenges to their authority, such as holding meetings and filing actions in the labor courts, with beatings, murder, and threats of murder, carried out by their privately contracted gunmen or by members of the local military police. It is for this reason that one of FETAPE's documents on the rural labor movement is entitled "Sugar with the Taste of Blood."

~◡ *7* ◡~

The Candidates
The Unions and Political Parties

The internal organization of Pernambuco's sugar unions, as chapter 5 explains, influenced their political role in the 1980s. In particular, tension between the leaders' welfare and workplace functions almost completely sidelined land issues as an area of concern and mobilization for the leadership. However, union leaders faced an external environment that also constrained their actions. Chapter 6 focused on landlord violence, a major disincentive to union activity. This chapter deals with a part of the political opportunity structure that had more ambiguous effects on union politics: the party system.

After 1979, Brazil's electoral politics became substantially more competitive than they had been in the previous fifteen years. The electoral system was transformed from a manipulated two-party system into a multiparty system, albeit one in which the dominant party of the military period, under a different name, retained considerable power. Despite the trade unions' influence on a large number of voters, they were unable to secure the consistent incorporation of their views by any political party. Trade union leaders therefore viewed party politics with suspicion. This outcome can be explained by the interaction of the union leaders' views of politics, the character of trade union–party relations, and the nature of political parties in Brazil's northeast.

Union Leaders' Political Attitudes

In general, union officials in Pernambuco's sugar zone did not see the right to vote and multiparty competition as the essence of democracy, but defined democracy instead in broader terms. These included material benefits and the right to participate in decision making beyond the electoral arena. The union officials seemed to hope for a democratic transition in which civil society played a large role in effecting substantive social change. They were thus critical of the transition that actually took place and the political parties that eventually dominated it.

Only one trade union leader of thirty-nine responded to the question, "What is democracy?" in terminology familiar to most political scientists, such as "government chosen by the people" (Dahl 1971). Far more frequent conceptions of democracy were material—as in "benefits for the suffering classes" (41 percent) and "agrarian reform" (21 percent). The unionists judged the transition to democracy in terms of the outputs and deliberative style of the new government and not just on the basis of the changes in the procedures used to establish it.

Political rights were important to them as well. Many trade union leaders distrusted the first civilian government after military rule, that of President José Sarney (1985–1990), because the president himself was a landowner and was perceived to be unwilling to allow workers meaningful political participation. Eighty-two percent of those surveyed replied no when asked, "Do you consider the Sarney government to be democratic?" When asked why, 54 percent of this group said that the president was not with the people and exploited workers (54 percent), he supported landowners (32 percent), he did not practice democracy (24 percent), he did not enact agrarian reform (12 percent), and he did not listen to the people (12 percent). Furthermore, many union leaders defined democracy as liberty (28 percent), as well as social justice and equal rights (31 percent).

Workers' rights formed the third element by which union leaders assessed the democratic qualifications of the government. Worker participation in government was listed as a defining feature of democracy by eleven of thirty-nine surveyed union officials. Similarly, the leaders' disapproval of the Sarney government revolved around a sense of workers' rights: Sarney "exploited" and "repressed" workers, while he "supported" landowners. Locked in a highly unequal struggle with landowners, the union leaders appeared to be seeking an activist state that not only allowed ordinary citizens to choose between competing elites, but also provided material benefits to the poor, defended equal treatment before the law, vigorously protected workers' rights, and allowed workers some kind of direct or corporatist participation in government. Understandably, within such a perspective, electoral institutions, party politics, and the right to vote were relegated to secondary status.

Perhaps for this reason, most of the trade union leaders in the Pernambuco sugar zone identified very little with the national government and accorded it scant legitimacy. While these officials helped elect the ruling party, the PMDB, at the state level in 1986, they made a sharp distinction between the state and federal administrations. Forty-one percent of those surveyed even claimed that, from their point of view, there was no difference between the military and civilian governments at the national level, despite the fact that the latter had been elected (albeit indirectly) and the former had not.

The union leaders' unwillingness to accord legitimacy to governments on the basis of their electoral credentials seems linked to their view of political parties, the main representative institutions in a consolidated democracy. They saw parties as a necessary evil at best. Because the democratic transition had not resulted in a social-democratic government that directly responded to union input and created peak bargaining institutions at the national level, parties and their candidates were needed as conduits to state resources and politics beyond the purely local level. Yet the parties the unions faced were unstable, frequently clientelistic, and programmatically incoherent. To understand the leaders' attitudes, we must briefly review local party politics.

Party Politics in the Sugar Zone

In the 1980s, Pernambuco was the seventh-largest electorate in Brazil with just under 5 percent of the nation's voters, or about 3 million people. Since World War II, it has had a bipolar party system with shifting parties.[1] During the 1945–1964 period, competition in Pernambuco was dominated by the two major national parties, the Democratic Nacional Union or UDN (União Democrático Nacional) and the PSD, although a local center-left coalition, the Recife Front (Frente do Recife), emerged in the 1950s and managed to get its candidate elected mayor of Recife in 1955, 1959, and 1963, as well as to elect Arraes governor in 1962 (Azevêdo 1990, 2).

Pernambuco has also had a sharply dualistic electoral geography. The capital city of Recife and the surrounding coastal sugar zone, which in 1986 contained 56 percent of the state's voters, had a tradition of oppositional and center-left voting. The interior regions of the *agreste* and the *sertão*, with 44 percent of the electorate in the same period, were largely controlled by landlords with a conservative mentality and clientelistic relations with the peasantry (Azevêdo 1990, 5–7).

Given this electoral configuration, center-left candidates for statewide office have often stitched together coalitions uniting conservative and landowning interests from the interior with labor and progressive middle-class groups from Recife. This type of alliance was the key to Miguel Arraes's gubernatorial victories in 1962, 1986, and 1994, and one reason why (especially after 1986) Arraes's performance in office did not match the expectations of many of his leftist supporters.

Pernambuco's electoral division also meant that center-left candidates that did well in the sugar zone frequently failed to win statewide. The electoral data showing this pattern is more meager than it might otherwise be. A year after the 1964 coup, the military regime banned all existing parties and engineered a two-party system with a token opposition party (the MDB) and a heavily advantaged ruling party (ARENA). For most of the military regime, there were no direct elections for governor; a 1966 decree provided that governors were instead elected indirectly by the state assemblies (Alves 1985, 70). In Pernambuco, there was no direct election for governor from 1962 to 1982.

However, in the latter year, as a result of political liberalization, governors were once more elected by popular suffrage, and in the Pernambuco sugar zone Marcos Freire of the opposition MDB party received a majority of votes. But his opponent in the promilitary PDS (Partido Democrático Social), Roberto Magalhães, because of his stronger support in the interior of the state, won the election. This pattern prevailed in the 1989 presidential election, when the candidate of the leftist Workers' Party won a majority of votes in the sugar zone but lost in the state and nation as a whole to Fernando Collor de Mello, the candidate of the right.

In the post-1982 period, Pernambuco remained essentially bipolar in its electoral configuration. Miguel Arraes won election for governor in 1986 and again in 1994 with an effective personalistic machine that included both landlord and trade union support in the sugar zone. In Arraes's first victory, the PMDB supplanted the PDS as the state's ruling party. However, allegiance to Arraes, and to many other politicians, was more personal than party-based. This was illustrated in 1990 when Arraes took his machine out of the PMDB when that party's fortunes were waning in 1990 and joined the socialist party PSB (Partido Socialista Brasileiro). Most of his supporters (including the sugar zone's rural union leaders, 94 percent of whom when surveyed said they voted for Arraes in 1986) followed him in this move, and Arraes won another term as governor with the PSB in 1994.[2]

Pernambuco's pattern of voting, and not just its electoral geography, is dualistic. Voters displayed different party preferences in gubernatorial and presidential elections, on the one hand, and congressional, state assembly, and municipal elections, on the other. Oppositional and center-left voting in the governor's and president's races did not correspond to the same kind of voting for municipal, state assembly, and congressional offices, indicating that much voting was for the candidate and not the party, and that right-wing parties retained considerable local appeal after the democratic transition.

The promilitary ARENA candidate, for example, won the 1966 Senate race both in Pernambuco as a whole and (by the narrowest of margins) in the sugar zone. ARENA candidates also outpolled their MDB rivals in the mata in the 1974 state assembly and congressional lower house elections, although the popular Marcos Freire of the MDB won the Senate seat by a fairly large margin. Similarly, the 1976 municipal elections saw ARENA winning handily in the sugar zone, while the PMDB only became dominant at the local level in 1988, when it had become the ruling party at the state level. Even in this latter election, the PMDB failed to win a majority of the municipal governments, with smaller parties winning significant numbers of mayoralties and seats on town councils. In the 1994 elections, Pernambuco's voters elected Arraes governor, but the majority of the representatives they sent to Congress were from the conservative PFL, the successor of the promilitary PDS and ARENA parties.

The explanation for this discrepancy is suggested by Nunes Leal, who argues in his classic *Coronelismo, Enxada e Voto* that because Brazilian municipal governments were dependent on higher levels of government for finance, true opposition to the government rarely developed at the local level (Nunes Leal 1949).[3] Thus, a strong critic of the military regime such as Marcos Freire could win a Senate seat in Pernambuco in 1974, while similar figures at the local level only began to emerge once the PMDB had a chance to control the state government in 1982 and after.

Another factor is the lack of ideological coherence in the parties at the local level. Parties were often nothing more than vehicles for local coalitions, without programmatic significance. After 1982, as the PMDB became the dominant local party, there were wholesale defections by ARENA politicians to the PMDB.[4] The explanation of one candidate for vice-mayor in a sugar zone town in 1988 is very revealing in this regard. Asked why he was running as a candidate of the democratic labor party PDT (Partido Democrático Trabalhista), he said that his initial preference was to run on the PT ticket, but he feared that the PT was not strong enough in the region to allow him to win. The local PMDB refused his candidacy; finally, after searching around for another party, he found that the PDT was willing to let him run as its vice-mayoral candidate. Clearly, this politician's selection of party had nothing to do with ideas or the stature of each party's state and national candidates (in fact, he claimed that ideologically he still identified with the PT). It was a pragmatic choice, and many local candidates in the sugar zone seemed to choose their party labels on the same basis.

There appeared to exist, therefore, considerable opportunism, both on the part of candidates and voters, within the political system of the sugar zone.[5] While old-fashioned clientelism declined, new forms of dependency seem to have emerged in the era of agricultural modernization.

Most commentators agree with Azevêdo that since the late 1950s "the ancient political oligarchies formed by the old *coronéis* and based on the latifúndio and private power began to decline and lose their exclusive power of political intermediation," especially in the coastal areas (Azevêdo 1990, 30). A comparison of the 1962 and 1986 gubernatorial elections supports this observation. In 1962 the third candidate in the race was Armando Monteiro Filho, a landowner and sugar mill owner based in the area of Rio Formoso, in the southern sugar zone. While Monteiro was heavily defeated throughout the sugar zone by his two opponents, João Cleofas and Miguel Arraes, he at least managed to win one county, his home base of Rio Formoso. Here he received 1,657 votes, compared to 741 for Cleofas and 682 for Arraes. While Monteiro did not have the resources to build an effective regional machine, he was able to use his position as local notable to mobilize client voters among the peasants in his local area.

Monteiro's nephew José Múcio Monteiro ran for governor in 1986 and was defeated by the same candidate who had won in 1962: Miguel Arraes. Múcio won in only one small county of the sugar zone, Belém de Maria. In his home base, Rio Formoso, he lost, receiving 5,036 votes to Arraes's 7,245.[6] Unlike his uncle in 1962, he had been unable to use his status and resources as a landowner and employer to mobilize local rural workers along clientelist lines.

Rio Formoso is illustrative of the decline in personalistic clientelism based on landlord-tenant relationships in the sugar zone. The tremendous expansion of the electorate due to population growth and the extension of suffrage to illiterates in 1985,[7] the shift in residence of most cane workers from plantations to towns, the replacement of the work-for-land arrangement of *moradía* by wages as the dominant form of labor relation, the spread of mass communications media, and the greater mobility of field workers because of better roads and bus service have all eroded this form of clientelism.

However, to some extent, the old clientelism has merely been replaced by a new, more anonymous version of it. Vote buying of various kinds was still common in the Pernambuco sugar zone in the 1980s. Despite economic changes and the spread of wage labor, low wages and unemployment remained a chronic problem. From 100,000 to 150,000 workers were routinely laid off during the six months of the "dead time" between harvests. These workers were susceptible to the kinds of inducements that political campaigns offered: free T-shirts and building materials, offers of jobs, money, and so on. The distribution of such benefits was an integral part of electoral campaigns in the northeast.

Roberto Aguiar (1988a) estimates that election campaigns in the Brazilian northeast are some of the most expensive in the world on a per capita basis, far more expensive than, for example, those in Britain. The Collor campaign in the 1989 presidential election was said to have spent a large amount in the sugar zone, especially in the crucial second-round contest against Lula. One rural union president reported that some 500 votes were bought by the Collor campaign in her town in the 1989 election. She recalled, "On election day they were giving money . . . placing it in the shirt pocket of the worker and saying, 'Look, our candidate is . . . .'"[8]

The type of vote buying described by the union president, although referred to as a "herd vote," is more impersonal, more contractual, and less certain than the *coronelismo* of an earlier era. The latter typically involved a landlord bringing his resident workers and day laborers to the polls, footing the bills for the trip, and expressly instructing them which way to vote (often providing them with completed ballots). The contemporary practice imposes fewer restraints on workers, involves far more fleeting tutelage, and depends more on their willingness to carry out their side of the bargain. Nevertheless, most workers do seem to respond to the obligation (or coercion) to vote for candidates from whom they have received something, and in this respect modern vote buying is similar to *coronelismo* in that it involves the use of economic power for electoral gain.

Patronage distributed by political machines probably affected more rural workers than outright vote buying. The Arraes machine, for example, rewarded its trade union supporters by instituting a Straw Hat (Chapeu de Palha) program after Arraes became governor in 1986. This program, run by the state labor secretariat (headed by a former FETAPE lawyer) was a jobs program for unemployed sugarcane workers. Workers were paid the minimum wage to work on road repair and other public works during the dead season. Selection of candidates was handled by local trade unions, in effect turning the unions into part of the government's social assistance program and into supporters of the Arraes machine.[9]

A review of electoral politics in the sugar zone thus leads to two conclusions. First, the region reflects the gradual rise of the electoral opposition to the military regime's coalition in the 1980s. However, the apparent simplicity of this two-party dynamic is belied by the instability in the parties actually competing, the tendency of politicians to switch parties, the parties' lack of programmatic consistency, and voters' tendency to vote for different parties at the local level than at the state and national levels. Most significant for understanding the nature of the transition in Pernambuco is the fact that a significant bloc of supporters from the old promilitary party, including many landowners, simply moved en masse into the PMDB, diluting its claims to be a genuine alternative to military rule.

Second, clientelism has changed in nature rather than disappeared. The role of parties as representatives of programmatic majorities and as conduits of opinion was significantly mitigated by the personalism and clientelism of electoral politics. The unions' relationship to parties and candidates in this system therefore tended to be opportunistic.

The Unions and Party Politics

The sugar zone unions had a complex and ambiguous relationship to political parties, not only because of the nature of those parties, but also the unions' limited ability to mobilize voters, internal divisions within the unions, and the peculiar nature of trade union ideology. This section will explore each in turn.

The Unions as Vote Banks

The unions functioned as vote banks in the sugar zone. As practically the only institutions that organized the rural poor aside from the Catholic Church and the evangelical sects, they were in a unique position to influence and mobilize voters. The Arraes machine was the most striking example of the effectiveness of the unions in this regard. In the 1986 governor's race, union leaders spread the word that Arraes, a leader revered for his actions as governor in the early sixties, would return and work new miracles. The almost mystical slogan, "Hope has returned" (*A Esperança está de volta*), circulated in the sugar zone, and when the ballots had been counted, 60.32 percent of the region's electorate had voted for Arraes.[10] Arraes's victory for the same office in 1994 was by an even higher margin.

No other political candidate in the sugar zone seemed to inspire the loyalty given to Arraes, whose bond with rural workers bordered on the charismatic.[11] Most candidates whom the trade unions supported were involved in closer races than the 1986 governor's election and needed every personal visit, every gift, every campaign advertisement that could be made on their behalf. For these candidates, the unions were not even close to being perfect vote banks, for reasons detailed below. These include the unions' limited ability to reach and influence members, their divergent interests vis-à-vis parties, and their incapacity to guarantee pay-offs to their members once the candidates they had supported were in office.

The first limitation on the usefulness of the unions to political candidates was the fact that a large number of the cane cutters in the sugar zone worked as illegals outside the union structure. Furthermore, the unions' participative core, whom the leaders saw frequently and on whom they could rely for voluntary effort and the donation of resources, was always rather small. The power of the unions to deliver their members' votes on behalf of candidates was thus not always high. Such capacity obviously varies from union to union and depends on the stature and effectiveness of particular leaders, the accessibility and political consciousness of members, and so on. But on average perhaps as few as a third of union members were really susceptible to the leadership's orientation, and even they might not follow the leaders' advice.[12]

If capacity was frequently lacking, so was will. In the final analysis, union leaders did not share the same interests as political candidates, and they were acutely aware of this. In the absence of charisma, strong ideological identification, or clearly specified benefits, many union leaders decided that it was simply not worth militating on behalf of a particular candidate. I observed an argument between a candidate for the Pernambuco state assembly and a trade union leader that illustrated this divergence very clearly. The candidate was a former union lawyer who had spent twenty years representing rural workers, and he had received the endorsement of the rural workers' state federation, FETAPE. The candidate felt that this particular union president was not supporting him strongly enough, and he complained loudly: Why don't you have my campaign sticker on your car? Why aren't you wearing my campaign T-shirt? and so on.

The candidate's biggest complaint, it turned out, was that this union president had rented out one of the union buildings to his political adversary. From the president's point of view, this rental had simply been good business, a way to earn money for his union. The rival candidate had come to him eight months before the election campaign, offered to rent the building, signed a contract, and paid cash when he occupied it. This infuriated the former union lawyer. "Why didn't you ask if I could rent the building?" he cried. He added that it was going to look as if the union was supporting that candidate.

This confrontation is an example of the clash between the needs of a union leader (to meet costs and run the organization efficiently) and those of a political candidate. It illustrates that the unions were first and foremost economic organizations tied up with the defense of their members' interests, and that this function could interfere with their role as supporters of political candidates. In addition, a union president owed primary allegiance to *his* members, not to all workers in his sector and certainly not to all workers. This is why the candidate's appeal fell on deaf ears. "Twenty years in the movement," he said disgustedly, "and I can't get your support. I'm not running for myself, I'm running on behalf of rural workers." But the union president did not represent all rural workers. He represented the workers in one county whose union would benefit economically if it rented its building out to a rival candidate (Field notes, 13 July 1990).

A similar reason why unions were reluctant to campaign strongly for, or even passively support, a candidate is that most candidates had only limited resources and thus limited ability to reward supporters. An example is the same candidate mentioned above. Before running for the state assembly, he was head of the state's Secretariat of Labor and a member of Governor Arraes's inner circle. As head of the secretariat, he was able to channel funds to unions whose support for him had been particularly strong and where he had worked as a lawyer. Other unions were left out. The president of a small union on the edge of the sugar zone in Pombos complained, "There are other regions where the union leaders at some point went to the secretariat and he did not give any help. . . . But he has to see that you can't have a commitment to A or B, you have to have a commitment to the movement, right?"[13]

Clearly, this particular union president felt that she had not received equal treatment. Particularly irritating was the way the Chapeu de Palha program—administered by the secretariat—worked. In her words:

> Last year the Straw Hat program gave work to about 800 workers and there were no layoffs by the mills and plantations, at least not many. This year [1990]) they laid people off like crazy, like they were throwing away garbage— "It's of no use any more, throw it away!" There was horrible need on the part of the workers, even in the sugarcane rum distillery, and unfortunately we had what? We had almost 150 jobs until today.[14]

Because this particular union was founded late, in 1987, was small (about 800 members in a region where the average union had 4,200 members), and had little clout within the state federation, it received few jobs from the Straw Hat program.[15] The union's leaders resented this because, among other reasons, it undercut their leadership. Consequently, they refused to support the former chief of the secretariat in his bid for a seat in the state assembly. Thus, even a relatively efficient political machine like that of Arraes could lose members when it appeared unable to make adequate or fair political payoffs.

For all the reasons discussed here—their limited ability to reach and influence members, their divergent interests vis-à-vis parties, and their lack of means to guarantee payoffs to their members once the candidates they supported were in office—the unions' capacity to provide the infantry of electoral warfare was decidedly limited. The union leaders' relationship to candidates and parties and their struggle to use the electoral arena to their advantage was thus fraught with ambiguity and uncertainty. For this reason, many trade unionists saw party politics as a confusing, divisive, and potentially destabilizing force within the union movement.

Internal Divisions Within the Unions

While the unions faced similar constraints in their ability to mobilize voters and pursue coherent strategies to get them through the electoral maze, their leaders were quite divided in their attitude toward parties and party politics. One such division appeared to hinge on religion. The survey, while based on a small sample size (forty Catholics and seven Protestants) indicated that party affiliation varies with religion. Protestants were less likely to declare party affiliation—71.4 percent of them said that they did not belong to a party, compared to only 37.5 percent of Catholics. Protestants who were affiliated with a party were less likely to be members of a leftist party such as the Workers' Party, Socialist Party, or Communist Party. In fact, no Protestant interviewed was a member of one of these parties.[16]

Catholics were also more likely than Protestants to agree with the statement that "the ideal is that union leaders belong to just one party, in order to achieve greater unity of action." Of the Catholics, 72.5 percent agreed with this statement, whereas only 57 percent of the Protestants did so.

However, the different views on the proper relations between unions and parties cannot be explained by religion alone. A sizable portion of the Catholics (37.5 percent) declared that they did not belong to a political party. And of twelve respondents who agreed with the statement, "It is preferable that union leaders are not affiliated to parties," ten were Catholics, one declared no religion, and only one was Protestant.

A narrow majority of the leaders belonged to a left or left-center party and believed that it was better for all leaders in the same union to belong to the same political party. However, many leaders diverged from this view, and unity over party affiliation seemed rarely to be achieved in practice. This could be seen in the 1988 municipal elections, when over 100 candidates from the rural labor movement ran for local offices in Pernambuco under a plethora of party labels. One even ran as a candidate of the conservative PFL.

Further evidence of schisms within the union movement was shown in a survey question, asked in 1988, about which candidate the leaders supported for president.[17] Admittedly, the question was asked before the campaign had begun, when many candidacies were purely speculative. But the responses reveal the diversity of opinion among leaders in what they must have regarded as a rather confusing and wide-open national political picture. Of the major candidates in 1988, Miguel Arraes was the most popular, with the support of 48 percent of the union leaders, followed by Luís Inácio da Silva (Lula) with 20 percent, Fernando Collor de Mello with 18 percent, and Leonel Brizola with 14 percent.[18]

Because of the diversity of views within the unions about trade union–party relations, the state federation could not successfully impose discipline on its members during elections. It could endorse candidates, persuade and advise its members to support them, but could not count on absolute fidelity. Adherence to the FETAPE line ranged from almost total, in the case of Miguel Arraes, to partial, as in the case of the candidate for state assembly mentioned earlier. Because the union movement was not monolithic, its relationship to political parties could not be simple and unambiguous and it did not speak with one voice at election time.

The Unions' Antipartisan Position

We have already reviewed unionists' attitudes toward democracy and electoral politics and have highlighted some features of the electoral politics of the sugar zone. Here we attempt to relate these to unionists' attitudes toward parties. Azevêdo asserts (1990, 2) that aside from Rio Grande do Sul, Pernambuco was the only state in Brazil in which the laborist ideology of *trabalhismo* survived the deaths of Vargas and Goulart and the long exile of Brizola. In 1994, Brizola's political machine collapsed in both Rio de Janeiro and Rio Grande do Sul, leaving Pernambuco as the only state appearing to fit that description. Among trade union leaders in the sugar zone, it would be more accurate to say that what prevailed was an antipartisan position. The *trabalhismo* of Goulart and Brizola, represented by the

PTB and PDT, respectively, involved a pact between trade unionists who pledged their support to professional, elite politicians. While this describes the Arraes machine as well, the rural union leaders of the sugar zone had a view of politics which was at once more radical and more alienated than old-style *trabalhismo*. Their position consisted of a mistrust of politicians and parties and a desire to maintain union separateness from them, a wish to be involved in local politics accompanied by considerable alienation from state and national politics, and a belief that their interests would be protected in the political system when their own kind—workers—represented them directly.[19]

It is not hard to find evidence of the first sentiment. One union leader described politicians simply as "enemies of the people." Another said that "the politicians want to take people only to use them as instruments" and that he "didn't want to be anyone's instrument." Similarly, a union official recognized that some politicians "have good speeches but they don't defend the workers" (Survey 1988). In these comments the union leaders were not simply echoing familiar complaints about politicians that exist within all Western democracies. They were expressing the view that politicians were not to be trusted because they were not *one of them* and because the legislative bodies that the politicians belonged to were inherently unable to represent their class interests. In the words of one official, "I don't believe in any politician . . . the situation of the worker is misery. Only the organization of the workers can win something" (Survey 1988).

The union leaders viewed parties as they did politicians. We have already seen how fluid the party system in Pernambuco was, and how, despite the continuity of a bipolar pattern, dominant parties—ARENA, the PDS, the PMDB—came and went in the space of thirty years. Such flux generated a corresponding wariness about parties among the populace that was shared by the union officials. Parties were not much more than vehicles for politicians and were often discarded for new ones. A common view, therefore, was that the union must stay separate from parties. Any *permanent* alliance between the union movement and a political party was to be avoided, for the same reason that multiyear contracts were not signed in the sugar zone. Both were too confining: things could change, a new opportunity to achieve gains could arise. So the preferred option was short-term commitments to specific candidates and parties at election time. In the words of one official: "Don't mix the union with politics. A party must not dictate to the union. But the union must have a party and candidates. It must give an example to the people" (Survey 1988). Such an orientation generated an instrumental attitude toward parties. One union leader said that "in this climate," the PMDB was the best party for his union (Survey 1988). The climate was capable of shifting, and it did.

However, there did seem to be a prevailing sentiment among leaders that they should unite around certain candidates and parties once those candidates and parties had been chosen. As noted above, two-thirds of the leaders felt it was better for all the leaders in a union to belong to the same party. The need for unity in the arena of party politics, and the fact that unity was hardly ever achieved, was a recurring theme in my interviews with trade union leaders. The lack of unity in practice was understandable because union leaders did not see any party as "theirs." They agreed that their duty as leaders was to support the candidates and party that best represented their members' interests. But it was not clear which was the best. Given the plethora of candidates and the confusing nature of their claims and counterclaims, there were divergences, and, as one leader said, the whole issue of whom to support at election time became a "hot potato" with which it was easy to get burned. The vagueness of many candidates did not help matters (Survey 1988).

The same skepticism and pragmatism about parties extended even to the most programmatic and explicitly worker-oriented party in Pernambuco, the PT. While fragile at the municipal level, with only three town councilors (vereadores) in the sugar zone in 1988, the Workers' Party managed to win the first round of the 1989 presidential election in the mata, with its candidate, Lula, getting 32.89 percent of the vote (Tribunal Regional Eleitoral de Pernambuco 1990). In the second round, Lula defeated his opponent Collor in the mata by 53.92 percent to 38.86 percent. Union support was important for Lula's victory; in July 1990, seven months after the election, Lula campaign material could still be seen covering the walls of rural union headquarters.

However, after this election result, there was some feeling among trade union leaders that, like other parties, the PT had been interested primarily in using the unions as instruments, that influence between party and union had flowed in only one direction. Frustration at this state of affairs was expressed by a trade union president:

> Our politics are the following: If the politician is on the left and has a commitment to the working class, we agree to help him, to fight, to struggle, to get him there on top . . . [and in] Lula's campaign, we worked here for the PT, we even founded a Commission. It was a struggle; we spent two years studying, studying the PT front and back, backward and forward . . . we'd meet once a month and . . . have debates, discussions, questions, and the worker participated actively. And then one day when we saw it was time to . . . [have] this

Commission elected by the workers [and recognized by the regional directorate of the PT] this was simply ignored by the PT at the state level . . . so the
PT . . . passed above us . . . passed over the decision of workers, didn't respect
what the workers did and this hurt us . . . really hurt those workers, who ended
up skeptical [about the PT].[20]

The union leaders' attitude toward parties, even the Workers' Party,
was thus skeptical. Parties tended not to listen, only to direct. Therefore,
union leaders were also opportunistic in dealing with parties. They felt
that unions should not be confined by incorporation into a party, but free
to look for the best deal at each election. This opportunism not only
reflected the opportunism of political candidates in northeast Brazil, but
also was based on the union leaders' concern not to divide their membership base along party lines.

Candidates readily changed parties. They used them as personal electoral vehicles; they liked to direct their supporters but rarely incorporated
their views into their own programs. The union leaders' self-reliant and
defiant antipartisanship was thus a defensive reaction to the personalism,
clientelism, and opportunism of the electoral politics surrounding them
and a strategy for maintaining corporate unity while seeking advantage in
the electoral arena.

However, the trade union leaders clearly were involved in local politics. Their alienation from politics did not extend to the local level. When
asked, "Who are the politicians with whom you have the most contact?"
the majority (56 percent) responded that they did have contact with mayors and mayoral candidates. In contrast, only 10 percent reported contacts
with representatives or candidates from the national Congress, while 28
percent said that they had contacts with state assembly candidates and
members. Local candidates could make face-to-face deals with union
leaders, such as promising them a municipal building or a health clinic.
Such deals were less likely to be made with state and federal campaigns.

Similarly, local candidates could be personal enemies of the union
leadership. As one official said, "The mayor hates the union because he is
a businessman—he has a plantation." Another said that the mayor "is of
the PFL, linked to the mill owner and is a cane planter" (Survey 1988).

The third component of the leaders' antipartisan position was their
belief that workers should be represented by workers. As one official said,
"The ideal is for the worker to vote for a worker" (Survey 1988). How
workers could properly be represented by workers was not really fully
considered; neither was the problem that once a worker became a member of a legislative body, he might cease to identify with workers.

In the absence of direct worker representation, union leaders had to make do with traditional politicians and parties. In thinking about union-party relations, it is useful to consider Offe's concept of opportunism, which he defines as the tendency for unions to orient themselves to established and recognized channels of political activity; to rely on parliamentary and electoral forms of action; and to accept the division of labor between economic and political campaigns. He adds that opportunism is a strategic self-limitation of the means and forms of struggle, a "reification of means which are, henceforth, considered to be ends in themselves" (Offe 1985, 214).

Offe's concept of opportunism, which is not intended to be pejorative, points to the rationality inherent in trade union political strategy. Using it, opportunism "no longer appears to be an organizational pathology that results from treason or external manipulation; it rather appears to be a perfectly rational strategy of transformation which . . . secures the chances for success while escaping the threat to survival" (1985, 217).

Summary

The inability of the unions to use their members' numerical superiority to vote for reforms in the sugar zone sprang from two sources. The first, external to the unions, lay in the nature of local political parties. Pernambuco's parties were personalistic and clientelistic, more adept at favors and exchanges than broad programmatic appeals. Candidates built up personal machines which they could temporarily attach to parties for opportunistic reasons. Therefore, no party became "the" party of the rural unions; rather, short-term electoral bargains were struck with individual candidates at each election. In addition, only a minority of Pernambuco's population lived in the sugar zone. Even leftist candidates such as Miguel Arraes tended to make alliances with conservative bosses from the interior (sertão) region in order to win elections.

A whole set of factors internal to the unions also accounted for their weakness in electoral politics. Union leaders had only a limited ability to mobilize and influence the votes of their members. On several key issues as well, the leaders were divided with regard to parties. And on other issues there was a conviction that parties and candidates were simply not to be trusted and that the best guarantee of trade union effectiveness and survival was its distance from party politics.

Trade unions' relations with parties in the sugar zone were "opportunistic," with all the advantages and limitations that the term implies. They seemed to view parties as necessary evils and defined democracy in ways that went well beyond the right to vote for competing elites. Given the nature of electoral politics in the sugar zone, it is perhaps not surprising that trade unionists were generally skeptical about the restoration of open party competition, fearing that it would not favor their interests. They seemed to want state institutions to reach around the electoral sphere, ignore the political power of large landowners, and attend directly to the demands of the rural lower classes. It is to one of those demands—agrarian reform—that we now turn.

~ 8 ~

The Struggle for Heaven on Earth
Unions and Agrarian Reform

The rural trade union movement in Pernambuco's sugar zone survived fifteen years of repression under the military regime, but it changed during those years. From a decentralized, free-wheeling set of organizations loosely tied to the state and strongly opposed by landlords, it evolved into a centralized and bureaucratic structure with strong ties to the state and a predictable, stable pattern of incremental bargaining with landowning employers. The movement gained state resources in return for limiting itself to a narrow range of reformist collective action. This familiar story has been told elsewhere with varying degrees of praise and condemnation—from Michels's account of the evolution of the German Social Democratic Party early in this century, to accounts of the success, bureaucratization, cooptation, incorporation, and opportunism (depending on the author's point of view) of trade unions and social movements.

The point of this book has been neither to lament nor to celebrate this trajectory, but to accept it as a historical event and to explain it. Such an explanation requires that we distinguish among four of the movement's features: (1) opportunities for action, (2) capacities to act, (3) ideology and program, and (4) strategy. This chapter deals mainly with ideology and stategy. As has been argued, FETAPE is tied to a national confederation, CONTAG, whose official platform calls for a wide-ranging agrarian reform, but FETAPE's union leaders in the sugar zone (as chapter 5 shows) spent almost all their time on wage and welfare issues, rather than land issues.

However, in 1985 the newly installed government in Brazil announced plans for a major agrarian reform. Responding to popular pressures for social change that had long been suppressed by the military regime, it promised to distribute millions of hectares to about 7.1 million of the rural poor between 1985 and 2000. It asked rural trade unions to participate in the reform by helping to select land for distribution.

In the Pernambuco sugar zone, the announcement did not return the region to the politics of the early 1960s, when numerous land occupations, violent clashes, and calls for immediate dispossession of the large landowners infused participants on both sides of the struggle for land with an apocalyptic fervor. Instead, the local unions agreed to participate in government commissions that were to draw up plans for the redistribution of local holdings. Some occupations of land did take place, but these were small and not officially supported by the trade unions. In the end, the commissions did not function as planned, and by 1988 less land had been distributed than had been distributed by the military regime in the 1970s.

This chapter explores some of the reasons for this outcome. The first part outlines the problem of landlessness in rural Brazil. The second section looks at the politics surrounding agrarian reform during Brazil's transition to democracy, both at the national level and in the Pernambuco sugar zone. In addition, it examines the breakdown of the reform plan, and why the unions were unable to prevent it.

The Rural Poor and the Struggle for Land

About 30 million people, or 73 percent of Brazil's total rural population, were considered poor in the early 1980s.[1] The majority of them were wage workers of one kind or another, the most numerous being seasonal workers (see table 8.1).

The rural poor struggled to survive in an agrarian system dominated by large estates or *latifúndios*. Brazil's pattern of land distribution, like its income distribution, was one of the most unequal in the world. Holdings exceeding 1,000 hectares or more accounted for only 1 percent of all rural properties but covered 45 percent of the total cultivated area. Those smallholdings of less than 100 hectares (*minifúndios*) equaled 90 percent of all holdings but had only 20 percent of the total area (MIRAD 1985, 4). Many small cultivators, an estimated 39 percent of all farmers, farmed the land under some form of "precarious" tenure.

The structure of Brazilian agriculture was dualistic (Prado 1953). On the one hand, large estates produced export crops requiring heavy capital investment and/or high levels of inputs (soybeans, coffee, sugar, tobacco, cocoa, citrus). On the other hand, *minifúndios* with under 100 hectares produced much of the domestically consumed food crops such as beans, rice,

Table 8.1 Workers Without Land or with Little Land in Brazil, 1978 and 1984

	No. of Workers (in thousands)	
	1978	1984
Smallholders		
Owners	1,469	1,872
Occupiers	505	644
Sharecroppers	273	433
Renters	122	180
Permanent wage workers	1,104	2,147
Temporary wage workers	2,560	4,260
Other nonsalaried workers	713	1,104
Total	6,746	10,640

Source: Ministério da Reforma e do Desenvolvimento Agrário (MIRAD) 1985, 13.

manioc, potatoes, and corn. Within this structure there was little room for medium-sized, capital-intensive family farms of the type that, until recently, played such a vital role in U.S. food production. The *empresa rural*, the Brazilian equivalent of the family farm, accounted for only 3.3 percent of all properties and 5 percent of the total cultivated area in Brazil in the mid-1980s.[2] Agricultural production in Brazil, therefore, was dominated by an elite of large landowners but also involved a great number of small landowners, tenants, and wage workers.

Despite the existence of acute poverty in rural areas, land in Brazil was not scarce. An estimated 160 million hectares of fertile land, or four times the total area occupied by the *minifúndios*, was unused (Kageyama 1987, 52). Much of this was held purely for speculative purposes.

The military government that came to power in 1964 passed a Land Statute in its first months of office whose ostensible goal was to eliminate the *latifúndio-minifúndio* complex and create a system of efficient family farms. In fact, the policies of the military regime (1964–1985) chiefly benefited the large landowners or *latifundiários*, who received a disproportionate share of the public goods provided to agriculture by the state and from whom taxes were often not collected.[3] Land concentration and rural poverty both increased during this time.[4] The government became highly involved in all stages of production on the large estates, from research on seeds and planting techniques to the management and subsidy of exports. Through a network of state-owned banks, large estates were granted cheap credit; rural credit increased fivefold in real terms between 1968 and 1978.[5] With credit, the *latifundiários* bought machinery, pesticides, fer-

tilizers, and other inputs. At the same time, the state built up rural infrastructure: roads, electricity grids, dams, and irrigation networks.

This policy of capitalizing large estates resulted in de-peasantization:
the large estates often displaced tenants, squatters, and smallholders.[6]
Toward the organizations representing these latter groups, rural unions,
the military adopted a policy of selective punishments and rewards. The
rewards included the welfare programs discussed in chapter 4, as well as
small-scale attempts to distribute land to the landless. In 1966, the first
national agrarian reform plan, based on the 1964 Land Statute, was put in
place. It amounted to a few colonization projects of symbolic significance.[7] In 1968, a second plan was promulgated; it focused primarily on
colonization in the Amazon as a substitute for land redistribution in settled areas such as the northeast. By 1985, the land reform institute INCRA
had given titles to 83,000 families in the Amazon (FAO 1988, 74). This was
a small number compared to the number of migrants settling in the Amazon without titles, and compared to the total number of landless in Brazil.
With the advent of the civilian regime in 1985, however, agrarian reform
became a much more important issue on the national political agenda
than it had been under the military.

The Transition to Democracy and Agrarian Reform

While land reform was a major rhetorical commitment of President
Sarney and the civilian regime that came to power in Brazil in 1985, the
reform itself quickly ran aground. At the national level, the weakness and
division of the reform's supporters was a major factor in its eventual
defeat. In Pernambuco, rural trade unions entered political coalitions with
landlords that made unequivocal support for land redistribution difficult.

The National Level

It is telling that the 1985 agrarian reform plan was issued as a decree-
law, in the style of the old military regime, rather than as a bill requiring
a majority of votes in Congress. The plan had been announced in May,
with much fanfare, at a CONTAG congress of thousands of rural unionists
in Brasília. It projected the expropriation of tens of millions of hectares
and the granting of land title to 7.1 million people by the year 2000.[8] The
plan was supported by the progressive wing of the Church, particularly its
Pastoral Land Commission (CPT), left-wing parties such as the PT, organizations of the landless such as the MST, and CONTAG.

But the plan officially approved on 10 October 1985 differed substantially from the May proposal. Whereas the plan presented to the CONTAG delegates made the reform the task of the central government, the October plan gave regional government agencies the right to select the land for expropriation, opening up the reform to all sorts of local pressures. Also, only properties that neglected their "social function" would be liable for expropriation. CONTAG issued an official note in response to the October plan, calling it a repudiation of the promises made to the workers' representatives in May. Among its complaints was the fact that sugar plantations were not made a priority for land redistribution. On 18 October, the superintendent of INCRA, José Gomes da Silva, and his entire staff resigned, alleging that the final text of the plan had disfigured the original proposal.

The revision of the plan between May and October reflected the power of agrarian interests and the opposition of the military within the national government, but it also revealed the weakness and division of the proreform movement. Ostensibly united in a national campaign, middle-class reformists, Church and left-party activists, the landless, and rural trade union officials formed an uneasy alliance. CONTAG, in particular, had a difficult relationship with other supporters of land reform. It regarded Church organizations of the landless such as the CPT as potential rivals to the unions.[9] In addition, CONTAG was affiliated with the CGT (Confederação Geral dos Trabalhadores), the General Workers' Central, the politically more moderate of what were then the two major central labor organizations. The other central, the CUT, heavily influenced by the PT, had a more radical strategy on agrarian reform.

That strategy was to encourage direct, and at times illegal, actions, such as the occupations of unused land and government offices, rather than to wait for government programs to distribute benefits from above. A CUT document published in 1986 declared that "the agrarian reform means to struggle against the New Republic, wresting victories in confrontations with the powerful and reaffirming . . . the power of the workers, the only type of power capable of . . . realizing a real agrarian reform under the control of workers" (Pandolfi 1988, 182). In contrast, the CGT favored a more legalistic approach, urging proponents of land reform to wait for the government's land management bureaucracies to do their work. It felt that illegal actions had provoked a violent rightist backlash and endangered the transition to democracy.

Church activists and PT members in the countryside tended to agree with the CUT's strategy, while union leaders most often sided with the CGT position and supported the ruling PMDB. Sometimes these differences would flare up during union elections, when leaders with opposing positions would compete, or during land occupations, when CONTAG officials kept a distance and Church and PT activists took up the cause of the occupiers.

The proreform lobby, while counting on the passive support of millions of rural poor, lacked strong urban and party-political support. Most parties of the left and center, including the PT, were based primarily on the support of the urban working and middle class, to whom land reform offered only indirect benefits. In rural areas, nationwide elections for state offices in 1986 meant that most left and center parties were subdued on the land reform issue, because they feared alienating landowners whose campaign contributions they wanted. One INCRA official, exasperated by the slowness of the reform, commented that "the mobilization of those interested in agrarian reform has to be . . . balanced, because any false step could serve as a pretext for a retrocession. It is like walking in a mine field."[10]

The reform as envisaged was expensive. Owners of expropriated land were to be compensated in cash for their homes and surrounding plots, and in agrarian debt bonds, TDAs *(títulos da dívida agrária)*, for all other lands. The federal government would also incur costs for mapping and surveying services, transport for staff, issuing land titles, and so on. The high cost of the plan, combined with the fiscal crisis of the government, bothered its supporters from the outset (Campanha Nacional Pela Reforma Agrária 1985a, 6).

In December 1985, twenty-five state agrarian reform plans were prepared by the regional directorates of INCRA and given to President Sarney. These plans were drawn up without the input of potential reform beneficiaries, rural workers, or their trade union representatives. Agrarian commissions to oversee the reform's implementation—three of the nine members were trade union officials—were set up in the states in August and September 1986. But this was long after the state plans had been approved by the president in May. Furthermore, the government minister who had first announced the plan to the CONTAG congress, Nelson Ribeiro of the Ministry of Agrarian Reform and Development (MIRAD, Ministério de Reforma Agrária e Desenvolvimento), was fired in May 1986. Ribeiro, linked to the Church, was replaced by Dante de Oliveira, a confidant of the president (Pessoa 1986, 108).

The land expropriation procedure employed by INCRA was complex and highly centralized, capable of being blocked by landlord pressure at numerous stages. Although the original plan had stressed that the "participation . . . of rural workers" was a "vital requisite" for the plan's success (MIRAD 1985, 26), such participation did not occur in practice. INCRA selected beneficiaries for land using surveys that collected personal information: the worker's age, experience in agriculture, number of family members, other trade skills, and so on. Points were given to each candidate in a number of categories by INCRA officials; a candidate needed 500 points or more to qualify for land. Land expropriation decrees always came from Brasília, where they required the signature of the president, and listed the number of parcels of land into which the expropriated plot had to be divided, without any local input. In many instances, local input would have been useful, because some crops require more land than others and the productivity of soil varies greatly from one area to another. Once granted a parcel, beneficiaries usually had to install themselves on the land at their own expense, although in some cases INCRA provided money for three months until the first harvest (Pessoa 1986, 115–16).

The state agrarian commissions, designed to increase participation in the reform, were short-lived and ineffective. A little over a year after their establishment, in October 1987, the federal government announced that it planned to abolish INCRA and transfer its responsibilities to MIRAD. CONTAG interpreted this as an abandonment of the reform by the government and withdrew its members from the commissions.

A vital blow to the reform was dealt on 10 May 1988, when the Constituent Assembly, then writing a new constitution, placed a clause in the document stating that "productive" land could not be expropriated. By withholding "productive" land from the reform, critics argued, any property with a few head of cattle or some machinery could be exempt from expropriation; land speculation would be protected. This was one of the most bitterly fought issues in making the new constitution. While CONTAG officials argued against the clause, the well-funded organization of landowners, the UDR, lobbied for it.[11] After seven separate votes, a majority was attained. The exemption of "productive" land was upheld 29 August 1988, in a second round of voting, with 83 of 168 PMDB congressional deputies voting for it (Folha de São Paulo, 11 September 1988). As one newspaper commented: before, the government had the law, but not the will, to enact agrarian reform; now, it lacked the law as well.

The rural unions considered the "productive" clause of the Constitution a betrayal. The federation in Pernambuco published posters with the title "Traitors of the People" after the August vote, showing pictures of congressional deputies who had voted for it. A union song with the same title was sung in meetings in the sugar zone. "The deputies who voted against agrarian reform betrayed the Brazilians," lamented the lyrics, "leaving the masses saddened, crushing us who are rural workers."[12]

By the end of 1988, it was reported that the agrarian reform plan had failed to meet its objectives. Of the 27 million hectares targeted for the period 1985–1988, only 7 percent had been expropriated. Of the 850,000 families slated to receive land, only 40,000, or 4.7 percent, actually had.[13] Furthermore, many smallholders involved in the program had been unable to retain the land given them due to insufficient credit, input, infrastructural, and marketing support, returning again to the ranks of the rural proletariat.[14] Nelson Ribeiro, the ex-minister of MIRAD, had written optimistically in 1987 that land redistribution, by "atomizing . . . [the] concentration of power" of the large landowners, would "give the most decisive contribution to the strengthening of democracy for all" (Ribeiro 1987, 30). Instead, the power of the large landowners, and the weakness of its supporters, had atomized the reform.

The Pernambuco Sugar Zone

In Pernambuco, a major effect of the democratic transition was the return of Miguel Arraes to the governorship. During Arraes's first brief administration in 1962–1964, rural workers had won significant rights which they had not forgotten. Arraes, simply by recognizing the unions' right to bargain on behalf of their members, had altered the balance of power in the sugar zone. Because of improvements in worker welfare under his administration, he won from many workers a loyalty and gratitude that bordered on worship, reflected in the popular saying, "God in heaven, Arraes on earth" ("Deus no céu, Arraes na terra"). On the other hand, he earned the enmity of many landlords, which led to his deposition by the military and fifteen years of exile.

The 1986 governor's race pitted José Múcio, a mill owner of the liberal front party (PFL), against Arraes of the PMDB. Campaigning on behalf of Múcio and running for federal deputy was Francisco Julião, the lawyer and politician who had helped found the Peasant Leagues thirty years before. Julião wrote an open letter to the sugar zone's mill owners urging them to set aside 10 percent of their lands and give it to their workers, out of a sense of Christian charity (*Diário de Pernambuco*, 18 May 1986). He later claimed that had Múcio been elected, he would have been appointed state secretary for agrarian reform, with the power to confiscate land from owners.[15]

Rural workers were generally unsympathetic to the Múcio-Julião campaign. Both candidates lost badly in the election. Of those trade union leaders surveyed, 94 percent said they had voted for Arraes against Múcio, and only 6 percent said they voted for Julião. The latter was widely seen to have "switched sides" since his days with the Peasant Leagues, allying with a mill owner for his own political advantage. FETAPE was also running its own candidates for the office Julião aspired to, that of federal deputy. It is indicative of the maturity of the rural workers' movement that in 1962, Julião, a landowner and urban lawyer, was elected as a spokesperson for rural labor, whereas in 1986, the trade unions had their own political representatives—both of whom, however, lost in the election.

The winning Arraes coalition in 1986, therefore, received the strong support of FETAPE, but it also received the support of a segment of the state's landowning elite. One of the PMDB candidates, for example, was Antonio Farias, a sugar mill owner who won a seat in the federal Senate. The rural union leaders knew, therefore, that this would be a different Arraes government from the one elected in 1962. Many were cautious, recalling those earlier days when activists had militated in favor of union rights and land reform and paid heavily for it after the 1964 coup. In the words of one leader, "A cat who has been burned with hot water fears cold water." Although the prospects of military intervention looked remote, union officials adopted a wait-and-see attitude toward the Arraes government.

Not all of that government's early appointments and policies met with the approval of the unionists. While the new secretary of labor was a former FETAPE lawyer, the important post of secretary of public security, in charge of the civil police, was a general and a holdover from the previous administration. Arraes's position on agrarian reform was also ambiguous. While rhetorically supporting the reform, he maintained that it was a federal matter and should not involve the state government. On 4 May 1986, when President Sarney met with the presidents of CONTAG and FETAPE at Recife's airport to discuss the state's newly drafted agrarian reform plan, Governor Arraes did not participate. Outside the VIP lounge where the leaders met, hundreds of rural workers carried signs and shouted, "Agrarian reform now!" ("Reforma agraria já!") (*Diário de Pernambuco*, 4 May 1986).

Reactions to the reform plan were mixed. FETAPE president José Rodrigues said, "The plan leaves much to be desired," and he accused the federal government of having caved in to landlord pressures and giving away substantial concessions in relation to the initial proposal (Pandolfi 1988, 180). The president of the state Cane Growers' Association said that the growers supported reform, but only if it were done on "unproductive" land. Governor Arraes, for his part, did not seem to involve himself with the federal reform, but initiated a local program of voluntary land donations on the part of the sugar mills. These donations, heavily publicized by the governor's press office, did not involve more than symbolic amounts of land or people.[16] Some in the trade union movement charged that mill owners only participated in the hope that it would obviate their need to participate in the national plan.

In the second half of 1986 the state agrarian commission was set up. This was a local body that included an equal number of landlord and trade union representatives and was supposed to pass expropriation requests on to INCRA, help select beneficiaries, and offer INCRA suggestions on the development and execution of the reform. However, in Pernambuco, so little land was redistributed that the commission never really exercised its function. When the plan to abolish INCRA was announced in October 1987, FETAPE withdrew its members from the commission and organized a protest march.

The union movement's frustration with the regime and its unfulfilled promise of agrarian reform is summed up by the lyrics of a union song circulating in the region at this time, "I Am a Cultivator." Part of the lyrics declare:

> I listen to the radio and am full of happiness
> When they say agrarian reform will arrive.
> I wait one year, I wait two . . . but they
> Only create false projects to deceive us.

In the narrative of these song lyrics, the workers had nowhere to turn after being betrayed by the federal government. Even the Church, once a protector and promoter of the rural union movement, could no longer be trusted:

> Even in the Church I have found deception.
> At times I don't know where to go.
> But either this God of shadow and cold water
> Is for everyone or will one day pass.[17]

These words suggest that some in the union movement sought refuge in the notion of a mystical egalitarianism rather than established institutions of church or state.

Meanwhile, some landless families, acting out of desperation, took matters into their own hands. On 23 August 1987, 199 families moved on to an area of unused land belonging to the powerful Lundgren family, about fifty miles from Recife on the border of Abreu e Lima and Igarassu Counties. They demanded title to the property. The case went to court, the squatters were ordered to be removed, and the state government settled the families on ten hectares of land in Igarassu belonging to the Ministry of Agriculture. However, the original plot of land, called by the squatters Pitanga II (a previous land occupation in another area had been called Pitanga I), became the focus of a legal and political battle that lasted for over a year.

The squatters were determined and patient, occupying the grounds of the MIRAD building in Recife three times during the ensuing year. They declared they had no faith that they would receive land in the official reform. They succeeded in getting some help from local trade unions and later, the state government, which sent food and provided medical care to the squatters on a weekly basis. Despite this, the squatters' leaders were critical of FETAPE. They claimed that the federation was not advocating their cause strongly, for fear of embarrassing the state government and alienating supporters in the ruling PMDB. The local Catholic CPT, based in Recife, became the squatters' most steadfast political ally.

In February 1988, FETAPE paid for a group of squatters and union representatives to go to Brasília for a meeting with MIRAD minister Jader Barbalho, who promised to recommend expropriation of Pitanga II to President Sarney. The squatters' leaders returned to wait with their companions at their bleak settlement, where eleven children died of illness between August and April.

On 11 April Governor Arraes declared himself against the expropriation of Pitanga II, citing the opinion of the Federal Forestry Institute, IBDF (Instituto Brasileiro de Defesa de Floresta), that settling the squatters on Pitanga II would cause unacceptable ecological damage. The next day he gave in to pressure from his secretary of labor and FETAPE President Rodrigues and sent a telegram to MIRAD asking for the "immediate expropriation" of the area. On 20 April, President Sarney signed a decree expropriating 1,120 hectares of Pitanga II. Rodrigues hailed the decision, crediting it to the "firm position of the state government" when, as has been shown, Governor Arraes only took action in support of the squatters' claims in April, a full seven months after they had first occupied the land (Jornal de Comércio, 22 April 1988).

On July 4, carrying pots and pans, mattresses, and food, the Pitanga II squatters occupied the MIRAD building as they had earlier in the year, this time to demand title to the expropriated land. They denounced the "lack of support from FETAPE" and declared that only the CPT was behind them (Diário de Pernambuco, 5 July 1988). The squatters were tired of oral promises (promessas da boca), and wanted a written guarantee that they could settle on the land. One squatter explained that "I don't understand laws, I understand right. The laws were made by men; right comes from God."[18]

Finally, on November 25, 1988, the federal government issued a title of 840 hectares for 102 families at Pitanga II (other families had abandoned the struggle or been resettled elsewhere). One year and three months after the initial land invasion, the squatters appeared to have achieved their goal.

The Pitanga II case illustrates several points about land reform in Pernambuco. First, the small amount of land that was redistributed was almost always the result of direct action on the part of the rural poor themselves, rather than the work of the unions or of the government's land reform bureaucracy. Second, because of his unwillingness to offend landowners, the state governor was reluctant to back the demands of the landless. He was willing to provide food, in part to avoid an embarrassing encampment in front of the Governor's Palace, but he did not push for federal expropriation until it seemed that the squatters simply would not go away. Finally, the trade unions, as supporters of the governor, shared his dilemma. Criticized by the squatters for not doing enough, they could not be seen to be doing nothing. They did provide essential help in the eventual resolution of the problem, but land for the landless was, throughout the period, a secondary issue for them. The wages and working conditions of the mass of their members remained their top priority.

Despite the transformation of agrarian reform into a national political issue during the transition to democracy, and the promises of the new civilian government, little change in the pattern of landownership in Pernambuco occurred. The original draft of the state plan envisaged expropriation in both the northern and southern sugar zone, but the final plan excluded the north from all but minimal reform. In the southern region, the government expropriated 1.78 percent of the land targeted in the plan, and granted land to 1.4 percent of the projected beneficiaries, by the end of 1987. In absolute terms, this amounted to 21 families receiving 400 hectares, a small number in an area containing hundreds of thousands of rural poor (CNBB 1987, 2–3). Ironically, the military regime's performance on the agrarian reform issue was better than that of the civilian regime in the sugar zone. Between 1971 and 1977, at least 279 families received land in the sugar zone under the military's PROTERRA program.[19] Pernambuco's weak performance on the land reform issue was mirrored by most, but not all, other states in Brazil. The government reported that in all of Pernambuco, 8,045.9 hectares, with a settlement capacity of 536 families, were expropriated between May 1985 and May 1988. But during the same period, the northeastern states of Bahia, Maranhão, and Ceará expropriated 373,712.6, 485,521.0, and 101,357.9 hectares respectively, with a total settlement capacity of 26,371 (INCRA 1988). Clearly, the weak reform in Pernambuco cannot be ascribed simply to the federal government's lack of commitment and politics at the national level. Governments in states with social conditions similar to Pernambuco's redistributed more land; state government therefore could make a difference. In Pernambuco, trade unions accepted a subordinate position in the state's ruling coalition, and neither they nor the state government was able to strike an effective blow for reform.

Summary

The weakness of the civilian government of José Sarney, and the fact that prior military governments had also made similar promises, resulted in a very cautious, wait-and-see attitude on the part of most Brazilian rural union leaders on the issue of land reform. That caution was justified: after raising the expectations of the rural poor on the issue, the civilian government redistributed less land in the sugar zone in 1985–1988 than had been redistributed between 1971 and 1977 by the military regime. Nationally, the picture was similar: the agrarian reform was hardly enacted. Landlord pressure in the form of a new and aggressive pressure group, the UDR, had been very successful. Furthermore, divisions within CONTAG were revealed and its moderate strategy of parliamentary and legal pressure without direct action was increasingly questioned by movement activists outside the unions. The organization's most dynamic elements were small farmers and wage workers, who were ambivalent toward agrarian reform. The organization of unions on the basis of the single category, "rural worker," failed to adequately represent the rural landless, who tended to affiliate with more radical organizations outside the rural trade union structure, such as the MST.

CONTAG suffered a serious political defeat with the Constituent Assembly's vote in October 1988. The provisions on agrarian reform in the new constitution made land expropriation more difficult, in legal terms, than it had been under the military regime's 1964 Land Statute. The UDR celebrated this result as a major victory, and CONTAG lashed out at the "traitors of the people" who had voted against them. Both sides knew that the vote was a watershed. In economic terms, redistributing land to small-holders was not unthinkable: France and Japan are two examples of industrialized countries that have preserved smallholder agriculture. But politically it appeared that large-scale land reform was not feasible in Brazil. Redistribution in itself, in any case, would not have been enough. In order to properly support smallholders who acquired land under any reform, a dense network of infrastructural support, in the form of credit, rural extension services, marketing networks, and so on, was necessary if those smallholders were to become viable farmers. And Brazil lacked that infrastructure. The state's agricultural programs had been oriented to the large capitalist estates for so long that any tilt of its policies toward smallholders was not possible without major political reform.

The 1988 constitution thus symbolized a turning point for the rural labor movement in Brazil. CONTAG's peasant populist language of "land to the tiller" had long obscured the fact that it was precisely in the areas where agricultural modernization had gone furthest that its unions were strongest. It did not reflect the real basis of CONTAG's struggle. The confederation had basically accepted the dominance of agribusiness in the countryside, but contested its hegemony in two issue areas: wages and working conditions for an increasingly proletarianized labor force and access to credit and marketing networks for those small producers able to survive in the evolving system. In short, CONTAG was no longer, as its predecessors in the early 1960s had been, a peasant movement challenging the fundamental basis of capitalist development in agriculture, the distribution of private property rights in land. It was a workers' and farmers' movement, striving to ameliorate the conditions of its members within a system whose basic framework it was no longer able or willing to challenge. CONTAG itself was the institutional embodiment of the "end of the peasantry."

~9~

Conclusion
The End of the Peasantry

T
he Brazilian rural labor movement mobilized hundreds of thousands of rural workers and small cultivators in the 1980s, emerging as an important political actor during the transition to a democratic regime. Among small farmers demanding price supports and credit in Rio Grande do Sul, rubber tappers confronting cattle ranchers to preserve the rain forest and their livelihoods in Acre, and wage workers seeking better wages and working conditions in São Paulo, rural trade union leaders played important roles as organizers, speakers, and negotiators. The national rural workers' confederation, CONTAG, was highly visible in the debates surrounding the new constitution. This phenomenon was not repeated in Brazil's southern cone neighbors, where rural unionism was relatively weak. Furthermore, unlike its predecessor from the populist period, Brazil's rural labor movement of the 1980s and early 1990s best represented wage workers and small farmers, rather than subsistence peasants.

Brazil's rural labor movement did not demonstrate "almost complete docility and patience," as one theorist of democratic transitions recommended for labor if democratic transformation was to succeed (Przeworski, in O'Donnell, Schmitter, and Whitehead 1986, 63). Instead, it struck preemptively, staging a successful strike in Pernambuco while the military was still in power, going on to mobilize subsequent strikes in Pernambuco and other parts of the country. Rather than destabilize the transition, these labor actions helped to convince the military leaders to arrange a transformation of regime. Rural labor thus was part of a broad range of forces in civil society that played a role in regime transition.

What explains the emergence of and character of Brazil's rural unionism? What was the relationship between the rural trade unions and the transition to democracy that took place in Brazil in the 1980s? This book argues that the dynamics of Brazil's regime transition may explain the timing of the movement's emergence, but they hardly explain its enhanced capacities and altered character in the 1980s.

This book argues that to understand Brazil's rural unionism, we need to distinguish four of the movement's features: (1) opportunities for action, (2) capacity to act, (3) ideology and program, and (4) strategy. It focuses on a leading segment of Brazil's rural labor movement, the unions of the Pernambuco sugar zone, to explain the movement's trajectory. Until the 1950s, rural labor in Pernambuco had neither the opportunity nor the capacity to offer a sustained, widespread challenge to the domination of the region's landed oligarchy. However, certain long-term structural and institutional changes favored the rise of rural unionism in Pernambuco, and with it the extension of democratic rights (to organize, to assemble, to bargain collectively, to strike, and to vote) to the rural majority. The rural labor movement was not created overnight, but was the result of a long struggle, numerous acts of repression by authorities, and countless negotiations. In Pernambuco's sugar zone, the rural workers' conquest of significant democratic rights was also an epic achievement, since the state's landed oligarchy, like its counterparts in the rest of the northeast, have denied those rights to rural labor for centuries.

Two powerful, related, and ubiquitous processes in modern society spurred the growth of Pernambuco and Brazil's new rural unionism. The first is agricultural modernization—the application of capital and technology to agricultural production. This raised the productivity of labor, changed the class structure, and led to the concentration of workers in small towns. Such a trajectory matches Paige's model (1975) of capitalist development in hacienda agriculture. The second process was not envisioned by Paige. This is the spread of the welfare state to the countryside— the implantation within the rural unions of a network of health programs that added new funds and strengthened the capabilities of the unions while limiting the possible political directions of their activities. Both of these changes added to the resources of the unions. In both, the state was a prime mover, even though some of the consequences of the welfare programs were clearly unintended. The unions' extension of rights in the countryside is not strictly equivalent to or synchronous with the implantation of a formally democratic regime at the national level. Clearly, the conflicts around each set of changes were related. But we have seen, for example, that the right to strike was regained in Pernambuco in 1979, six years before a civilian replaced a general as head of state and ten years before the first direct election for president following the military coup.

The "little world" of the rural trade union leaders clearly had a dynamic of its own that was not perfectly encapsulated by the homogenizing, official story of national regime change.[1] Union politics in Pernambuco were part of a broad series of conflicts in Brazilian society in which groups at the local level claimed the rights embodied by the democratic transition, and where the concrete local meaning of the transition was created. These conflicts were generally more rough-and-tumble affairs than the clean, elite-level games described in the literature on transitions (Tilly 1995, 367).

After the unions were founded in the early 1960s, tutelage over the rural labor movement by social elites (the Church, renegade landowners, Communist Party activists) was gradually replaced by state tutelage, as the unions were incorporated into the federal labor bureaucracy and rewarded with state-funded welfare programs begun in the early 1970s. These added resources then enabled leaders to push beyond the limits of union activity envisaged by the military regime. Using traditions of past mobilization and solidary networks among workers, union leaders engaged in a cultural struggle to increase worker militancy and transform the increased resources wrought by agricultural modernization and state patronage into weapons that could be used to confront landlords and the state. In the later years of the military regime, the rural labor movement headed by CONTAG achieved an uncommon degree of unity in the face of repression.

The case study of Pernambuco helps to explain why rural labor was reactivated in the 1980s. Agricultural modernization and expansion of the welfare state into the countryside strengthened the classes that CONTAG represented best, wage workers and small farmers. CONTAG was able to channel rural protest toward a common enemy, the military regime, and the political opening of that regime in the late 1970s provided a political opportunity for unions throughout the country to mobilize and express long-suppressed demands.

The Pernambuco case also suggests sources of variation among Brazil's rural labor unions. The degree of solidarity among the rural lower classes varies from place to place. In the Pernambuco sugar zone, these networks were unusually strong, due in part to extensive and briefly successful mobilization in the early 1960s. Common residence in towns by many workers also built up a solidarity that often did not extend to migrants from the nearby interior regions of the state. Finally, CONTAG leadership and financial resources were directed heavily toward Pernambuco, enhancing the region's natural advantages as a locus of strike activity.

Pernambuco's annual rural strikes in the 1980s demonstrate that long-standing patterns of exploitation and dependence were not immutable. If, as Putnam puts it, "the North Americans inherited civic traditions, whereas the Latin Americans were bequeathed traditions of vertical dependence and exploitation"[2]—a generalization open to question—those traditions were grounded in particular institutions of the state and the local political economy. And they could be changed by those most oppressed by them. When agricultural modernization and state expansion altered those institutions, the boundaries of what was politically possible were altered and rural workers rushed into public spaces to demand their rights. Relationships of exploitation and vertical dependence, if not obliterated, were substantially modified by new bargains that recognized labor's right to a political voice. The new deal was born of successful protest and resistance.

However, the politics of Brazil's democratic transition revealed the limits of official rural trade unionism. Despite CONTAG's declared commitment to agrarian reform, the internal organization of unions and the logic of member-leader relations caused union leaders to be more focused on wage issues than on land issues. Furthermore, widespread landlord violence, especially in areas such as Pernambuco with large numbers of small landowners burdened by high labor costs, dampened union militancy. Finally, the absence of coherent, stable, programmatic political parties meant that union leaders were unable to arrange something like a social-democratic pact for labor at the national level, as the grass-roots energy of civil society was gradually supplanted by the wrangling of elected politicians in Brazil's transition.

The 1980s revealed deep contradictions within CONTAG. Able to unite a wide variety of interests against the dictatorship in the 1970s, the confederation found itself torn internally once that common threat had disappeared in the mid-1980s. The fiscal crisis of the state squeezed the welfare programs on which unions had depended. CONTAG president José Francisco remarked despairingly in 1987,

> Before, in the darkness of the dictatorship, we . . . would end up finding a way, some space. Today we are having difficulty finding the way to this space within the democratic transition. It is such a complicated, illogical transition that we ask if we are living in a transition to democracy or incorporating the behavior of the dictatorship. (*O Trabalhador Rural*, November 1987)

Francisco's frustration was compounded in 1988 when a broad conception of agrarian reform was not included in the 1988 constitution. The 1988 decision thus marks a watershed for the unions, a major defeat for CON-

TAG, and symbolizes the exclusion of the peasantry from Brazil's political transition.

Theoretical Implications

The study presented here suggests some broad conclusions about state-society relations and labor movements. As I argue in the introduction, neither a purely state-centered nor society-centered analysis is justified by this case. Clearly, the state was central to the processes of agricultural modernization and welfare provision that undergirded the union movement. But we do not find the continuous growth of the state's capacity or infrastructural power in all areas of the study (Mann 1993, 59). State capacity declined with the fiscal crisis of the 1980s, eroding labor's bargaining position. In addition, the state's tendency to replace the "dispersed domination" of landlords with an integrated domination of its own bureaucracies was clearly not complete in the Pernambuco sugar zone, where landlords retained considerable autonomous control over coercive power and where state regulation was weak.

Equally, Mann's metaphor of the state increasingly "caging" the society is only sometimes apt (1993, 734). Sometimes social forces overwhelmed state institutions. The union bureaucracies replaced landlords as providers to the rural poor in the countryside, with the state replacing landlord power. But the collective action of workers transformed state programs into something more than welfare programs that did not affect the political status quo. In institutions that represented landlord interests such as the IAA, this transformation of state institutions by social interests was even more pronounced. Rather than representing the project of a coherent, centralized, and expanding state, the IAA was a bureaucracy captured by the sector it was supposed to regulate and at odds with the logic of other state bureaucracies.

This study also reflects a need to go beyond the initial wave of theorizing about democratic transitions that were focused on short-term, contingent interactions between strategic decision makers. In such studies, the conditions under which such decisions are made are obscured. As we have seen, a change in political opportunities explains the timing of the emergence of Brazil's rural union movement, but not the movement's increased capacities nor its altered composition. For these factors, we must turn to a historical, path-dependent approach that links broad structural changes with the outcomes of particular regime transitions and shows how these outcomes were embodied in political institutions that subsequently shaped post-transition politics. My emphasis on the labor-managment bargaining system that was devised after the 1979 Pernambuco strike is an example of how a labor movement transformed by structural changes emerged at a moment of political liberalization and forged a pact that endured well beyond the period of democratic transition. There are countless other examples for other places and actors. This, then, is the story of what democratic transition meant to a particular set of grass-roots actors.

This research also bears on recent theorizing about new social movements. Some studies of new social movements seem to suggest that, once linked to the state, movements are inevitably coopted and neutralized and that only those that arise and remain completely outside the state are capable of achieving significant social change. These studies, derived from societies with strong states, must be applied with caution to Latin America realities. In Latin America, the state is extensive but weak, especially in the countryside (O'Donnell 1993). Its ramshackle institutions allow for considerable representation of popular interests, conflict, and compromise. Brazil's rural labor movement began apart from the state, in the demands of peasants and workers, and was led by social elites. However, this dependence on elites was traded for dependence on the state, a process that began under Goulart's presidency and was consolidated under the military regime. This did not mean, however, that the unions were condemned to political quiescence. Despite state controls, and in part because of state resources, rural labor played a significant role opposing the military regime and won significant gains. Old corporatist unionism, not just new social movements, played a role in the Brazilian transition.

Most of this study's findings relate more specifically to the role of rural labor in democratic transitions. One is that rural workers, in general, are unlikely to play a major role in democratic transition in most places. In industrialized countries, the political weight of the rural working class is usually minimal, due to the small proportion of rural workers in the economy and their lack of a fixed connection, through stable rural communities, to the land. In agrarian societies, peasants are generally politically controlled through traditional mechanisms of some kind: patron-client relations with landlords, conservative political parties, ethnic or kinship ties, or monarchical institutions. Only in countries where capitalist development in agriculture has begun to disintegrate the peasantry, but has not gone so far that the rural proletariat has become insignificant, will rural labor have the capacity to play an important role in democratic transition.

Several Latin American countries occupy just such an intermediate position between advanced industrialization and agrarianism. In

Argentina, Uruguay, and Venezuela, rural labor has already been diminished to a role comparable to that in industrial countries, and in countries such as Bolivia, the Dominican Republic, Paraguay, and most of Central America, peasants are still numerous. But in countries such as Brazil, Chile, Colombia, Costa Rica, Cuba, Ecuador, Mexico, and Panama, a sizable rural proletariat exists alongside a large class of small farmers, making the kind of rural unionism analyzed here possible, but certainly not inevitable.

The example of Chile shows that agricultural development may produce capital-intensive farms that employ migrant labor seasonally and sparingly, hindering labor organization. The Pernambuco case suggests that special circumstances are required for the structural conditions of depeasantization and a sizable rural proletariat to result in the creation of a militant and successful rural workers' movement. In this instance, state protection and promotion of the sugar industry also played a large role in guaranteeing an organizational base to labor. State-supervised negotiations gave labor representatives a place at the bargaining table. The sugar sector had a heavy demand for labor that concentrated the work force, creating an unusually propitious environment for union organization. In Pernambuco, the existence of stable working-class communities outside the direct control of plantation owners gave union organizers an added resource. Sugar workers in Pernambuco thus formed a nucleus of resistance that was unusual in Latin American agriculture, an incubus of labor militancy comparable to the industrial peripheries of São Paulo and Buenos Aires. In comparative terms, what appears truly distinctive about Brazil is not agricultural modernization per se. In other countries in the region, the use of capital, technology, and (increasingly temporary) wage labor increased under authoritarian regimes (Diaz 1993). However, unlike that in the other southern cone countries, the authoritarian regime in Brazil accepted the need for a controlled, welfare-type unionism in the countryside; it was this unionism that slipped off the yoke of the welfare state and became more militant in the 1980s.

There is thus something different about the military regime in Brazil that is concealed beneath the generic label *bureaucratic-authoritarian* that has been applied to most of the South American regimes of the 1960s and 1970s (O'Donnell 1973). A relative independence from large landowners; a lower degree of peasant threats from below on the land reform issue in the populist period; a relatively "soft" authoritarianism capable of engaging in populist forms of incorporation, even of segments of the lower class; a greater degree of continuity with the populist regime; the preservation of the basic features of the union structure across regimes, in which union-state relations were more important than union-party relations: these are some of the special features that stand out when one compares Brazil with Chile, for example, on the issue of rural labor. Brazil's rural welfare programs were certainly unique.

A second conclusion concerns the continuity of authoritarian power relations in the countryside. The reintroduction of elections for the highest political offices certainly opened up previously unavailable political space for unions. But in the northeast, rural labor unions were not able to extend democratic rights as far as they might because landlords continued to dominate politics through new electoral mechanisms. Despite the unions' acquisition of some countervailing power, a landowning oligarchy enjoyed privileged access to the state. The alcohol policy that so drastically changed Brazil's pattern of energy consumption and land use, for example, was decided by a small coterie of state managers and sugar industry representatives, without any input from representatives of labor or small farmers. The policy was maintained in the 1980s despite the democratic transition.

The rural labor movement's slogan, "No democracy without agrarian reform," refers to the idea that the extension of democratic rights in Brazil's countryside required a curb on the political power of the landed upper class, which is most deeply entrenched in the northeast. Social scientists reach a similar conclusion when they observe that liberal democracy does not occur without the destruction of the political hegemony of the landed aristocracy (Moore 1966; Rueschemeyer, Stephens, and Stephens 1992). The corollary of this insight is that large landlords engaged in labor-intensive production, even when their power is regionally rather than nationally based, pose a serious threat to the establishment of democratic rights in those regions where they are located.[3]

The vigorous rural labor movement in Pernambuco in the 1950s and early 1960s met with a violent response from many landowners, who completely denied workers' basic democratic rights such as the right to assemble, organize, strike, and vote in elections. Only as capitalist development continued in the 1960s and 1970s was the stage set for a democratic resolution of labor conflicts in Pernambuco. While many large estates were still not models of capitalist efficiency—in the late 1980s about half of Pernambuco's sugar mills could not compete without state subsidies—their more capital-intensive production methods allowed them to make pacts with labor that traditional landlords would not make. This, in turn, meant that the democratic transition would not fundamentally

threaten big agriculture. However, because many labor-intensive producers still remained, the rights won in labor negotiations were not universally respected.

Another general conclusion of this study derives from the analysis
above: that de-peasantization may be a neglected causal factor in democratic transitions. This would not be the first time that de-peasantization
has been linked to regime change. Lenin used the term in his polemical
attack on Russian populists, who argued that the traditional peasant com-
mune *(mir)* could serve as a microfoundation of a new socialist regime.
Against the populists, Lenin argued that peasants were not just experienc-
ing increasing differentiation among themselves, but that they were dis-
appearing, most becoming wage laborers and a few becoming small farmers under the pressures of commercialization. Lenin exaggerated the
extent of class polarization in Russia in 1905 for political purposes, but his
basic insight was correct. The beginning of the end of the Russian peasantry undermined a crucial basis of support for the czarist regime, while
a newly emerging proletariat became a pillar of support for Bolshevik rule
(Lenin 1982, 112–21).

De-peasantization is a more appropriate term than proletarianization,
because not all peasants become full-time wage workers in this transformation. While the transformation of labor into a commodity that is
bought and sold on the market corrodes old solidarities based on ties to
the land, it offers the potential for new forms of solidarity and collective
action and the achievement of democratic rights. This potential is often
unmet. Many peasants in Brazil, for example, migrated to cities, where
their citizenship rights remained unrealized in urban slums marked by
violence, repression by police and drug traffickers, and poverty. Other
former peasants stayed in the countryside, underemployed or unemployed, migrating from one seasonal job to the next. But sometimes new
working classes arise that are capable of demanding and obtaining some
degree of political inclusion. When this happens, a new kind of rural politics occurs in which old forms of patrimonial control are no longer
viable. This conclusion has important implications for other countries
undergoing processes of agricultural modernization. Under certain circumstances, de-peasantization can lead to the rise of a militant rural
unionism such as Pernambuco's. The extension of welfare programs to the
countryside can be a contributing factor in this transformation.

An additional theoretical point to be drawn from this case study is that
the form of the local political economy and of the state shapes the way
interests are represented in a democratic transition.[4] In Pernambuco,
organizations representing peasants and expressing their desire for land

have been marginalized not because peasants there have completely ceased to exist, but because organizations of this type were violently abolished by the military regime. Subsequently, the implantation of welfare programs in the unions raised the costs of entry into the "market" of rural labor representation, deterring competitors to the unions. The welfare programs also empowered a new category of professional union leaders, connected to the state, who had considerable influence over their members and the responsibility of representing rural labor as workers, but little interest in challenging the distribution of property rights; they became in a way analogous to their counterparts in urban unions. These union leaders directed what was now an "old" social movement that repeatedly used a single repertoire of collective action—the strike—in a stable, ritualized pattern of annual class conflict. The unions helped those workers who could benefit from wage increases—in particular, permanently employed field hands—to achieve some measure of citizenship, dignity, and economic improvement.

The analysis in chapters 5–8 suggests a theoretical insight about the divergence between elite and popular conceptions of democracy. These chapters analyze various aspects of the political role and impact of rural unions in Brazil's long transition to a new regime, from the opening of 1979, through the inauguration of a civilian president in 1985, the adoption of a new constitution in 1988, and direct elections for president in 1989 and 1994. Understanding this role necessitates an analysis of the links between the unions and external forces and institutions: the national union bureaucracy, landlords, political parties, and the coalition for agrarian reform.

The crisis of Brazil's development policies in the 1980s made the role of rural labor leaders increasingly difficult during the regime transition. The union movement was revitalized at a time when state subsidies to agriculture were slashed and the import-substitution policies of the past were replaced by a more open, export-oriented (and less successful, in terms of growth) model of development. This meant that labor's new freedom to organize was exercised in an increasingly lean environment, as the state attempted to ride out the debt crisis by curbing domestic demand, ratcheting down wages, and increasing trade surpluses that provided the foreign exchange needed for debt repayment.

In Pernambuco, given the sugar workers' lack of access to land and alternative employment, the employers' flat demand for labor and lack of need for strong labor discipline, and continued population growth and hence surplus labor, workers were not in a strong bargaining position vis-à-vis employers. Sugar workers in richer and more industrialized economies, such as those of Hawaii and Louisiana in the United States, had a stronger bargaining position than Pernambuco workers and earned far higher pay.[5]

Large landowners continued to retain substantial political power, even over populist machines such as that led by Miguel Arraes, and made labor's construction of an alternative political base problematic as well. The best that rural union leaders could accomplish was attachment to Arraes's clientelistic machine in return for a slightly better climate in which to negotiate than the one offered by other parties and candidates. Ironically, the new bargaining freedoms won by the unions in 1979 were used primarily in a losing battle to halt the slide in real wages. The post-1985 civilian regime, presiding over a disastrous loss of control over inflation, became associated with impoverishment in the sugar zone.

Experience shapes attitudes. The union leaders' expectation of the democratic transition was that it would provide an opportunity to meet long-frustrated material wants. However, most union leaders did not see the post-1985 civilian regime as greatly improving their members' economic position, nor were they willing to curb their economic demands in order to preserve the stability of the transition.[6] Some leaders were openly nostalgic for the military government of President Figueiredo (1979–1985), when the biannual salary adjustments had kept up with inflation, in contrast to the 1986–1989 period, when inflation raced ahead of wage increases.[7]

More important, the conception of democracy shared by most Pernambuco trade union leaders was material and procedural, as distinct from the institutional definition preferred by most political scientists. In other words, the trade unionists were interested in substantive changes in policies that affected their members, and the way those policies were made, not just in the restoration of open party competition (of which, in fact, they were generally suspicious). The study therefore suggests that, among subordinate groups, democratic legitimacy may be as much a function of substantive outputs as it is of procedural reforms. In Adam Przeworski's words, people want "to eat and to talk—to be free from hunger and from repression" (1991, ix). In northeast Brazil, state repression was lifted (although repression by landlords remained a problem), but for many, freedom from hunger had not yet been attained.

These findings have important implications for the study of Latin American democracy. Just as recent economic studies show that growth alone will not solve the problem of poverty,[8] greater electoral competition is unlikely to increase citizens' attachment to new regimes, nor is it likely to generate the kind of civic fraternity necessary for democratic consolidation. The latter may require new formulae for decision making, procedures that incorporate not just the traditional, corporatist entities such as trade unions but new social movements that have grown up outside the state as well.[9]

Possible Futures in the Pernambuco Sugar Zone

In Pernambuco, the state federation of rural workers is inextricably bound up with the sugar sector, whose condition looks uncertain due to reductions in state subsidies. The possible future of Pernambuco's sugar sector includes at least two different scenarios: maintenance of some subsidies and the continuation of modernization of production; or major cuts in subsidies, a sharp drop in local sugar production, and the diversification of land use into new crops.[10]

The first scenario derives its plausibility from the fact that the Brazilian northeast is strongly represented in the administration of President Fernando Henrique Cardoso, elected in 1994. The Liberal Front Party (PFL), based primarily in the northeast and with substantial backing from landlord interests, is an important pillar of the Cardoso presidency, and it is unlikely that Cardoso can risk this alliance by cutting the subsidies completely. In 1995, when a bank in the northeastern state of Bahia, Banco Econômico, went bankrupt, strong pressure from northeastern politicians in Congress influenced the eventual decision of the Central Bank to intervene and cover Econômico's losses in August of that year (*Veja*, 22 November 1995). Similar pressures are likely to keep at least some northeastern sugar producers afloat for some time.

Therefore, the Proálcool program may well be maintained in some form, and the state will continue to finance, on a more limited basis, the modernization of sugar production. Because the IAA is virtually moribund, this would result in more vertical integration of production, more mechanization, and declining employment levels in Pernambuco. Reductions in subsidies will mean that some mills and plantations will go out of business.[11] The plantations that remain will become highly mechanized.[12] Demand for labor in the fields will fall sharply, and manual cane cutting will become as quaint and folkloric as it is in present-day Louisiana, in the southern United States.[13] The development of the sugar industry will result in more "modernization and poverty," to borrow the title of a book evaluating the Brazilian sugar industry (Andrade 1994).

In a declining but still state-supported sugar industry, the tactics of the trade unions will probably continue to be pragmatic incrementalism. After the 1964 repression, union leaders learned from the mistakes of the early 1960s and built a more cautious union movement, free of the revolutionary utopianism and illusions that flourished under the populist republic. The new movement played down the zero-sum conflict over land and concentrated on the incremental goal of annual wage increases. However, if FETAPE maintains this position, clinging to its corporatist role and bargaining only for higher wages, it might eventually find itself eclipsed by new movements, outside the corporatist labor structure, claiming to speak on behalf of the growing pool of workers marginalized by capitalist development in agriculture. While the space for such movements is easy to imagine, their particular forms could be quite varied. For example, in July 1994, representatives of an organization called the Movement for Land, Work, and Liberty (Movimento por Terra, Trabalho, e Liberdade) vowed to organize land invasions on northeastern sugarcane plantations that are indebted to the government.[14]

The second scenario for the sugar zone envisages not a projection of current trends, but a major change: a sharp reduction in sugar production and the diversification of the land to other crops. Petrobrás, the state oil firm, is reported to be unhappy with the Proálcool program. A 1996 review of the program noted that alcohol costs twice as much as gasoline to produce and that the production of alcohol-fueled cars had almost completely ceased (Brazil Watch, 13–27 May 1996, 10). The Brazilian government's efforts to curb deficit spending and reform the state are likely to put pressure on the alcohol program. If the Proálcool program were reduced or eliminated, the relatively inefficient northeastern producers would probably face the possibility of collapse and go the way of many Caribbean sugar producers.

The implications of such a collapse for workers would depend on whether viable alternative crops to sugar could be profitably grown. If such crops could be developed, they might require year-round employment of the workers, breaking the current vicious cycle of work at harvest time and unemployment and hunger in the dead season. Such a diversification is more possible than it was in the past because the current generation of planters are not wedded to the land, as previous generations were. Increasingly, they live in Recife rather than on the *engenho* itself. Their attachment to their property is purely commercial; they are no longer the traditional *senhores de engenho*, who saw land as a symbol of social status and sugar production as a way of life. If the economics of the business should change, these new planters are likely to be flexible and adapt the land to new uses rather quickly.

However, if new crops cannot be found to substitute for sugar, the rural labor movement might return to the "politics of despair" that has afflicted the northeast in past eras. The democratic consensus that prevailed between landowners and union leaders after the 1979 strike would collapse. As in the 1960s, demands for land could surface and spontaneous incidents of direct action on the part of an idled labor force could occur. These demands would come not from a marginalized segment of the labor force, as in the first scenario, but from the majority of workers. In such a setting, rural laborers might create something that looked much more like a new social movement than the current network of unions does. Glimpses of such a possibility could be seen in March 1993, when 1,000 sugarcane workers occupied the state agricultural secretariat in Recife. They demanded that the state redistribute uncultivated land to workers and create more public works jobs.[15] The federal government's response was to create some public works jobs on a temporary basis while leaving the land issue untouched. In the absence of a major economic crisis, as projected in scenario 2, neither of FETAPE's demands for land redistribution and extensive public works programs seems likely, given the power of Pernambuco's landed oligarchy and the fiscal crisis of the Brazilian state. Furthermore, it has become increasingly clear that the unions cannot effectively represent the rural lower classes on their own. They need the help of other organizations devoted to representing groups that they cannot easily help. If labor-saving technology continues to reduce the work force, for example, the unions' membership and representativeness will decline. Already, the unions' ability to help those outside the wage labor system—squatters and smallholders of various types—is minimal. This has given space to new social movements, such as Church organizations, associations linked to political parties such as the PT, and NGOs with international contacts, that supplement and sometimes compete with unions in the struggle to represent the interests of the rural poor within Brazil's political system.

Problems of Representation in the Countryside

As the outcome of the debate about agrarian reform in the 1988 constitution showed, the "agrarian problem" was not solved in Brazil along the lines envisioned by reformers in the 1960s. Land was redistributed, but mainly through market transactions rather than state programs. Vast inequalities in landholding and the distribution of credit remained. The *latifúndio* was transformed into a capitalist, agro-industrial estate, and no matter how inegalitarian and repressive were the policies that nurtured it, this agribusiness now dominated production. It was too well entrenched, too productive, and too useful to any future government to be dismantled.

At the end of the 1980s, landlessness and underemployment at the bottom of the social hierarchy were on the increase (Abramovay 1992, 256). More than 6 million wage workers toiled in agriculture's "factories in the fields" (Venceslau 1989, 64). Modernization continued apace. Despite the halving of government subsidies and no net increase in the area under cultivation, farm production in Brazil increased by 47 percent between 1980 and 1995, compared to an increase in industrial production of 11 percent. Huge investments in mechanization drove this phenomenal growth (*New York Times*, 26 April 1995).

It is in this context that we can speak of Brazil's new rural unionism as representing the "end of the peasantry." It is a largely secular, self-led movement that, although it challenges the state to fundamentally overhaul the agrarian system, is itself very much a product of that system.

Land reform, even within a party committed to radical change such as the Workers' Party, has become a solution at the margins. It is presented as a cure for the worst cases of rural poverty, capable of preventing the rural-urban migration from being larger than it already is, within an agricultural structure basically divided between capitalist farmers and wage workers. In the 1994 elections, the Workers' Party candidate, Lula, proposed a redistribution of land to 800,000 rural families during his four years as president (a lesser number than the 1 million he promised land to in 1989). Fernando Henrique Cardoso, Lula's main rival for the presidency and the winner of the election, claimed to plan to settle 280,000 families on the land during his administration (*Folha de São Paulo*, 8 August 1994; *O Estado de São Paulo*, 25 August 1994). Both figures pale next to the grandiose promise of the 1985 agrarian reform to give all 7.1 million landless rural families in Brazil access to land in fifteen years.[16]

In this context, land reform has become a necessity even to administrations, like that of Fernando Henrique Cardoso, that gave only lukewarm rhetorical support to the idea. The end of the peasantry presents a paradox: as the number of peasants declines, the less threatening talk of land redistribution becomes even to large landowners. Eventually, even governments that receive significant support from such landowners come to accept the rationale for spending some money on settling the landless, if only to avoid the costs and pressures associated with continued rural-urban migration. Thus, the Cardoso government's redistribution of land to roughly 20,000–30,000 families in 1995 reportedly far exceeded the average number of families settled each year since 1980.[17]

The redistribution came as a result of pressure from below as well as the logic of a declining peasantry. It came mainly from outside the rural trade unions. The Cardoso government faced a militant landless workers' movement, the MST, whose slogan was "Occupy, resist, and produce." The organization was partially responsible for the reported 25 percent increase in squatters in Brazil in 1995 (*Manchester Guardian Weekly*, 7 January 1996). Originating in the dense rural social networks of the southern state of Rio Grande do Sul, the MST was said in 1995 to operate in 22 of Brazil's 26 states and claimed responsibility for some 89 land occupations throughout the country in 1995.[18] The organization's militant tactics often provoked severe repression from landowners and military police, but they got the government's attention and, sometimes, results—results that would not have come from merely waiting for the slow agrarian reform bureaucracy to distribute land.[19] In September 1995, MST coordinator Gilberto Portes warned the government of Fernando Henrique Cardoso that if it did not keep its promise of settling 40,000 landless families on land by the end of the year, the MST would double the number of land invasions (Villar 1995, 6–7). The government, for its part, did not meet the target, in part because landowners could easily delay and block expropriations in court.[20] But the MST's threats and militant stance in defense of the landless families contrasted with the more moderate position of CONTAG, whose president in 1995, Francisco Urbano de Araújo Filho, was a member of President Cardoso's own party.

The MST, like the Peasant Leagues of the 1950s and early 1960s, succeeded in putting land redistribution on the national political agenda. But it is unlike the Peasant Leagues in many important respects. While both the Leagues and the MST took direct action in an attempt to redistribute land, the Peasant Leagues arose in an area that was agriculturally relatively backward. Furthermore, the Leagues started as an organization devoted to the communally based, local defense of tenants who were being evicted from the land by a landlord. The MST, in contrast, arose in a state with some of Brazil's most capital-intensive and mechanized agriculture. Rather than defending traditional rights to land, the MST organizes landless people in land invasions all over the country. It carefully selects estates where the owners' claims to title are dubious, the chances of victory are high, or where the land seems unproductive, and organizes people from many different areas into squatter camps. Unemployed factory workers, not just peasants with backgrounds in land cultivation, are said to be members of these camps and to take part in land invasions (Villar 1995, 7–8). Furthermore, whereas the Peasant Leagues' actions were not coordinated on a national scale (the Leagues had no presence outside the northeast), those of the MST are nationally coordinated from headquarters located in Brazil's largest city, São Paulo. Like the trade unions, therefore, the MST reflects the decline of the peasantry.

Despite past gains, the political position of the official rural labor movement in the post-1988 period is a difficult one. CONTAG constructed its major political demand—agrarian reform—as a broad political plank that would unite farmers, workers, and the landless; it includes the notion of price supports and other subsidies to small farmers, land redistribution to the landless, and labor policies beneficial to workers. But land redistribution, the most highly charged aspect of agrarian reform, is more difficult under the 1988 constitution than it was under the military's 1964 Land Statute. Any "productive" land is exempt from expropriation, and all expropriated owners must be paid by a government drowning in debt.

In addition to political defeat on agrarian reform, CONTAG faces powerful new challenges from continuous agricultural modernization that marginalizes more and more of the rural poor; from heavily armed landlords ready to use violence in defense of their interests; from state bureaucracies unable, even when willing, to protect the rural lower classes; and from dynamic, newer organizations like the MST that are willing to break the trade unions' monopoly on the representation of the rural poor.

These newer organizations include the Church's Pastoral Land Commission (CPT) and myriad local associations such as those of the landless, rural dwellers threatened with relocation by dam projects, women, indigenous groups, human rights organizations, and environmentalists. All of these associations had some claim to membership in the rural workers' movement, although they were outside the corporatist labor structure and did not enjoy CONTAG's official recognition by the state. Many of them challenged CONTAG's claim to a monopoly on representation of rural labor. Like the CUT, the labor central formed in 1983, they criticized CONTAG's insistence on a hierarchical approach to action that gave primacy to the confederation, its defense of the corporatist labor system, its stance on agrarian reform which insisted that the reform could be carried out merely by applying existing law and supporting the government's cumbersome land reform bureaucracy, its reluctance to support illegal direct actions such as land occupations, and its attempt to get key players in the democratic transition to recognize certain demands of rural labor at the national level, at the expense of a more grass-roots approach (Ricci 1994).

CONTAG's defeat on agrarian reform in the Constituent Assembly in 1988 gave added impetus to these criticisms. The profile of new social movements that advocated direct action by the landless rose. CONTAG hegemony over the rural labor movement, once very tight, looked vulnerable. If, under the military regime, CONTAG had represented the "politics of the possible" (Maybury-Lewis 1994), it was clear that in the more pluralistic conditions of post-transition politics, many grass-roots activists believed that more was possible than CONTAG was willing to allow and that their cause could be furthered by using different methods. The gap between CONTAG's successful mobilization on behalf of its bedrock constituency, wage workers and small farmers, and its somewhat ineffectual advocacy of the rights of the landless, became more apparent. The unity of the movement unraveled, with the peasantry increasingly represented outside the official union movement.

Such unraveling is understandable. No urban labor confederation faces problems of coordination comparable to those of CONTAG, which is supposed to speak for small landowners, colonists, renters, sharecroppers, and temporary and permanent workers all over the country. The confederation's leaders were somewhat ambivalent about land redistribution, because the majority of them were themselves small landowners who, while not directly threatened by plans for land redistribution, sometimes identified more with owners than with the landless. Discussions within the labor movement and the wider society about the need for more pluralism in the representation of labor's interests threatened still further the cohesion and central control of the confederation.[21]

New forms of interest representation in the countryside are vital if the negation of citizenship rights by economic marginalization, landlord violence, and misery is to be curbed. The rural unions are part of Brazil's corporatist labor structure, with its trinity of *unicidade*, the mandatory union tax, and the labor court system. This structure, while originally built to enhance the central state's control over unions, served as a focal point for rural opposition to the military regime in the 1970s. Beneath its protective canopy, a wide coalition of the rural lower classes was forged. This coalition could agree on minimal demands: the extension of rights to bargain and strike in the countryside, the return of the competition of party politics, the enactment of more favorable policies for small farmers. But as these liberties were restored and minimal demands were met, the rural union movement's inherent pluralism became more manifest. It became increasingly clear that the single category "rural worker" did not adequately represent the divergent, sometimes contradictory, interests of the three distinct classes in the movement: small farmers, wage workers, and peasants (sharecroppers, tenants, squatters, the landless). These classes are themselves highly heterogeneous (Venceslau 1989). One union cannot effectively represent all of them in what are often complex negotiations with state institutions and landlords. This is one reason why organizations representing the landless poor have sprung up largely outside the official union structure.

In sum, the organizational form that proved so effective in resisting the military regime became a liability after the democratic transition. CONTAG's centralized and unified hierarchy of leaders, its cautious, legalistic approach to mobilization, and its determination to demand only what the most progressive of the transition's top players were themselves willing to concede, increasingly made it irrelevant to grass-roots groups impatient with the inertia of the new civilian governments. Increasingly, grass-roots groups engaged in small-scale direct action on behalf of people whose very survival was in question, people who did not want to wait for legal or parliamentary actions to churn slowly through the state bureaucracy. Even the rural trade unionists among the rubber tappers of Acre—whose most prominent leader, Chico Mendes, died a martyr's death at the end of 1988—were most effective when they went outside the CONTAG hierarchy to form direct alliances with indigenous groups and environmentalists.

The paths to reform of the structures that represent interests in Brazil's countryside are numerous. One way would be to simply divide the "rural worker" category into several new categories, allowing separate unions for wage workers, small farmers, and peasants in the same area. The rural labor legislation on the books from 1962 to 1965 actually permitted unions to organize along lines very similar to these, although it was little used in practice (Venceslau 1989, 63).

A more radical reform was endorsed by President Fernando Henrique Cardoso: the end of *unicidade* and the mandatory union tax. This would allow workers freely to form unions representing the same category of workers in the same area. It would wipe out the sixty-year monopoly of representation enjoyed by Brazil's official union leaders. Such a reform contains significant advantages. It would do away with unresponsive leaders who do little for their membership because their finances are automatically extracted from workers by the state. It would allow for the more spontaneous creation of unions at the local level, and a more pluralistic kind of bargaining between employers and employees.

The danger is that such a reform would weaken existing unionism without putting anything in its place. Nowhere is this fear greater than among rural unions. Chile illustrates what can happen: the old labor structure was dismantled by Pinochet and replaced by a much more "flexible" and decentralized system that resulted in very few unions at all in the countryside. In short, the end of *unicidade* could be a positive change if it gave resources for organization and coordination to the new unions that would be allowed to form. On the other hand, it is hard to see how the extension of democratic rights in the countryside could result if the reform served as a pretext for the atomization and marginalization of rural unions.[22]

In Pernambuco, one solution (albeit an improbable one) to the conditions of violence and marginalization that exist there would be to involve trade unions and other organizations in a creative adaptation that ends the 450-year-old stranglehold of sugar and employs the land in new and more socially productive ways. In highlighting the Pernambuco labor movement's modest victories, we should not forget all those who are frequently excluded from the current, dominant forms of popular representation in rural Brazil: women, children, migrants, landless peasants, squatters, illegal workers. The union song "I Am a Cultivator" eloquently expresses the dilemma of citizenship for the millions of rural poor who have not been effectively granted the right to political consultation: "I am a Brazilian only when it is time to vote." Barrington Moore's tranquil assertion that democracy is best served by the disappearance of the peasantry (1966, 429) reflects the developed world's comfortable history, in which the acceleration of capitalist development in agriculture occurred at a time when surplus labor could readily be absorbed by industry. Those conditions do not exist in contemporary Latin America, and the peasantry is not quietly shuffling off the political stage to accommodate "modernity."

The fact that the official rural trade union movement cannot fully represent these displaced people, refugees within their own country, is its Achilles' heel. That is why new movements have grown up around it and increasingly question its right to speak for all the rural poor. The trade unions were vital opponents of authoritarian repression under the military dictatorship, but the cultivators whose interests have been neglected by their monopoly of representation are becoming increasingly vocal. Involved in intricate and intense local conflicts, they criticize the union structure for being too large, hierarchical, centralized, and unrepresentative. Almost four decades after its birth, Brazil's rural union movement faces complex problems of representation for which there are no easy answers. Its dilemma shows that there is a price to pay for success as well as for failure.

Appendixes
Notes
Glossary
Bibliography
Index

APPENDIX I
Survey Method

The survey cited in this book was conducted between 18 March and 25 November 1988. The survey sample consisted of members of the directorates of the forty-five trade unions who had signed the 1987 collective contract in the sugar zone (signed on 28 September of that year). Since most union directorates consisted of three people (president, treasurer, and secretary), the size of the relevant population was roughly 135 (a little more, as some unions had vice-presidents).

Several pretests of the survey were conducted in Recife and the backlands region *(sertão)* of Pernambuco state in order to refine the questionnaire. Then, in the coastal sugar zone of the state (as shown on the map at the beginning of this book), fifty members of trade union directorates were surveyed. The sample included twenty-seven presidents, fourteen secretaries, seven treasurers, and two vice-presidents. These leaders came from a total of forty-two of the targeted forty-five trade unions. (Three unions who had signed the 1987 collective contract—those from Catende, Condado, and Chã Grande—were absent from the survey.) The unions listed below were visited; those at which two members of the directorate were interviewed are followed by a (2). As indicated, all except the last two of these unions are located in the sugar zone:

Southern Sugar Zone (Mata Sul)
Twenty-nine Interviews

Agua Preta
Amaraji
Barreiros
Bonito
Cabo (2)
Cortês
Escada
Gameleira
Glória do Goitá

Ipojuca (2)
Jaboatão (2)
Joaquim Nabuco
Maraial
Moreno (2)
Palmares
Pombos
Ponte dos Carvalhos
Quipapá
Ribeirão
Rio Formoso
São Benedito do Sul
São José da Coroa Grande
Sirinhaém
Vitória de Santo Antão (2)

Northern Sugar Zone (Mata Norte)
Nineteen Interviews

Aliança
Camutanga
Carpina
Ferreiros
Goiana
Igarassu
Itambé
Itaquitinga
Limoeiro
Macaparana
Nazaré da Mata (2)
Paudalho (2)
São Lourenço da Mata
São Vicente Ferrer (*delegacia sindical*)
Timbaúba (2)
Vicência

Intermediate Zone (Agreste)
Two Interviews

Bom Jardim
Canhotinho

Contact was made with the union officials in various ways. Sometimes I telephoned first and explained that I was a North American student conducting research on trade unionism in the sugar zone. Because many unions had no telephones, I often had to make preliminary trips to meet the union leaders. Sometimes, several visits to a union headquarters were needed before respondents would agree to be interviewed. Respondents sometimes voiced skepticism about why I was conducting this kind of research.

All interviews were conducted at union headquarters in the towns listed. Each interviewee was asked a set of sixty-three questions, responses to which were then written on the questionnaire. The interviews were sometimes interrupted while the respondent dealt with requests and questions by union members visiting the headquarters. Interviews took anywhere from ninety minutes to four hours. I personally conducted thirty-eight of the interviews; the other twelve were done by two student research assistants from UFPE (the Federal University of Pernambuco), working under my close supervision.

A translation of the questionnaire used for the survey appears below.

Questionnaire for Members of the Directorates of the Unions of Agricultural Workers in the Sugar Zone of Pernambuco, Brazil

1. Position
2. Name of this union
3. How old are you?
4. Were you born in:
    a.   a city
    b.   a town
    c.   the countryside
5. Were you born in Pernambuco?
    Yes   County
    No   State
6. Can you read and write?
    Yes
    No
7. How many years of schooling do you have?
8. What is your religion?
    When was the last time that you participated in a religious activity?
9. When did you join the union?
10. For how long have you participated actively in the union?

11. What is your professional category?
    small landowner
    sharecropper
    rural worker
    other
12. What are the principal crops grown in this county?
13. How many years ago did the current union president join the directorate?
    Was he reelected in the last union election?
14. Did your directorate have opposition in the last union election?
    Yes
    No
15. What was, roughly, the level of participation in the last union election?
16. Do you plan to run in the next union election?
    Yes
    No
    Why?
17. How many members, more or less, does the union have?
18. How many members, more or less, are current with their union dues?
    Why aren't more members current with their dues?
19. What are the most common demands or complaints that your members bring to you? (Cite them in order of frequency.)
20. How much time do you spend outside the union headquarters each week?
21. Do you consider illegal workers (*os clandestinos*) a problem for the union?
    Yes
    No
    If "yes," is the union trying to cut down on the incidence of this problem?
22. Does the union directorate have women members?
    Yes   How many?   Positions
    No
23. Is there some type of violence against rural workers in this county?
    Yes
    No
    Why or why not?
24. What are the principal problems faced by the union? (Cite them in order of importance.)
25. Do you know a union member who lost his or her job because of his or her union or political activity?
    Yes
    No
    If "yes," what happened to this person or these persons?

26. Do you know a union member who was jailed for his or her union or political activities?

> Yes
>
> No

If "yes," what happened to this person or these persons?

27. Does the union receive help from the Church in this county?

> Yes
>
> No

28. Do you think that the situation of the union improved when direct elections for governors began again in 1982?

> Yes
>
> No
>
> Why or why not?

29. In your opinion, was the political change marked by President Sarney's inauguration in 1985 important and positive for the unions here in the sugar zone?

30. Is it important to consider the consequences for the government when the union makes demands?

31. In your opinion, what is the function of the union?
    a. Provide social assistance
    b. Struggle for agrarian reform
    c. Help the government
    d. Win better salaries for the members
    e. Work with the employers
    f. Struggle against the government
    g. Other

32. Why do people join the union?
    a. Medical and dental services
    b. Retirement benefits
    c. Agrarian reform
    d. To defend their rights
    e. Other

33. In the experience of this union, how is communication between the directorate and the membership carried out?
    a. Via bulletins and newspapers
    b. Via general assemblies
    c. Via other meetings of workers
    d. By members visiting the union office
    e. Other

34. Do you think that the standard of living of workers today is:
    a.   lower
    b.   equal
    c.   higher than the standard of living of workers during the first gover-
         norship of Miguel Arraes (1963–1964)?
         Why?
35. What was the level of participation in the last FETAPE strike in this county?
36. Are the gains from the last strike respected in this county (wages and other
    provisions of the current collective contract)?
37. Do you consider the Sarney government to be democratic?
         Yes
         No
         Why or why not?
38. In your opinion, what is agrarian reform?
39. Do you think that the Sarney government has the will to carry out an agrar-
    ian reform?
40. Is there a country in the world that you admire, in political terms? If "yes,"
    which one?
41. Are you a member of the Landless Rural Workers' Movement (Movimento
    dos Trabalhadores Rurais Sem Terra)?
         Yes
         No
42. Are you a member of a political party?
         Yes   Which one?
         No
43. Whom did you vote for:
    a.   In the 1978 federal Senate election
    b.   In the 1982 federal Senate election
    c.   In the 1982 governor's race
    d.   In the 1986 federal Senate election
    e.   In the 1986 governor's race
44. Did you vote for Dr. Francisco Julião for state deputy in 1986?
    a.   Yes
    b.   No
         Why or why not?
45. Who are the local politicians with whom you have most contact? And state
    politicians?

46. Which candidate do you prefer for president of Brazil?
    a. Franco Montoro
    b. Leonel Brizola
    c. Luís Inacio da Silva (Lula)
    d. Ulysses Guimarães
    e. Antonio Ermírio de Morais
    f. Fernando Collor de Melo
    g. Aureliano Chaves
    h. Miguel Arraes
    i. Other
    j. No preference
        Why?

47. In your opinion, what should be the relationship between union leaders and political parties?
    a. The ideal is that a union's leaders all belong to the same party, so as to achieve greater unity.
    b. It would be better if the leaders belonged to various parties, so as to better reflect the political tendencies of the membership.
    c. It is preferable that the leaders are not affiliated with a party.

48. How do you see the current labor legislation in Brazil?
    a. It should remain as it is.
    b. It should be reformed in some details.
    c. It should be profoundly reformed.
        Why?

49. What is your opinion about the right to strike?
    a. In favor
    b. Against
    c. In favor but with limitations of this right
        Why?

50. Right now, Brazil has a unitary system of one trade union per professional category. Some people think that the law should permit the existence of one or more trade unions per professional category (in other words, a pluralistic trade union system). Which system do you prefer?
    a. One union per category
    b. One or more unions per category
    c. No opinion
        What are the reasons for your preference?

51. How do you see the performance of the union in helping workers at the level of the workplace?
    a. For us, this is important
    b. It is important, but conditions are unfavorable.
    c. For us, this is not of great importance.
        Why?

52. Does the union directorate maintain contacts with the employers or repre-
     sentatives of the employers to deal with problems that arise at the work-
     place?
     a.   With frequency
     b.   Sometimes
     c.   Rarely

53. If the union directorate does not have frequent contacts with the employers
     or their representatives, to what do you attribute this lack of frequency?

              Yes   No
     a.   Contacts are made at the federation level
     b.   Because the employers refuse to enter into contact with the union
     c.   Because not many problems arise at the workplace
     d.   Because the workers don't bring their problems to the union
     e.   Because the problems are resolved at the workplace, without the
           necessity for union intervention
     f.   Other

54. What are the problems that are dealt with in contacts with the employers or
     their representatives?

             Frequent   Infrequent   Never
     a.   Firings of workers
     b.   Conditions of work (security, piece-rates, etc.)
     c.   Threats of removal from the land
     d.   Access to land
     e.   Worker demands involving strikes or threats of strikes
     f.   Other

55. The employers take the initiative in maintaining contacts with the union to
     discuss the problems mentioned in question 54:
     a.   Frequently
     b.   Sometimes
     c.   Rarely or never

56. What is the behavior of the employers' representatives in the negotiations
     over problems that arise between them and the union directorate:

             None   the Majority   a Minority
     a.   They are willing to find negotiated solutions
     b.   They are very rigid in their positions but they negotiate
     c.   They never make concessions to other points of view
     d.   They are sympathetic and polite, but in reality they do not take
           account of the union point of view

57. What are the tactics used by employers to impede union activity at the workplace?

	the Majority	Some	None
a. The most active union members are fired			
b. The most active union members are denied access to plantation land			
c. Information on activists is sent to the police			
d. Only those who help management control the work force are promoted			
e. Other			

58. At the current time, what is the union doing to fulfill its responsibilities?
59. In your opinion, what is democracy?
60. Have you noticed a change in the willingness of employers to recognize the union in the last few years?
61. How do you see the military regime in comparison to the current civilian regime? Is there a great difference between them?
62. Have there been political changes in the last few years which have given you hope that the situation of the unions would improve?
63. Which political changes of the last few years have most disappointed you?

Appendix II

Who Are the Union Leaders?

This book would be incomplete without some personal information about who the rural trade union leaders are. While generalizations about people within a social category are always fraught with the dangers of reductionism and oversimplification, the survey does reveal some important characteristics of the leaders.

All fifty officials surveyed were men. Men dominated the leadership of the unions and also predominated in the rural work force in the sugar zone. Only one of the forty-five unions surveyed had a woman among the three top leadership positions (president, secretary, treasurer), although I later discovered that one union had a woman president and interviewed her in 1990, after the survey had been completed. The leaders' median age was 45 years. At the time of the interviews, six of them were 20–29 years of age, thirteen were 30–39 years, thirteen were 40–49 years, twelve were 50–59 years, five were 60–69, and one was over 69 years.

Ninety percent of the leaders were born in the countryside, 10 percent in towns. Of the fifty, forty-six had been born in Pernambuco (twenty-one in the same *município* where they currently worked), three in the neighboring state of Paraíba, and one in the neighboring state of Alagoas. The union leaders were thus overwhelmingly rural people who sprang from the communities which their unions represented. They were not "outside agitators," as the landlords sometimes alleged, but part of the local work force.

Professionally, forty-six of the leaders listed their occupation as *trabalhador rural*—rural worker. Two called themselves *agricultores* (a word roughly equivalent to *trabalhador rural*, but which can imply some sort of land tenure arrangement); one was a small landowner, and one a renter. The vast majority, therefore, had begun their careers as cane cutters in the sugar fields; many, especially those over age thirty, had begun their working lives as early as eight, nine, or ten years of age.

However, while only one declared himself to be a small landowner, twelve leaders indicated that their family owned land, and four mentioned that they had the use of a small plot on a plantation. This confirms the insight of Eric Wolf (1969), whose "middle peasant thesis" pointed to the importance of landownership as a basis for an independent and politically active rural population.

On the whole, the union leaders had little formal education. While only seven admitted to not being able to read and write, the median time in school was only three years, and most leaders had not completed primary school. Only eight had completed more than five years of school, and only three more than eight years.

Older leaders were generally less educated than younger ones. Ninety percent of the leaders age forty-one or more had undergone four years or less of formal education, whereas only 62 percent of those younger than forty-one years fell into this category.

In the area of religion, forty of the respondents were Catholic, seven Protestants, two had no religion, and one gave no response. Of those who responded, twenty-six said they had been to church the week before they were interviewed, fifteen, between one month and one year ago; of the remaining eight, two "never" went, four went so infrequently that they said they had been "within the last five years," one "more than five years ago," and one "sometimes." These results show that while professions of religious faith are common amongst the union leaders, church attendance is variable, with only half of those surveyed describing themselves as regular churchgoers.

In general, leaders had many years of experience in their union jobs. The average leader had spent a median of nineteen years as a union member, and had participated actively in the union's affairs for eighteen years. While no hard data are available on why these leaders became involved in the union, anecdotal evidence suggests that a family member previously active in the union was often a key factor in their decision to get involved. Given the tight family networks in the sugar zone, such connections are quite plausible entrance networks for many officials. At forty-two unions where the question was asked, the president's average length in office was ten years, or longer than three three-year mandates. Once elected, union officials in the sugar zone could therefore count on relatively long spells in office. Competition in union elections was not intense—only fifty-eight percent of the forty-two surveyed said that they had faced opposition in the last elections.

The leaders usually wanted to keep their jobs. Despite the long hours that many of them put in, with meetings on weekends and at night, they were able to earn more than they could as simple field workers. Union salaries varied depending on the dues that the union received, but they were always higher than the minimum wage, and often two to four times the minimum wage (a field hand's minimum salary was 10 percent above the national minimum wage in 1988). Also, union leaders' jobs were secure for the duration of their three-year terms, unlike those of field workers who faced the threat of unemployment at the end of each sugar harvest.

Perhaps the immediate benefit that a worker experienced when he became a union leader was the freedom from back-breaking, closely supervised work in the fields. Union leaders had the privilege of working behind a desk, traveling by car, and eating at restaurants in town. They were usually better fed, more energetic, and more alert than the average field worker.

In addition, union leaders had access to union resources for their personal use. Most leaders used a union vehicle, and union headquarters could serve a variety of purposes. The temptation of corruption may have offered further opportunities for material gain. Some union leaders owned new or nearly new cars, rumored to be the fruit of payoffs from local landowners. Others had much more well-appointed homes than those of most sugar workers, and some dressed in relatively expensive clothing.

Aside from the material perquisites, union leaders enjoyed considerable prestige in their communities. While the landowners often resented and threatened them, they at least acknowledged and dealt with them to some extent. Union leaders were often sought out by local political candidates because of their ability to deliver votes and were usually welcomed into workers' homes as persons capable of dispensing largesse. Officials spoke frequently before groups of workers and were often asked to give talks and make appearances at nonunion functions. They became noted in the towns where they lived. They also had opportunities to work their way up the union hierarchy, into the state federation and even the national confederation, where they could enjoy even greater material rewards and prestige.

Given the advantages of union leadership over work in the fields, it is not surprising that most union leaders habitually ran for reelection. Out of the fifty officials surveyed, only nine said that they would not run in the next union election. In the "don't know" category, twelve (a large number), said that they would run "if the people wanted them to"; this was probably in deference to the democratic rights of their members rather than from any lack of desire to stay in the job.

Most leaders (62 percent) said that they divided their work time equally between staying in their headquarters and making outside visits to plantations and other places; 14 percent said they spent more than half their time away from their offices; 18 percent that they spent less than half their time away. Observation and informal conversations with leaders gave me the impression that for many unionists the 50–50 division was an ideal rather than something actually practiced. Some leaders often spent all day in their offices, signing papers, attempting to resolve the problems of individuals who came to them, and so forth. But there seemed to be a feeling among almost all officials that a good leader could do his job properly only if he visited the work sites and tried to find out the actual working conditions of his members.

No data on race were overtly collected in the survey. However, the leaders were overwhelmingly black and mulatto. This applied to the state federation as well as to the local unions. Admittedly, racial classifications are different in Brazil from those in the United States. Almost all union leaders would be called black in the United States, whereas only a few would be called *preto* (black) in Brazil, with most probably referred to as *(moreno)* or *(pardo)*, all terms to designate a "brown," or black-white mixed-race identity.

I believe that it makes sense to refer to the trade union leaders in the sugar zone as a specific social category. The leaders formed a coherent group with similar characteristics, backgrounds, life experiences, and expectations. This is not to deny, however, the considerable differences among individual leaders, nor the importance of human agency in union activities.

Appendix III
Archival Research

Many different archival materials were consulted in the research to produce this book. These materials related to three main topics: the unions themselves, the immediate socioeconomic and political environment in which they operated, and the national political scene of which they were a part.

For the first topic, I consulted newspapers containing information about the rural trade unions and the Peasant Leagues. For the early 1960s, the best source was *Última Hora* (1962–1964). This was a popular leftist-populist newspaper owned by a Vargas supporter, Samuel Wainer, that was closed down in the 1964 coup (Leite 1987). *Última Hora* had a daily column of trade union news that gave a good picture of labor conflict in the Pernambuco sugar zone in that period. This column was supplemented by occasional articles in Recife's two mainstream newspapers, the *Diário de Pernambuco* and the *Jornal de Comércio*. All of these papers were located in the Pernambuco State Archive (Arquivo Estadual) in Recife. I also read through some articles in *A Liga*, the Peasant League newspaper, which I found in the Leuenroth Archive at the São Paulo state university at Campinas (UNICAMP). In the Government Documents section of Widener Library at Harvard University, I examined the Communist Party's newspaper *Novos Rumos* for the 1959–1964 period.

Pernambuco's rural unionism is virtually undocumented in the state's local press in the post-coup period until the 1979 strike. However, for 1979–1988, I found many articles, mostly about the strikes, in the *Diário de Pernambuco* and the *Jornal de Comércio*. I also consulted CONTAG's newspaper *O Trabalhador Rural*, at the research institute CEBRAP (Centro Brasileiro de Analise e Planejamento) in São Paulo, as well as CONTAG documents from their headquarters in Brasília. Finally, I looked at Ministry of Labor reports on the Pernambuco unions, especially election results, at the Union Division Archive at the Regional Labor Delegation, part of the Ministry of Labor in Recife.

The second type of archival research I engaged in was that of local demographic, economic, social, and political conditions in Pernambuco's sugar zone. This included reviewing demographic and agricultural census data (for various decades), found in the Government Documents section of Widener Library. I analyzed reports on Pernambuco's economy, including the distribution of landholding, in each county *(município)* in Pernambuco's sugar zone, as well as more state agricultural census data from 1950 and 1980. These documents were in the library at the Pernambuco Development Institute (CONDEPE) of the Secretariat of Planning (SEPLAN), part of the Pernambuco state government in Recife. These reports were supplemented by documents supplied by the sugar mill owners' and cane planters' associations. In addition, I gained access to the archives of the state legislative assembly and obtained transcripts of sessions of the state legislature for various years relevant to this study. Finally, I gathered election data at the Regional Electoral Tribunal in Recife and compiled tables on election results in the sugar zone and Pernambuco, from 1962 to 1994.

In researching the national political scene, I relied largely on the National Archive in Rio de Janeiro, where I reviewed transcripts of the council of ministers during the Goulart presidency, Ministry of Labor documents, and the personal archives of former foreign minister San Tiago Dantas and former president Carlos Castelo Branco. While in Rio, I drew on the transcripts of interviews with Pernambuco political figures such as Cid Sampaio, Francisco Julião, João Cleofas, Padres Melo and Crespo, Pelopidas da Silveira, and Osvaldo Costa Lima at the Center for Research and Documentation of Brazil's Contemporary History (CPDOC) at the Getúlio Vargas Foundation. Also consulted were the Octavio Brandão archive and the *Hispanic American Report*, 1961–1964, both at UNICAMP, the Nucleus for the Documentation and Information of Regional History at the University of Paraíba in João Pessoa, and transcripts of the Brazilian Senate and House of Deputies in the early 1960s, both of which were housed in the Government Documents section of Harvard's Widener Library. For more contemporary events, I relied on reports published by the Rio de Janeiro–based nongovernmental organization, IBASE, as well as reports and pamphlets from the Pastoral Land Commission (CPT) office and the extensive archives of the state rural labor federation, FETAPE, the last two located in Recife.

NOTES

Introduction

1. Whereas 253,000 rural workers had been unionized in 1973 (Loveman 1976), only 30,000 out of 450,000 agricultural workers were unionized in 1989 (Petras, "Chile's Exploited Farm Workers," *Christian Science Monitor*, 11 April 1989, 18).

2. I owe this distinction between the *end* and the *ends* (in this case, of the peasantry) to Perry Anderson, who uses it in "The Ends of History" (1992, 279–375).

Chapter 1. From Peasant Leagues to Unions in Rural Brazil

1. Field notes, 15 October 1988.

2. The literature on new social movements sees the latter as different from "old," class-based movements in that they represent "a multiplicity of social actors" bearing diverse local gender, ethnic, neighborhood, and other identities; and they compete within "a fragmented social and political space" (Escobar and Alvarez 1992, 3). While I question some of the imputed attributes of new social movements ascribed to them in this literature, it is clear that labor in Brazil became enmeshed within the state's hierarchical and monopolistic state corporatist institutions established in the 1930s, while newer social movements have tended to remain more clearly outside the state.

3. IBGE 1991, 425. In 1994, according to confederation president Francisco Urbano de Araújo Filho, the number of unions in CONTAG reached 3,000 (interview with author, Brasília, 17 November 1994). However, membership figures for those unions are not always reliable because names of people listed in the registry who have died, moved away, or changed jobs are rarely removed. Also, absolute membership figures do not indicate rates of active participation in the unions, in which, for example, participation in elections is relatively low.

4. There is a large literature on why and how peasants should be defined. One tradition identifies peasants primarily in cultural terms as "part societies with part cultures" (see Forman 1975, 247). I here define peasants in economic terms, as rural cultivators who have access to land and who engage in small-scale subsistence production, mainly with family labor. Workers, on the other hand, derive most or all of their income from wages. In the Pernambuco sugar zone, tenants, sharecroppers, and small landowners are peasants; wage workers are permanent or temporary employees on the sugar estates. The *moradores*, resident workers on the sugar estates discussed later, are between the peasantry and the proletariat, with both a land and wage relationship to the landowner.

5. McAdam 1995. McAdam distinguishes between "initiator" social movements, which begin a cycle of protest and are the first to use a given repertoire of collective action, from "derivative" movements which copy these repertoires and sustain a cycle of protest. Strictly speaking, the initiators of Brazil's strike wave in the late 1970s were the metalworkers' unions in São Paulo's industrial periphery. However, because of the major differences between urban and rural unions, the Pernambuco strike of 1979 was important in showing the replicability of strikes in the countryside.

6. The ABC region of São Paulo, a major manufacturing center, derives its name from the neighboring cities of Santo André, São Bernardo, and São Caetano.

7. From Rueschemeyer, Stephens, and Stephens 1992, 43–44. For similar definitions of democracy, see Weiner and Ergun 1987, 4–5; Goran Therborn, "The Rule of Capital and the Rise of Democracy," in Held et al. 1983, 262. For comparisons of this elite or empirical definition with more participatory conceptions of democracy, see Cohen and Arato 1992, 8–10; Bowles and Gintis 1986, 182–83; Chauí 1994, 431–32.

8. This literature is large and growing. Some representative works include Alves 1988; Bacchus 1987; Diniz 1986; Garreton 1988; Handelman and Sanders 1981; Jonas and Stein 1990; Mainwaring et al. 1992; Malloy and Seligson 1987; Munck 1994; Przeworski 1991; Schmitter 1993; and Weffort 1992.

9. Valenzuela 1989. Important exceptions are Rueschemeyer, Stephens, and Stephens 1992; Fishman 1990b, the latter an excellent study of labor in the Spanish transition.

10. The notion of a peasantariat, discussed more fully in chapter 4, can be found in Cohen 1991, 24, 73–74.

11. Paige's explanation of rural politics in terms of a typology of local forms of production in export agriculture is deservedly influential. However, the typology, while conceptually clear, is difficult to apply in practice, because most regions contain characteristics of more than one type. I use here the hacienda type because it most closely fits the Pernambuco sugar zone. For a useful analysis of Paige's work, see Wickham-Crowley 1992, 11.

12. Paige 1975, 24, 49–51. However, contrary to Paige's account, that process is neither ineluctable nor purely market-driven. Heavy state intervention in agriculture is common in most countries, and different patterns of intervention produce different development paths. These development paths, in turn, influence labor movements in the countryside. Paige thus underemphasizes the role of the state in the process he analyzes. He also analyzes only structural change that makes reformist mobilization and democratic landlord-labor pacts possible, without exploring the political mechanisms through which such potential might be realized.

13. Land productivity is usually measured in output per hectare, labor productivity in output per worker (Grigg 1992, 3). Productivity could also be measured per unit of capital. In using the term *modernization*, I do not mean to evoke the assumptions or teleology of modernization theory. I am using the term in a technical way to refer to the movement of agriculture away from labor-intensive, subsistence cultivation toward more capital-intensive, mechanized, and commercial forms of production.

14. For example, in the contemporary United States, fewer than 4 percent of the labor force works in agriculture, while fewer than 10 percent of workers are on farms in Western Europe (Suits 1990, 1).

15. A study of 114 developing countries estimated that there were more than 600 million landless peasants in these countries, and that landlessness continues to spread at a rate of from 3 to 5 percent per year. Aside from agricultural modernization, other causes of landlessness include population growth, exhaustion of ecosystems, inequitable patterns of land inheritance, and the adoption of structural adjustment programs (Jazairy et al. 1992, 47–50). For an argument that, as agricultural modernization continues, 2 billion of the world's 3.1 billion rural people may be driven off the land, see James Goldsmith, "Economic Disaster Called GATT," *Manchester Guardian Weekly*, 16 October 1994, 21.

16. An early use of the term can be found in Lenin 1982 [1899], 113.

17. Researchers at the University of Brasília's Sociology Department have produced many excellent studies analyzing the affects of macroeconomic change on Brazilian agriculture and rural workers. These include Figueiredo 1982; Figueiredo and Teixeira 1989; Figueiredo, Teixeira, and Araújo 1985; Teixeira 1989; Porto 1992 and 1993.

18. CONTAG eventually affiliated with the CUT in 1995.

19. For a somewhat different conception of the relationship between structural change and the rural labor movement, see Maybury-Lewis 1994, 26−37. I agree with most of his well-researched arguments but differ with Maybury-Lewis on several points: he sees structural change in Brazil's rural political economy as one of five variables explaining the emergence of the rural labor movement, giving less weight than I do to agricultural modernization. His analysis also sees class polarization as more pronounced, and political representation as less contested, than the one offered here.

20. For comments on Brazil's inequality, see Sarney 1986, 106−07; Mainwaring, O'Donnell, and Valenzuela 1992, 41−42. For a useful review of the vast literature on poverty and inequality in the northeast, see Scheper-Hughes 1992.

Chapter 2. The Past as Prologue

1. Scott 1991. Unlike Scott, I do not refer here to *the* hidden transcript, because the various interests of the rural unions' thousands of members constitute not a single transcript, but many.

2. There appears to be evidence of the existence of a mill on the island of Itamaracá, in what is now Pernambuco, as early as 1526 (Schwartz 1985, 16).

3. As late as 1583, two-thirds of the slaves on Pernambuco plantations were Indians. Galloway explains the indigenous people's eventual replacement by Africans with reference to Church and crown opposition to Indian enslavement, the high cost of Indian slaves due to their scarcity, and their lower productivity (Galloway 1989, 72). Another important factor mentioned by Schwartz (1985, 28), as well as by Galloway, was the susceptibility of the Indians to Old World diseases.

4. The frequency of slave runaways is suggested by this verse: "My lady, sell me / Enjoy your money / Don't come saying later / That I escaped from slavery" (Carvalho 1994, 8).

5. These runaway slaves are called maroons in the English-language literature on the subject. In 1827 a bounty of 100,000 réis was put on the head of Malunguinho, a leader based at the Quilombo do Catucá who was particularly feared by white planters (Carvalho 1994, 13−14).

6. A ditty popular in Pernambuco in the late 1840s captures this reality. It refers to the Cavalcantis, an elite family, and plays with the similarity between their name and the term *cavalgado* (ridden): "Who lives in Pernambuco / Must not be deceived / One has to be either a Cavalcanti / Or one has to be ridden" (Lopez 1987, 61).

7. Between 1836 and 1840, Pernambuco produced a yearly average of 26,743 tons of sugarcane per year (Carvalho 1994, 2). In the 1980s, production was around 25 *million* tons of sugar per year; see table 3.1.

8. The Brazilian saying that a slave needed three p's—*pau, pão e pano* (the stick, bread, and clothing)—reveals the stark brutality of this institution. The saying is reported by André José Antonil, an Italian Jesuit priest who lived in Brazil, primarily Bahia, from 1618 to 1716, and who published a book in 1711 (Keith 1977, 84).

9. Eisenberg (1974, 186) calculates that the real wage of cane cutters on Pernambuco sugar plantations declined by 23 percent between 1876 and 1896.

10. Pernambuco abounds with stories of rural workers receiving gifts such as shirts, shoes, building materials, and food in return for their vote. Many rural folk feel that once they have accepted these kinds of gifts from a campaign, they are obliged to vote for its candidate, because "Minha palavra é minha honra" (My word is my honor). One story about rural vote buying, probably apocryphal, concerns a candidate in the *sertão* (interior) who

offered those who voted for him sets of dentures—the lower set before the vote, the upper set afterward.

11. The 1980 census lists the sugar zone's population of 1,093,936 as 25 percent white, 6 percent black (*preto*), and 69 percent mulatto or brown (*pardo*). These racial categories, and the methods used to assign people to them, are different from those used in the United States.

12. In the contemporary sugar zone there is a clear racial division between the principal classes. It appeared from my observation that the mill owners are all white, the planters a mixture of whites and mulattos, and the cane workers a mixture of blacks and mulattos, with some whites.

13. In 1988 one trade union official reflected this counterideology when he said to me: "For you I am an illiterate, but I can hear and decide things for myself" (interview in Agua Preta, November 1988).

14. For explanations of the role of regionalism in Latin American politics, see Tannenbaum 1960, 21−34, 126; Stein and Stein 1970, 75.

15. Of the ten presidents from 1894 to 1930, five were from São Paulo and three from Minas Gerais. The other two were Hermes da Fonseca, an army candidate (1910−1914) and Epitácio Pessoa (1919−1922), a compromise candidate from Paraíba (Flynn 1978, 34−35, 53).

16. Juan de Castellanos wrote about Cuba, "A plantation is a great estate" and "each of these is a domain" (quoted by Fernando Ortiz, in Smith 1966, 173).

17. Coffee, rather than sugar, accounted for two-thirds of all Brazilian exports in 1889, the first year of the Old Republic (Burns 1980, 193). In 1907, an American diplomat wrote, "All the Northern States are bitterly opposed to the hold the coffee planters have over the Government and complain that their legitimate needs are being sacrificed in favor of the planters. The Executive, however, clings to its purpose of doing everything to please the coffee interests. The President fully realizes that he was elected by the planters and that he must now return the favor" (ibid., 305).

18. In the 1987−1988 harvest, some 5.6 million tons of cane, out of a total of 14.1 million tons crushed, were grown by the mills themselves (IAA 1988).

19. There is evidence that some of the old regionalism was preserved after the revolution of 1930. In the 1934 Constituent Assembly, for example, there were no proposals to change the Brazilian system from a federal to a unitary one. There was a "consensus on the necessity of a certain amount of political and administrative decentralization" (Gomes 1980, 391). For an argument which disputes the assertion that 1930 saw the creation of the modern state in Brazil, and that this actually took place much earlier with the founding of the Republic, see Saes 1985.

20. Letter from Lindolfo Collor, first minister of labor, to President Vargas, 6 March 1931 (Arquivo Nacional, Secretaria da Presidencia da República, Ministério do Trabalho, Indústria e Comércio, Box 46, Folder 1931). Another Ministry of Labor document from the same archive lists 251 unions recognized by the Ministry; none is rural.

21. One hectare is approximately 2.5 acres. For aggregate statistics on landownership in Latin America as a whole (using 1960 data), see Burns 1990, 228.

22. The average family size in the sugar zone is 5.4 persons. The fifteen-hectare family minimum was set by the National Institute of Colonization and Agrarian Reform, INCRA.

23. In the late 1940s, São Paulo sugar producers fought to abolish the IAA because it was attempting, under pressure from the northeastern sugar sector, to curb their expansion of output. This dispute was resolved when São Paulo was allowed to increase its production (Ramos and Belik 1989, 197, 207).

24. In this case, a materialist explanation coincides with one emphasizing status because, for peasants and workers who had resided on plantations, loss of access to land was devastating in both status and material terms.

25. The *imposto sindical* was discounted in March from all legal workers' pay, and divided as follows: 60 percent for the union, 20 percent for the Ministry of Labor, 15 percent for the state federation, and 5 percent for the confederation.

26. Of fifty trade union leaders surveyed in 1988, forty-one were ten years or older at the time of the 1964 coup, six were younger than ten, and three were not yet born. Their mean average age was forty-five, so that the mean average age at the time of the coup was twenty-one. When asked, "When did you join the union?" seventeen of the fifty said that they joined a rural union before 1964, twenty-eight between 1964 and 1979, and five after 1979.

27. Cerqueira 1986, 27−30. These figures do not include the union in Barreiros, which was founded in 1953. In its official history, CONTAG claims that the rural workers' unions of Rio Formoso and Sirinhaém had also been founded in the Pernambuco sugar zone before 1960 (CONTAG 1993b), although I could not confirm this from other sources. The figures presented here refer to the time the unions were founded, rather than when they were officially recognized by the Ministry of Labor, typically several years later.

28. The parties of this period included the Socialist Party, PSB (Partido Socialista Brasileiro), of which Julião was a member; and the Social Democratic Party, PSD; the Socialist Labor Party, PST (Partido Socialista Trabalhista); the Labor Party (PTB); and the United Democratic National Party, UDN (União Democrático Nacional) (Morães 1970, 501). All faded into oblivion when they were abolished by the military regime in 1965, with the exception of the PTB and the PSB, which reappeared as quite different entities in 1982.

Chapter 3. Structural Change and Conservative Modernization

1. *Diário de Pernambuco*, 13 May 1964; Lessa 1985, 80. Some of the information in this paragraph was culled from an interview with FETAPE president, José Rodrigues, in August 1988, and from the *Jornal de Comércio*, 2 April 1964. A further insight into the traumatic nature of the 1964 coup for Pernambuco's rural unions is revealed by the fact that only one member of the FETAPE directorate in May 1962 was still on the directorate in May 1964 (Lessa 1985, 94).

2. The concentration of landholding in Brazil increased from a Gini coefficient of .858 in 1970 to .871 in 1980 (Passos and Khan 1988, 27). In a 1975 survey, sugarcane had the highest average concentration of land (with a Gini of .929) of nineteen major crops, including soybeans, coffee, and wheat. Interestingly, this same study found that the concentration of productive assets in Brazilian industry exceeded those in agriculture (Hoffman and da Silva 1986, 153, 155).

3. In 1989, São Paulo had an average yield of 73,962 kg per hectare, compared to Pernambuco's 54,140 kg per hectare. Pernambuco had a higher yield than Rio de Janeiro, Bahia, or Alagoas (IBGE 1991, 511).

4. Nunberg 1986, 70. Shortly before PLANALSUCAR was initiated, in 1970, a report by the IAA saw three major structural problems as plaguing the sugar sector, giving us an insight into the rationale for the program. These were chronic overproduction; low productivity on the agricultural side (due to a relatively low level of mechanization and use of new varieties of cane); and low industrial productivity caused by the proliferation of undersized *usinas*, which often had obsolete plants (Nunberg 1986, 67).

5. The world sugar market is particularly volatile. In a study of the price instability of thirty-two commodity exports over the period 1980−1989, the World Bank found that sugar had the highest instability rating. Sugar prices are not only volatile; historically they have declined over time. One study found that the terms of trade for Brazilian sugar (the price of Brazilian sugar divided by the price of a basket of manufactured goods imported from more industrialized countries) declined by an average of 4.4 percent per year between 1870 and 1990 (Goldszal 1992, 45, 115).

6. Schneider 1991, 18. Itaipú absorbed $15.3 billion in investment capital in the same period. In what must be an underestimate, CONTAG (1993b, 19) reports that the federal government invested $4 billion in Proálcool between 1975 and 1993.

7. According to *Correio Popular* (Campinas), 11 August 1994, 94.6 percent of new cars produced in Brazil in 1985 ran on alcohol. The share of alcohol-fueled cars in the new car market fell considerably in the early 1990s, to 16.5 percent in the first half of 1994, according to *Correio Popular*, and 3.5 percent in 1995, according to *Brazil Watch*, 13−27 May 1996.

8. IAA 1987. Years refer to the year in which the harvest was complete.

9. Barzelay 1986; Demetrius 1990. In recent years, only about 10 percent of Pernambuco's sugar production has been exported (U.S. Department of State 1993, 20).

10. A report by the Ministry of Industry and Commerce (MIC) and the IAA showed that government subsidies, in the form of negative-rate loans and high sugarcane prices for Pernambuco producers, rose by 58 percent between 1979 and 1981 (*Situação Econômico-Financeira da Agro-Indústria Açucareira nos Estados de Alagoas e Pernambuco*, an MIC-IAA report quoted in *Diário de Pernambuco*, 26 September 1982).

11. Anderson 1990. Permanent employment actually declined between 1960 and 1970, but rose considerably in the 1970s, making the overall trend positive. It declined again in the 1980s.

12. Data show that in Pernambuco between 1966 and 1979, average real wages for permanent agricultural workers increased by 4.4 percent per year (compared to 4.5 percent for the same category of Brazilian workers as a whole), while those of temporary workers increased by 5.6 percent per year (compared to 6.3 percent in Brazil as a whole). The gap between urban and rural wages closed considerably during this time (Barros, Amaral, and Amaral 1983, 315−16). The extent to which these wage gains were actually captured by Pernambuco's sugar zone workers, whose earnings were often reduced by employers' manipulation of the piece-rate system, is unclear.

13. Maybury-Lewis downplays the contradictory nature of the demand for agrarian reform—and the considerable ambiguity the FETAPE leadership seems to feel about making it—in the Pernambuco sugar zone. See the chapter on Nazaré da Mata in Maybury-Lewis 1994.

14. In 1982−1983, for example, many basic crops declined in production from the previous year. Rice was down 28.2 percent, beans 74.6 percent, manioc 18.6 percent, corn 87.4 percent, and tomatoes 54 percent. But sugar, of which there was a domestic glut, rose in production by 11.6 percent in Pernambuco (Governo do Estado de Pernambuco 1987a, 35).

15. The landholding figures discussed here are clearly not definitive indicators of *ownership* of land, because they do not show who owns the listed properties. One person may own many different properties listed in the agricultural census, but this is difficult to discover unless information on private wealth is available. Examining data on landholding is therefore one of the best ways to discern the class structure of an agricultural economy. Landholding tells a lot because the chief basis of wealth, status, and control over labor in the northeast and many other agricultural regions is the control of land. Whenever possible, of course, landholding data should be supplemented with other indicators of class structure. For more on the problem of using statistics such as these, see Asad 1994.

16. Labor achieved a more active role in decision making within other sectors in Brazil. Unions in Brazil's auto sector, for example, negotiated over prices for automobiles, levels of employment, and many other issues beyond the conventional ones of wages and working conditions in the early 1990s (Martin 1994).

17. CGT 1991, 16−17; 60 percent of Pernambuco's sugar zone has a slope of 15 to 30 degrees, and 15 percent of the land has a slope of over 30 degrees, in contrast to the flat terrain of São Paulo (CGT 1991, 17).

18. Werneck Vianna, quoted in Diniz 1986, 65. Other commentators have made similar remarks: "The transition . . . has not been caused by either government or opposition, but rather by the relationship between these" (Sanders, in Bruneau and Faucher 1981, 194); "The regime was also shaped somewhat by opposition forces" (Mainwaring 1988, 97); and Chauí writes of two transitions to democracy, one public, involving mass demonstrations, and one secret, involving elite politicians in negotiations (1984, 10).

19. Skidmore 1988, 172–73. The total vote tallies were: for the lower house of Congress, ARENA, 11.87 million, and MDB, 10.95 million, and in the Senate, ARENA, 10 million, and MDB, 14.6 million. After the election, ARENA still controlled Congress, with 199 deputies in the lower house and 46 Senate seats, compared to the MDB's 165 deputies and 20 Senate seats.

20. The AIFLD county director in Brazil from 1968 to 1976 told me that he had nurtured the career of José Francisco, who became CONTAG president in 1968, by putting him in charge of a union center and sending him to training sessions in São Paulo and in Front Royal, Va., in the mid-1960s. He also claimed that he encouraged Francisco to run for the CONTAG presidency. Interview by the author, 8 February 1991. For a critique of AIFLD, see Spalding et al. 1988.

21. A *pelego* is a sheepskin cover placed between a saddle and a horse; in the labor context, it refers to a labor boss who sides with management and/or the government, neglecting his members' interests. For more on the São Paulo strikes, see Keck, in Stepan 1989; Cohen 1989, chap. 7; Humphrey 1982, chaps. 6–7.

22. Assemblyman Mansueto de Lavour made this statement in the floor debate of the Pernambuco Legislative Assembly, 8 October 1979. On the career of de Lavour, who became a federal senator, see Chilcote 1990, 278–81.

23. Reflecting the continuity of the Brazilian transition, Sarney had been a member of the promilitary ARENA party. In 1966, when governor of Maranhão, Sarney wrote to President Castelo Branco praising "the example of work, efficiency, and administrative probity offered by Your Excellency's government" (letter dated 9 February 1966, Arquivo Castelo Branco, CPDOC).

24. *Jornal de Comércio*, 22 December 1989. Total votes were 35,089,998 (42.75 percent) for Collor, 31,076,364 (37.86 percent) for Lula.

25. *Estado de São Paulo*, 13 October 1994. The three parties supporting Cardoso's candidacy were his own Social Democratic Party, PSDB (Partido Social-Democrático Brasileiro); a successor of the PDS, the Liberal Front Party, PFL (Partido Frente Liberal) and the Labor Party, PTB (Partido Trabalhista Brasileiro).

Chapter 4. The Regulation of Conflict

1. On the relationship between objective structures and the practices or representations that accompany them, see Bordieu 1977, 21.

2. Becker 1985, 88–90. The basis of these welfare programs was established earlier—in 1960 (ibid.), and in the 1963 Rural Workers' Statute (Maybury-Lewis 1994, 39). Poor enforcement and the absence of an entity to administer the programs meant that they were not effectively established. But decree-laws 276 and 61,554 in 1967 changed the financing of the programs and created an autonomous structure to administer them. Legislation in 1971 created the Program for the Assistance of the Rural Worker, PRORURAL, which considerably broadened the benefits of the programs (ibid., 39–45). Coverage to rural workers who suffered accidents at work was extended by law 6195 in 1974 (Becker 1985, 89).

3. The union figure for 1963 (Price 1964, 68); the figure for 1980 (Keck, in Stepan 1989, 261). CONTAG had 9.4 million members and 2,732 unions in March 1985 (Maybury-Lewis

1994, 12). Another source lists CONTAG as having twenty-two state federations and 2,747 unions in the late 1980s (IBGE 1991, 425).

4. Cerqueira 1986, 27-30. Six of these were created before 1965, five in the period 1967-1971; no others were established until one was set up in 1979 and another in 1987. Although there were forty-six unions in the sugar zone, only forty-five signed the 1988 collective contract, as one union was not recognized by the Ministry of Labor. The sugar zone here refers to all areas of coastal Pernambuco state where sugar is grown for the mills; some unions listed here are technically in the *agreste* (intermediate) region rather than the *zona da mata*.

5. Maybury-Lewis 1994, 43-44. The military regime's attitude toward popular participation in politics is reminiscent of the declaration of Brazil's first emperor, Dom Pedro I, on 6 April 1831 that he would "do everything for the people, but nothing by the people" (Bushnell and Macaulay 1991, 166).

6. Similarly, 71 percent of rural unions collected voluntary dues from fewer than 40 percent of their members, whereas in urban unions the equivalent figure was 16 percent (IBGE 1991, 426). Consequently, rural unions were much more dependent upon the state-collected union tax than urban unions were and therefore often more cautious in defying government policies. The São Bernardo metalworkers' union actually devolved the *contribuição sindical* to its members in 1993 (Martin 1994, 17-18), an action unheard of among rural unions.

7. I use the term *cultural struggle* rather than *identity politics*, often used in the new social movements literature. The latter can have misleading connotations. It may imply that the individuals involved in conflicts in this kind of politics are not driven by material interests but are simply expressing or defending some notion of collective identity. However, material interests can be part of identity politics, and class identity has a material as well as a symbolic or ideological content (Slater 1985, 55-59). *Identity politics* may also suggest that its participants' engagement in collective action stems from deep-seated and permanent self-conceptions, rather than from contingent, temporary, and perhaps incongruent interests and ideas.

8. Gramsci, in Forgacs 1988, 225-30. I use the Gramscian distinction between war of maneuver and position loosely but in a way consistent with the original meaning. Whereas war of maneuver suggests the strike's battle for territory and the control over labor, the war of position suggests the slow, imperceptible struggle to change cultural values and perceptions.

9. Other scholars use similar categories. Lancaster refers to *urban peasants* (1988, 215). Jeffrey Gould (1991) refers to a *situational class* of peasants and rural workers who engaged in collective action against large landowners producing for export in Chinandega province, Nicaragua. Some scholars do not distinguish between wage workers and smallholders in the countryside; Charles Brockett uses *peasant* loosely to describe "any rural cultivator who is low in economic or political status" (1990, 8).

10. Rural workers' unions in the Brazilian countryside include as members any landowner who does not employ wage workers on his property. Those who do are members of the rural employers' trade union.

11. These are just two stanzas of the eight in the song, which was sung at a union assembly in Nazaré da Mata, 2 October 1988, when about 600 members of the union came to discuss and to vote on the strike. The union had printed the lyrics and distributed them to those at the meeting; this song (and others) were sung with musical accompaniment.

12. Inflation data for 1980-1985 are from Baer 1989, 135; for 1986, UN *Economic Survey of Latin American and the Caribbean*; for 1987 and 1988, IBGE 1987 and 1988; for 1989, *Wall Street Journal*, 29 January 1990, A12.

13. Interview with José Rodrigues, FETAPE president, August 1988.

14. In 1980, sixteen independent unions accused FETAPE's leaders of being "totalitarian" because they centralized the bargaining over salary in their own hands and told the unions to "return to the interior and wait for the result of the negotiations." This split within FETAPE was, on this occasion, eventually papered over (*Diário de Pernambuco*, 24 September 1980). However, similar complaints about the federation were heard in union headquarters in the sugar zone in the late 1980s.

15. For example, Agápito Francisco dos Santos, president of the São Lourenço union, said, "The strike is the means which the worker has to resolve, united, his problems. A law exists for this, but the landowners, since 1964, don't use it because the law had been suspended" (*Diário de Pernambuco*, 3 October 1979). This is very different from the more militant language of the metalworkers.

16. Bezerra also said, "Your problem is being watched by the whole of Brazil. You are not alone." Other observers made similar comparisons. During the 1980 Pernambuco strike, an ex-member of the metalworkers' union in São Bernardo, Enilson Simões de Moura (known as "Alemão"), observed the strike at the invitation of FETAPE leaders. He said that the problems of the two groups of workers were very similar (*Diário de Pernambuco*, 27 September 1980).

17. Interview with José Bento di Santi, first treasurer of FETAESP, the São Paulo rural workers' federation, 3 July 1990.

18. *O Trabalhador Rural*, 7 October 1993. The state federations that asked for unified negotiations were Rio Grande do Norte, Pernambuco, Paraíba, Alagoas, and Sergipe. Interestingly, only the Pernambuco employers agreed to the union proposal—indicating that the degree of modernization, and the relatively high wages in Pernambuco probably made the proposal less threatening to employers there.

19. According to numerous press reports, in June 1990 the real minimum wage was lower than it had been at any point since its creation in 1943. One study revealed that the real value of the minimum wage had declined 45 percent during the 1980s (*Boletim DIEESE* 9 [July 1990], 8). Furthermore, the economic journalist Joelmir Beting states that in the 1970s, salaries accounted for roughly 60 percent of Brazilian national income, whereas in the 1980s this figure had fallen to about 35 percent (*Folha de São Paulo*, 30 June 1990).

20. For example, I estimated that a meeting in Nazaré da Mata to vote on the 1988 strike had about 600 participants at most, well below the number legally required for a quorum. The *Diário de Pernambuco* reported that 3,000 members were at the meeting (Field notes, 2 and 8 October 1988). This tendency to exaggerate participation in union activities can also be found in an otherwise comprehensive and engaging article by Sigaud 1986.

21. The strikes in the Pernambuco sugar zone are usually interpreted as an unambiguous sign of worker strength and militancy (Gryzbowski 1987, 35−36; Keck, in Stepan 1989, 261; Sigaud 1986, 320−32).

22. The strike—or salary campaign—was planned six months in advance by FETAPE, with meetings of union presidents, discussions of strategy, and so on. The strike is also analyzed afterwards, at local meetings and at an annual FETAPE conference in December, with an eye to improving performance the next year.

23. That is, twelve of fifty union leaders reported that they or their family owned a parcel of land. Anecdotal evidence also suggests that small landowners were important to the establishment of unions in the *zona da mata*. In 1990 I visited a small property in Buenos Aires, Pernambuco, which belonged to the family of a union organizer. I was shown a large tree, which looked like a weeping willow, and told that under it union organizers had hidden from landowners in the early days of union organizing in the early 1960s. An independent smallholder in this case provided refuge to workers who dared to challenge the *patrão*.

24. IBGE 1991, 430. The term for small landowners is *pequeno proprietários*. In contrast, only

13.5 percent of CONTAG presidents were wage workers *(assalariados)*; 8.7 percent, tenants *(arrendatários)*; and 9.2 percent, sharecroppers *(parceiros)*. These data are from a survey of 2,729 rural unions, only 18 of which did not respond.

Chapter 5. Sons of Cane: Leadership Dilemmas Within the Unions

1. Information on the strike comes from interviews conducted by the author in 1988; the *Jornal de Comércio* and the *Diário de Pernambuco*, October 1979; and Sigaud 1980 and Linhart 1980.

2. The mechanism was accurately called the *imposto sindical* from its establishment in 1940 until 1964, when the military government gave it the euphemism *contribuição sindical*. Its status is uncertain. It was formally abolished by presidential decree in 1990, but Congress obtained a five-year postponement of the decree's implementation (Gomes and D'Araújo 1993, 317-51; "CGT Proposes New Labor Policy," *AFL-CIO Bulletin of the Department of International Affairs*, 1990, 5).

3. Morães Filho 1952, 316-17. See also Holanda 1956, 209-19, and Freyre 1978, who write about the privatism and isolation of the plantation in colonial Brazil and how this resulted in a lack of social solidarity.

4. For an interpretation which defends much of existing labor law for the reasons described here, see also Rodrigues 1981, 77-80. However, Rodrigues differs from Morães Filho by ultimately judging Brazilian unions to be out of touch with contemporary national reality.

5. Consistent with this interpretation is the view of Brazilian history as one of steady, peaceful evolution from colony to monarchy to republic, without violence, class conflict, or repression from above. Even an institution like slavery is seen as benign by this school, involving *carinho* (affection) on the part of masters and slaves, with slaves fully integrated into the master's household (Freyre 1978).

6. Erickson expressed this view in 1977; see in particular his remarks on the social service orientation of unions (37) and their lack of rank-and-file protection (41).

7. Morães Filho 1982, 182. For the view that the *imposto sindical*, as it was called before 1964, was one of the strongest elements of union dependence on the state, see Alves 1985, 86. For the argument that it destroyed union representativeness, see Troyano 1978, 62.

8. The new unionists in the ABC region often called themselves *autênticos* (authentics). For a description of the corporatist labor institutions and their capacity for cooptation, see Costa 1986, 87.

9. This is a point that Cohen 1989 does not adequately address.

10. In the words of Romeu da Fonte, a FETAPE lawyer, "There are highs and lows depending on the degree of organization of each union" when it comes to pressure for enforcing the collective contract. "The enforcement [of the contract] in Pernambuco goes from *municípios* with a note of ten to *municípios* with a note of one" (CEDI 1985, 38).

11. The union in São Vicente Ferrer, a small town in the northern sugar zone, is an example. It did not have its own headquarters, which is a requirement for Ministry of Labor recognition of a union. Instead, it used its president's barber shop as a makeshift headquarters. FETAPE signed the 1987 collective contract on its behalf (Field notes, 18 November 1988).

12. There were about twenty-five plantations in São Lourenço, which also accounted for some employment.

13. In the United States, "wage rates tend to vary systematically and directly with the size of the enterprise . . . large firms pay higher wages than smaller firms" (Dunlop 1988, 1060). The same seems to be true in the Pernambuco sugar zone.

14. In 1987 the *taxa assistencial* (as listed in the collective contract) was 40 cruzados per

worker. At the then black market rate of 65 cruzados to the dollar, this would have meant $56,923 to FETAPE if all 185,600 legal workers in the sugar zone were covered by the *taxa*.

15. An extreme case of internal apathy is that of the rural union in Nazaré da Mata, which held its first contested election in twenty-six years in September 1989. Despite the unprecedented competition for leadership within the union, only 1,110 (less than the legal quorum) of the approximately 8,000 members bothered to vote. The union federation had to get both sets of candidates to sign an agreement setting aside the lack of a quorum and honoring the election result.

16. Adversarial democracy refers to the competitive, Western model which assumes that members' interests are in constant conflict and in which the point is not to convince the other side that one is right but simply to defeat it electorally by capturing a majority of the membership. Mansbridge contrasts this with "unitary democracy," which is more common in the unions and which assumes a common interest among members. Here, the goal is to discuss and debate political options so that a consensus, approved of by everyone or almost everyone, is reached (Mansbridge 1983, esp. chaps. 1−3). Many union leaders, for example, think it is better to achieve unity among members and nominate only one set of candidates for union offices, rather than have competition.

17. As one union leader said, many workers in his area did not participate in the strike because "if they stopped [working] they would die of hunger" (Field notes, 1988).

18. The work of James Scott on "everyday resistance" and "infrapolitics" (1985, 1991) provides important insights into circumvention as a form of resistance.

19. In the late 1980s, a provision in the sugar zone's collective contract guaranteeing employment to the unions' *delegados* on the plantations was struck down by the regional labor court (interview with Geraldo, president of the Ipojuca union, 21 June 1988).

20. Field notes, 1988. The strong attractiveness of individual incentives in the context of stagnant living standards for a class as a whole is cogently discussed by Cohen in Roemer 1986, 237−59.

21. Field notes and interview with Amaro, president of the São José de Coroa Grande rural workers' union, 13 July 1988.

22. For example, I witnessed a union strike committee finding a worker in the fields, breaking the strike, who the day before had eaten a free lunch at the union. Although he was forced to stop work, he was treated good-humoredly and made to ride in the union pickup truck with the rest of the strike committee (Field notes, October 1988).

23. This tendency is borne out by other research. Hirata, for example, reports on a 1977 survey of São Paulo workers that found that unskilled workers were more likely to agree (33.7 percent) that the "union is good because it gives medical assistance, et cetera" than semiskilled workers (31.6 percent) and skilled workers (17.1 percent). Thus the unskilled Pernambuco cane cutters' attitudes toward their unions seem similar to that of unskilled workers elsewhere (Hirata, in Coletivo Edgar Leuenroth 1980, 90).

24. Field notes, 1988. Hirata reports that dissatisfaction with union performance also increased with workers' skill level. In a 1977 study, the tendency to agree with the statement "the union is dominated by a clique (*panelinha*)" was as follows: unskilled workers 12.3 percent, semiskilled workers 25.3 percent, and skilled workers 33.4 percent. Unskilled workers such as the Pernambuco cane cutters seemed to be less critical of union leadership than other workers (Hirata, in Coletivo Edgar Leuenroth 1980, 90).

25. This is perhaps the single biggest difference between North American and Brazilian union leaders. The U.S. union leader may act as grievance server, meeting chairman, plant-level organizer, candidate for office, strike leader, and contract negotiator, but not as welfare administrator.

26. Union officials' salaries, which are paid year round, depend on the revenue base of the union, and are frequently the equivalent of two minimum salaries. A rural worker typically earns one minimum salary.

27. Interview with the president of the Paudalho rural workers' union, 18 July 1988.

28. This problem was not limited to Pernambuco. In a 1985 meeting of rural trade unionists in the neighboring state of Paraíba, union leaders complained that the collective contract was not published in the federal government's official publication, the *Diário Oficial*, until December, two months after it had been signed, and near the end of the sugar harvest. Presumably this was the only way they could get a copy of it (CEDI 1985, 27).

29. One union leader in Paraíba called this situation "diseducative" for unions. Their leaders know that the negotiation really doesn't depend on them, so they tell the federation that everyone in their area went on strike, even though they (and the federation officials) know that this is not the case. The union leaders try to fool the federation the way employees try to fool the *patrão*. On this problem, see the comments of Wanderley Caixe in CEDI 1985, 40–41.

30. The failure of state officials to enforce labor law is an additional important contributing factor to this problem, which is by no means restricted to northeast Brazil. Jan Breman writes movingly and eloquently about this in his book on a regional labor market in rural south Gujarat, India (Breman 1985, xxii).

31. Breman finds the same kind of exploitation in Gujarat (1985, xxiii).

32. Córdova 1985. Some observers in Brazil have therefore recommended the preservation of the single-union system on the grounds that, while it was imposed by the authoritarian Estado Novo, it is now a legitimate tool of the workers and can be used by them as a kind of boomerang against the state and employers.

33. Landlords are legally obligated to transport sick and injured workers, although they often seemed to avoid this obligation in the sugar zone. Sometimes, the welfare function did challenge the landlords indirectly. Some landlords held parties with free beer, or arranged trips to the beach, for their workers on Sundays when the union had a meeting or party, just to lure people from the union.

Chapter 6. Sugar with the Taste of Blood: Landlord Violence

1. Maxwell 1991; U.S. Department of State 1994. In 1993 the men escaped from prison, probably with the connivance of local authorities, but were recaptured in 1996.

2. The first law permitting the organization of labor was decree 979 of 6 January 1903, as implemented by decree 6532 of 20 June 1907. It was enacted primarily to reassure foreign governments that immigrants who came to Brazil to work on coffee estates would enjoy legal protections comparable to those in their home countries, such as Italy (Price 1964, 5).

3. In my 1988 survey, the majority of workers, both young and old (80 percent of those over forty, and 85 percent under forty), said that their standard of living had declined since 1963, when most workers had lived on plantations.

4. In my survey, 57 percent of those who said they were in favor of the right to strike (92 percent of all respondents) justified their stance by saying that landowners made concessions only in the face of strikes or threats of strikes.

5. On the dualistic view of the state among rural workers in São Paulo state in the early 1970s, see Martínez-Alier and Boito 1977, 160.

6. Few workers seemed to consider the danger that union officials might abandon their roots once they were in local government, developing new interests and bases of support, that is, that one of "us" might turn into one of "them" if given the chance. The fact that this

danger was a real one is reflected in the rueful remark of one union official, commenting on the performance of a former union president who became mayor: although "we had access" to him, "he wasn't the mayor we had hoped for."

7. I was given these lyrics and those of other songs at a union meeting in Nazaré da Mata, 2 October 1988, held to vote on the strike. Other song lyrics were gathered from the FETAPE headquarters in Recife.

8. Interview in Vitória de Santo Antão, Pernambuco, 2 May 1988.

9. Rural worker in Maraial, Pernambuco, 30 November 1988 (Field notes).

10. Pernambuco's total population doubled from 1950 to 1980, from about 3 to 6 million. During the same period, the number of Protestants rose from 80,000 to 325,000 (IBGE 1950b, 1980b).

11. For the difference between representative and participatory theories of democracy, see Pateman 1970.

12. This was an open-ended question to which most respondents gave more than one answer; therefore, percentages do not add up to 100.

13. The n for this question was thirty-nine—lower than for most of the other questions in the survey.

14. This is the point made by de Janvry and Sadoulet 1989, 22. The authors suggest that the rural poor can only win politically if positive gains from a particular policy also accrue to the nonpoor. Groups from the latter category can then take the initiative in mobilizing the poor in support of the policy. In the case of Brazilian land reform, the nonpoor did stand to benefit from land redistribution, in the form of cheaper food prices and perhaps also lower rates of urban crime, but these benefits were quite indirect. This may well account for the relatively low level of political pressure for the policy by the nonpoor.

15. These data come from an informal survey of rural violence from clippings from local newspapers in 1987–1988; most come from the *Diário de Pernambuco*, but also the *Jornal de Comércio* and *Folha de Pernambuco*. For murder data, Amnesty International 1988 was also a source.

16. The president of the union complained about this veiled threat, because the state secretary had been appointed by Governor Miguel Arraes, who had received strong support from rural workers. "We find the position of the secretary very strange," he said, "because all the rural workers voted for Arraes, and it isn't possible that his police now line up against us" (*Diário de Pernambuco*, 14 May 1988).

17. The Cabo union president told me on 22 September 1988 that a legal action was pending against the policemen thought to be responsible for the abduction of Batista, but it is not clear whether this was brought by the union or by another party.

18. Sources of these data are Movimento dos Trabalhadores Rurais Sem Terra 1987; Confederação Nacional dos Bispos do Brasil (CNBB) 1987; FETAPE 1988; Amnesty International 1988, 6. Data on rural violence vary according to the source. Deaths listed may include some rural workers killed by other workers and by some landlords. All tables I have seen (compiled by organizations in favor of land reform), indicate an upsurge in violence since the early 1980s.

19. Article 48 of the 1941 Cane Cultivation Statute (Estatuto de Lavoura Canavieira) prohibited northeastern mill owners from taking over all the land of the *fornecedores*. On the other hand, no such prohibition was applied in São Paulo, where the *fornecedores* ceased to be a significant political factor at the state level (Ramos and Belik 1989, 203).

20. In another study, FETAPE claims that sixty-seven rural workers were killed in Pernambuco between 1981 and 1991 (CGT 1991, 21).

21. CONTAG 1993b, 40–43. Because Pernambuco was better represented within CONTAG than the federations of other states, these figures could be partly an artifact of better report-

ing from Pernambuco. However, even if we allow for some distortion because of this, it seems clear that Pernambuco had a far greater problem with rural violence against unionists than did São Paulo and most other states. Even Pará, which had more rural violence in general than Pernambuco, lost fewer rural trade union leaders—twenty-three as opposed to tenty-six—than Pernambuco. In another publication, it was reported that seventy-three rural union leaders or their assistants were killed in Brazil in the first ten months of 1985—and not one was from São Paulo (*O Trabalhador Rural*, October–November 1985).

Chapter 7. The Candidates: The Unions and Political Parties

1. All electoral data in this chapter are from Pernambuco's Regional Electoral Tribunal (Tribunal Regional Eleitoral), unless otherwise noted.

2. In 1988, one trade union president said that he would follow Arraes into any party except the conservative PFL.

3. This pattern may well have changed after the promulgation of the 1988 constitution, which transferred some control over revenue from federal to local and state governments.

4. These defections took place in many states, not only in Pernambuco. They are analyzed in greater detail in Hagopian 1990, 159–60.

5. By opportunism I mean the practice of "seizing tactical opportunities without any regard for principles" (Offe 1985, 214). For a fuller discussion of opportunism as it pertains to trade unions, and a five-stage model of opportunistic behavior, see ibid., 214–20.

6. Lavareda 1987, 139–41. The numbers of votes given here have been deduced from the percentages presented in this source. I owe to Cecília Mariz the information about the family link between Monteiro and Múcio.

7. The expansion of the electorate before 1985 was primarily the result of increasing levels of education and thus the number of people able to qualify as literate in order to vote. Granting the right to vote to illiterates in 1985, of course, removed this barrier completely and further swelled voter rolls.

8. Interview with Elisete, the only female rural union president in the sugar zone at that time, in Pombos, 17 July 1990.

9. Arraes has been called a "*coronel* of the left" by the São Paulo press, emphasizing the importance of clientelism and elite bargaining to his political style.

10. As part of the 1986 campaign, the Arraes forces published a pamphlet written by a local lawyer entitled *Arraes: A Brief History of a Popular Government* (Cavalcanti 1986). This pamphlet described Arraes's interrupted term as governor in the 1962–1964 period, to revive both memories of that period and expectations that a new Arraes administration would result in benefits for the common people.

11. *Charisma* here refers to "a certain quality of an individual personality by virtue of which he is considered extraordinary and treated as endowed with supernatural, superhuman, or at least specifically exceptional powers or qualities" (Weber 1978, 241).

12. This is my own very rough estimate based on following a union president around for a few days and observing the people with whom he came into contact.

13. Interview with Elisete, president of the Pombos rural workers union, 17 July 1990.

14. Ibid.

15. The union membership figure is from an interview with the Pombos union secretary, 24 November 1988.

16. It is interesting that Protestants are disproportionately represented in leadership positions in the rural unions. While they formed 7 percent of the sugar zone's total population, they were 14 percent of the sample of leaders I interviewed.

17. The question was asked during the period between 18 March and 25 November 1988.

The surprising PT victory in São Paulo in early November may have influenced the responses of those who were interviewed after that time.

18. Of the fifty respondents to this survey question, some gave more than one answer.

19. A union president's anguished calculation that a Congress member's salary (excluding benefits such as free travel, housing, mail, telephone, and other services) was more than 100 times that of a rural worker in the sugar zone, exemplifies the sense of injustice and illegitimacy that colors union leaders' thoughts about politicians within the national regime. At the time of my interview, a cane cutters' salary in Pernambuco was the minimum wage of Cz$ 6,800 per month. Congress members (whose absentee rate was something of a scandal among the public) received Cz$ 722,000 per month, or over $70,000 per year (interview with Timbaúba union leader, 8 April 1988).

20. Interview with Elisete, president of the Pombos rural workers' union, 17 July 1990.

Chapter 8. The Struggle for Heaven on Earth: The Unions and Agrarian Reform

1. FAO 1988, 17. Figures are from 1980. The FAO defines poverty as the "incapacity to become inserted into the socio-economic environment in a way that continually allows for the satisfaction of basic necessities of life." For measurement purposes, absolute poverty is "that income below which a set of basic necessities cannot be afforded" (FAO 1988, 7).

2. Kageyama 1987, 50. The data are from a 1978 INCRA study that was not released until 1985.

3. The value of the debt of *latifúndiarios* who hadn't paid the land tax *(imposto territorial rural)* between 1980 and 1985 was estimated in the latter year at 3.6 trillion cruzeiros (Campanha Nacional Pela Reforma Agrária 1985a, 11).

4. Between 1970 and 1980, the number of rural poor rose from 27.6 to 28.8 million (FAO 1988, 7). Brazil's Gini coefficient for land concentration went from 0.85 in 1960 to 0.86 in 1980 (FAO 1988, 48–49). Properties of more than 1,000 hectares increased their share of the cultivated land from 47 percent in 1967 to 58 percent in 1984. Small properties of less than 100 hectares had their share of land decrease through these years, from 19 percent to 14 percent (MIRAD 1985, 4).

5. Goodman et al., in Finch and Munslow 1984, 198. According to the 1975 agricultural census, rural properties of 100 hectares or more got 68.1 percent of all credit; some of this credit was not used for agriculture at all, but invested instead in urban property (IBASE 1981, 3–4).

6. Many of these displaced peasants went to the cities; rural-urban migration is estimated at 30 million for the period 1960–1980.

7. An FAO mission that came to Brazil to monitor the reform in 1968 reported that the number of families which had received land up to that date did not exceed 329 (IBASE 1985, 1).

8. Francisco Graziano Neto, an agronomist who worked for then Senator Fernando Henrique Cardoso and later briefly became head of INCRA in 1995, claimed (unconvincingly) that the 1985 plan was based on inaccurate land data and that there was much less land available than the government thought. See "Reforma no Brejo," *Veja*, 7 November 1990, 5–7.

9. At the fourth CONTAG Congress in Brasília in May 1985, delegates expressed the fear that religious groups had the objective of "dismantling the union movement" in the countryside (Chaloult 1985, 12).

10. Pessoa 1986, 121–22. For the author of those words, the minefield exploded. In September 1987, he and three other INCRA officials were killed in a plane crash in southern Pará under mysterious circumstances. Although the official government investigation of the crash ruled out foul play, southern Pará is an area of intense land conflict, and some commenta-

tors believe that the INCRA plane was sabotaged by landowners who felt threatened by the agency's apparent commitment to land redistribution in the area.

11. The UDR, formed almost immediately after the announcement of the 1985 agrarian reform plan, grew spectacularly. In 1986 it reported membership of 50,000 landowners, but by 1988 the figure was 250,000 (*Veja*, 11 November 1987, 30). The UDR was invited to establish a center in Pernambuco by the Cane Growers' Association in January 1988, but it was not a strong presence in the sugar zone, with only a few hundred members by the end of that year. After the conflict over agrarian reform was settled by the 1988 Constitution, the UDR declined in importance, but it remains a key political actor in areas where land redistribution is a political issue.

12. "Traidores do Povo," union song lyrics distributed in Nazaré da Mata, Pernambuco, 2 October 1988.

13. *Manchester Guardian Weekly*, 29 January 1989. INCRA data uses a longer time frame and differs slightly from those presented here. Between May 1985 and May 1988, it reports that 2,966,902.4 hectares (11 percent of the target) were expropriated, and this land was capable of sustaining 78,229 families, or 9.2 percent of the beneficiaries planned for settlement by the end of 1988. There were no data on how many of this latter figure had actually been settled on land (INCRA 1988, 1).

14. his conclusion came out of a 1988 study by Brazil's National Bank for Economic and Social Development, the BNDES (Banco Nacional de Desenvolvimento Econômico e Social), which examined 1,517 small farmers who received land in 12 different states (*Relatório Reservado*, 24-30 July 1989).

15. Interview with Francisco Julião, Cuernavaca, Mexico, 24 May 1988.

16. *Primeira Pagina*, a newspaper published by the state government, reported that 1,200 hectares had been donated in the program as of 4 April 1988. Given that INCRA defined the minimum plot size to sustain an average family in the sugar zone as fifteen hectares, this would allow eighty beneficiaries to receive land. Yet there were said to be 100,000 to 150,000 unemployed cane cutters in the sugar zone during the slack season.

17. Song lyrics collected at a union meeting in Nazaré da Mata, 2 October 1988.

18. *Jornal de Comércio*, 7 July 1988. The difference between *leis* (laws) and *direito* (right) is an important one among Brazil's rural poor. *Leis* are the state's laws: unfair, arbitrary, easily manipulated and stretched, obscure to everyone except lawyers. *Direito* is what is right in accordance with popular notions of justice and credited with divine origin. There is a parallel between *lei* and *direito* and E. P. Thompson's "market" and "moral" economy (1971).

19. Becker reports that 31 percent (279) of the 900 families which received land under PROTERRA were settled in the sugar zone county of Paulista. It is not known where the other families were settled; if some of them were also given plots in the *mata*, then the overall land redistribution figure for the military period would be even higher (Becker 1985, 71).

Chapter 9. The End of the Peasantry

1. For the distinction between the "big world" of national politics and the "little world" of peasant land occupations and rural worker mobilization, see Hobsbawm 1974.

2. Putnam 1993, 179. While not discounting the importance of cultural traditions and the "social capital" that Putnam focuses on in his book, my point here is that such traditions are not static but linked to institutional arrangements that are unlikely to be permanent. The erosion of the "civic culture" in the United States since the 1970s illustrates my point.

3. Rueschemeyer, Stephens, and Stephens (1992, 163) prefer *labor intensivity of agriculture* as

the key variable rather than Moore's term *labor repressive landlords*, arguing that in many systems landlords use some type of coercion to guarantee a supply of cheap labor for their plantations.

4. For a similar conclusion about political transitions in Africa, see Bratton and Van De Walle 1994.

5. Labor organizer Conrad Abadie said that Louisiana field workers received between $4 and $5 an hour in 1988. In Hawaii, workers in the ports, sugar mills, and cane fields negotiated together and in that year enjoyed wages of between $8 and $9 an hour. In Pernambuco, the average wage was 25 cents an hour in 1988, which, ignoring relative costs of living, is less than 1/32 of the Hawaiian wage (interview, 17 May 1988).

6. This seems to be common. Karen Remmer writes in a different context that "democratic political regimes may fail to equalize access to political power and may even have negative consequences for subordinate groups" (1984, 112).

7. Interview at the Goiana union headquarters, 2 May 1988.

8. An article in the *International Herald Tribune*, 8 September 1994, quoted a United Nations study predicting that although steady economic growth would continue in Latin America through the 1990s, poverty would not be reduced, but instead increase slightly.

9. For an analysis of new forms of popular interest representation in Latin America, see Chalmers 1997; Eckstein 1989; Escobar and Alvarez 1992.

10. A third scenario for the sugar zone is that contemplated by Clifford Geertz for workers in Modjokuto, Java (Indonesia) in the 1950s. Geertz recommended the delinking of sugar cultivation from its processing and marketing, allowing rural workers themselves to cultivate sugar and to sell it to the mills, working out mutually beneficial arrangements that combined capital-intensive techniques and scientific management with the maximum possible freedom and progress for rural workers (1984, 435). In such a scenario, the trade unions would be the logical institutions to carry out such a "new deal" in Pernambuco agriculture. This democratic outcome, however, seems utopian, given the very firm control that large landowners, and especially mill owners, have on the process of sugar cultivation, and their reluctance to contemplate any solution to the present crisis which would entail large-scale changes in property relations. I therefore exclude the scenario from consideration in this discussion.

11. In the 1980s, many plantation owners already felt under enough economic pressure to engage in ostentatious acts of public protest. On 11 April 1988, for example, about 5,000 cane planters from various northeastern states protested against low federal prices for sugarcane. They blocked the main highway between Alagoas and Pernambuco with hundreds of cars, tractors, trucks, and buses. A confrontation with the military police resulted in one shooting incident but no injuries (*Diário de Pernambuco*, 12 April 1988).

12. Conrad Abadie, secretary of the International Sugar Workers' Cooperative, a Louisiana-based international labor organization, believes that mechanization is the wave of the future in Pernambuco, as it has been in many other sugar-growing regions. This is especially likely if the unions continue to win wage increases. He foresees the use of mechanical harvesters which can negotiate Pernambuco's hilly terrain (interview, 17 May 1988). Mechanization of the harvest is also likely to increase elsewhere in Brazil; in 1996, only 10 percent of the sugar crop was harvested by machine (*Brazil Watch*, 13-27 May 1996, 12-13).

13. In the early 1930s, the Louisiana sugarcane industry employed around 500,000 field workers. In the 1980s, due to the use of mechanical harvesters, the labor force was down to 75,000 people (Butler 1980, 18). Interestingly, those workers enjoy far better working conditions than the mass labor force ever did—including a guaranteed working year of fifty weeks, something that would be revolutionary in Pernambuco.

14. *Folha de São Paulo*, 3 July 1994. The movement was reported to be an offshoot of the MST linked to a faction of the Workers' Party.

15. The occupation took place 29 March (*New York Times*, 8 April 1993). In the same month, in the interior of the northeast, the situation was much worse. Hungry peasants and workers looted food supplies in dozens of towns. In response, President Itamar Franco allocated $180 million to create 1 million public works jobs—a fraction of the $1.2 billion in federal credit that went to sugarcane growers for the 1993 harvest (*Veja*, 24 March 1993; Business Monitor International Ltd. 1993, 118−19).

16. That this plan was presented cynically by at least some members of the new civilian government as a way of garnering support is revealed by Senator José Sarney's reflections on his presidency: "To govern is like playing the violin. You take it with your left [hand], and you play it with your right" (*Veja*, 3 January 1996, 8).

17. *Manchester Guardian Weekly*, 7 January 1996. The article cited reports that the average was 9,000 per year, but this type of statistic is often unreliable.

18. Villar 1995. The organization's roots are in a 1979 land occupation at Encruzilhada Natalino in Rio Grande do Sul, and it was formally founded in the mid-1980s: in 1984 (*Folha de São Paulo*, 3 July 1994); or in 1985 (Villar 1995, 6−7).

19. An account of the massacre of at least nine landless people by military police in Corumbiara, Rondônia, on 9 August 1995, is given by Mônica Bérgamo in "Executados, Torturados e Humilhados," *Veja*, 6 September 1995, 38−41.

20. According to the Economist Intelligence Unit 1995, 10−11, the government of Fernando Henrique Cardoso had settled 22,000 families in the first ten months of 1995. Minister of Agriculture and Agrarian Reform José Eduardo de Andrade Veira declared that his ministry had expropriated 1 million hectares for settling 31,000 families in 1995 and that this was a record for Brazil (*Veja*, letters, 27 December 1995, 12). However, these figures were challenged by the MST, which argued that the government manipulated the data to exaggerate the extent of redistribution that had taken place.

21. It seems likely that the transition to democracy will eventually result in an overhaul of Brazil's corporatist labor structure. The Ministry of Labor's right to intervene in unions and replace leaders was abolished by the 1988 constitution (Gomes and D'Araújo 1993, 317−51). For an argument in favor of the effective abolition of the *contribuição sindical* and *unicidade*, see Boito 1991; Gomes and D'Araújo 1993; for the contrary view in support of more modest modifications of the system, see Unger 1990, 332; Gacek 1994; Martin 1994.

22. For an article against the end of *unicidade*, see Antonio Neto, "Unicidade versus Pluralidade Sindical," *Folha de São Paulo*, 21 October 1994. Neto was president of the CGT, the weakest of Brazil's three central labor organizations. Of the other two centrals, the CUT, linked to the Workers' Party, has officially supported the end of *unicidade* for over ten years, while the Força Sindical, generally seen as more conservative than the CUT, is divided on the issue (*Folha de São Paulo*, 11 October 1994).

GLOSSARY

abertura: opening; second phase, begun in 1979, of a process of political liberalization undertaken by the Brazilian military regime.

agrarismo: rural ideology based on the concept of land to the tiller and advocating land redistribution as the primary solution to problems of the rural lower classes.

agreste: intermediate zone of Pernambuco, devoted mainly to the production of cotton, tobacco, and food.

assistencialismo: welfarism; union posture in which leaders relate to members mainly by providing them with medical and other benefits rather than strongly representing them in labor disputes.

braça: unit of length, about six feet, used to assign work quotas in the cane fields.

cabo: plantation foreman.

camponês: commonly used to describe anyone who works on the land; often used interchangeably with *trabalhador rural*.

cana arrumada: sugarcane arranged into bundles.

cana solta: sugarcane arranged loosely in a pile after cutting.

carregador: machine with clawlike front end used for picking up loose cane.

clandestino: worker who works illegally without papers and benefits; called *bóia-fria* in the south.

companheiro: comrade or colleague; used frequently within the union movement.

convenção coletiva: collective contract signed every October between FETAPE and employers, usually after a TRT ruling on the wage increase.

coronel: traditional political leader, usually a landowner, with ability to mobilize lower-class voters in the countryside, as a rule on the basis of patronage; derives from the fact that many such leaders were colonels in the national guard.

cruzado: Brazilian currency in use between 1986 and 1990.

cruzeiro: Brazilian currency before 1986 and from March 1990 to July 1994.

delegado: union representative on the plantation, similar to a shop steward in an industrial union.

dissídio coletivo: ruling by the Regional Labor Court (TRT) on wages and other issues dividing employers and FETAPE. If a compromise was not reached in employer-employee negotiations, the dispute was automatically assigned to the TRT.

distenção: decompression; process of political liberalization initiated by Brazil's military regime in 1974.

empreiteiro: labor contractor, also known as a *gato*, who organizes teams of workers for temporary work on plantations.

engenho: sugar plantation.

entresafra: "dead season" when sugarcane is not being cut and unemployment is very high, roughly between February and August.

Estado Novo: "New State" established by President Vargas between 1937 and 1945. Under the Estado Novo, Brazil's labor law and labor structure were established.

foice: two-foot-long implement with a straight handle and wide blade, used by workers to cut cane.

fornecedores: cane planters; literally, suppliers of the mills.

hectare: unit of land measurement used in Brazil; roughly 2.5 acres.

imposto sindical: obligatory check-off of workers' wages by the state in order to finance trade unions; also known as *contribuição sindical.*

interventor: substitute leader appointed to a union leadership post by the Ministry of Labor after original leaders are removed; interventors were numerous within trade unions after the 1964 military coup. The 1988 constitution removed the power of the Ministry of Labor to appoint them.

latifúndio: traditional, labor-intensive large estate.

mata: coastal zone of Pernambuco (literally, forest) devoted almost entirely to sugarcane, further divided into humid (southern), and dry (northern), zones, with Greater Recife between the two.

moradía: traditional labor arrangement in which a worker on a plantation would be granted the use of a plot of land in exchange for agreeing to provide a certain amount of labor to the landowner.

município: county; also refers to the main town in a county.

new unionism: trade union movement that arose in Brazil in the late 1970s, and advocated more authentic, grass-roots union representation, reform of the corporatist labor structure, removal of *pelegos*, militant defense of workers' interests, and curbs on *assistencialismo.*

patrão: common term for employer used by workers; could refer to either a plantation owner or mill owner.

peasantariat: rural labor force characterized by mixed peasant and proletarian features, so that many of its members have access to both land and temporary wage employment.

pelego: traditional union boss who refuses to engage in militant action on behalf of his members and who prefers instead to work within the union bureaucracy; often associated with *assistencialismo*.

real: Brazilian currency since July 1994.

safra: cane harvest, which lasts roughly from August to February, with its peak in late September and early October.

sertão: dry, interior area covering most of Pernambuco, where the chief economic activity is cattle ranching.

sítio: plot of land on a plantation on which a worker has been granted use rights by the landowner.

tabela das tarefas: list of specific duties in the cane fields with corresponding wages, part of the piece-rate payment system. First established in Pernambuco in the Accordo do Campo, signed in August 1963.

tarefa: duty or job of the rural worker, for which he can earn the daily wage.

trabalhador rural: rural worker.

trabalhismo: rural ideology based on the promotion of labor rights and advocating higher wages, better working conditions, and strong enforcement of labor law as the primary solution to the problems of the rural lower classes.

unicidade: system of union monopoly in which only one union per category of worker is allowed in a given territory, usually a *município*.

usina: sugar mill.

usineiro: sugar mill owner.

BIBLIOGRAPHY

Abramovay, Ricardo. 1992. *Paradigmas do Capitalismo Agrário em Questão*. Campinas: Editôra da Unicamp.

Aguiar, Roberto. 1988a. Os Custos da Campanha Eleitoral. Manuscript for the *Folha de Pernambuco*, March.

———. 1988b. Os Financidores das Campanhas. Manuscript for the *Folha de Pernambuco*, March.

Alves, Maria Helena Moreira. 1985. *State and Opposition in Military Brazil*. Austin: University of Texas Press.

———. 1988. Dilemmas of the Consolidation of Democracy From the Top in Brazil. *Latin American Perspectives* 15 (summer): 47–63.

Alves, Vania Malheiros Barbosa. 1984. *Vanguarda Operária: Elite de Classe?* São Paulo: Paz e Terra.

Amnesty International. 1988. *Brazil: Authorized Violence in Rural Areas*. London: Amnesty International.

Anderson, Julie. 1990. Legislation, Development and Legislating Development in Brazilian Rural Labor Markets. Cambridge, Mass., unpublished.

Anderson, Perry. 1992. *A Zone of Engagement*. London: Verso.

Andrade, Manuel Correia de. 1980. *The Land and People of Northeast Brazil*. Albuquerque: University of New Mexico Press.

———. 1994. *Modernização e Pobreza: A Expansão da Agroindústria Canavieira e seu Impacto Ecológico e Social*. São Paulo: Editôra Unesp.

Araújo, Braz José de, ed. 1979. *Reflexões Sobre a Agricultura Brasileira*. Rio de Janeiro: Paz e Terra.

Araújo, Paulo Fernando Cidade de. 1983. Agricultura Brasileira Sem Subsídio. *Revista de Economia Rural* 21 (July–September): 295–303.

Asad, Talal. 1994. Ethnographic Representation, Statistics, and Modern Power. *Social Research* 61, no. 1 (spring): 55–88.

Avelar, Lucia. 1990. As Clivagens do Voto: Eleições Presidenciais de 1989. New Hampshire: unpublished paper delivered to the New England Latin American Studies Association Meeting.

Azevêdo, Fernando Antônio. 1982. *As Ligas Camponesas*. Rio de Janeiro: Paz e Terra.

———. 1990. *A Dinamica Política e a Competição Partidária em Pernambuco: 1945–1989*. São Paulo: IDESP.

Bacchus, Wilfred A. 1987. Controlled Political Transition in Brazil: Abertura as a Process for a Gradual Sharing of Political Power. In *Liberalization and Redemocratization in Latin America*, edited by George A. Lopes and Michael Stohl. New York: Greenwood Press.

Baer, Werner. 1989. *The Brazilian Economy: Growth and Development*. 3rd ed. New York: Praeger.

Banfield, Edward. 1951. *The Moral Basis of a Backward Society*. New York: Free Press.

Barreto, Leda. 1963. *Julião, Nordeste, Revolução*. Rio de Janeiro: Editôra Civilização.

Barros, Geraldo Santa'Ana de, Cicely Moitinho Amaral, and Vera L. Barros Amaral. 1993. Análise do Mercado de Trabalho na Agricultura Brasileira. *Revista de Economia Rural* 21 (July–September): 305–21.

Barros, Henrique Osvaldo Monteiro de. 1983. Relações de Trabalho e Produtividade na Lavoura Canavieira Pernambucana. *Boletim Sobre População, Emprego, E Renda No Nordeste* 2 (September–December): 421–43.

Barzelay, Michael. 1986. *The Politicized Market Economy: Alcohol in Brazil's Energy Strategy*. Berkeley: University of California Press.

Bastos, Elide Rugai. 1984. *As Ligas Camponesas*. Petrópolis: Editôra Vozes.

Becker, Bertha K. 1985. Brazil: Rural Development Problems, Policies and Perspectives. In *Rural Development: Capitalist and Socialist Paths*, vol. 2, edited by R. P. Misra. New Delhi: Concept Publishing Co.

Becker, Bertha K., and Claudio Egler. 1992. *Brazil: A New Regional Power in the World-Economy*. Cambridge: Cambridge University Press.

Boito, Armando, Jr. 1991. *O Sindicalismo Brasileiro nos Anos 80*. São Paulo: Paz e Terra.

———. 1994. The State and Trade Unionism in Brazil. *Latin American Perspectives* 21, no. 80 (winter): 7–23.

Bordieu, Pierre. 1977. *Outline of a Theory of Practice*. Cambridge: Cambridge University Press.

Borges, Francisca Neuma, et al., eds. 1986. *Antologia de Literatura de Cordel*. João Pessoa: Universidade Federal da Paraíba.

Bowles, Samuel, and Herbert Gintis. 1986. *Democracy and Capitalism*. New York: Basic Books.

Brass, Tom. 1991. Moral Economists, Subalterns, New Social Movements, and the (Re-) Emergence of a (Post-)Modernised (Middle) Peasant. *Journal of Peasant Studies* 18 (January): 173–205.

Bratton, Michael, and Nicolas Van De Walle. 1994. Patrimonial Regimes and Political Transitions in Africa. *World Politics* 46 (July): 453–89.

Breman, Jan. 1985. *Of Peasants, Migrants, and Paupers: Rural Labour Circulation and Capitalist Production in West India*. Delhi: Oxford University Press.

Brockett, Charles. 1990. *Land, Power and Poverty*. Boston: Unwin Hyman.

Bruneau, Thomas, and Philippe Faucher, eds. 1981. *Authoritarian Capitalism*. Boulder, Colo.: Westview Press.

Buchanan, Paul. 1995. *State, Labor, Capital: Democratizing Class Relations in the Southern Cone*. Pittsburgh: University of Pittsburgh Press.

Burns, E. Bradford, ed. 1966. *A Documentary History of Brazil*. New York: Alfred Knopf.

———. 1980. *A History of Brazil*. New York: Columbia University Press.

———. 1990. *Latin America: A Concise Interpretive History*. 5th ed. Englewood Cliffs, N.J.: Prentice Hall.

Bushnell, David, and Neil Macaulay. 1994. *The Emergence of Latin America in the Nineteenth Century*. New York: Oxford University Press.

Business Monitor International, Ltd. 1993. *Brazil 1993: Annual Report on Government, Economy, and Business Environment*. London: BMI Ltd.

Butler, W. E. 1980. *Down Among the Sugar Cane: The Story of Louisiana Sugar Plantations and Their Railroads*. Baton Rouge: Moran Publishing Co.

Cabral, Pedro Eugênio Toledo. 1986. O Processo de Proletarização do Trabalhador Canavieiro de Pernambuco. *Revista Pernambucana de Desenvolvimento* 11–12 (July 1984–June 1986).

Callado, Antonio. 1980. *Tempo de Arraes*. Rio de Janeiro: Paz e Terra.

Camargo, Aspásia Alcantara de. 1979. Authoritarianism and Populism: Bipolarity in the Brazilian Political System. In *The Structure of Brazilian Development*, edited by Neuma Aguiar. New Brunswick, N.J.: Transaction Books.

Cammack, Paul. 1991. Brazil: The Long March to the New Republic. *New Left Review* 190 (November–December): 21–58.

———. 1986. A Questão Agrária: Crise de Poder e Reformas de Base: 1930–1964. In *História Geral da Civilização Brasileira*, vol. 3: *O Brasil Republicano 3, Sociedade e Política (1930–1964)*, edited by Boris Fausto. São Paulo: Difusão Editorial.

Campanha Nacional Pela Reforma Agrária. 1985a. *Reforma Agrária, Para Que?* Rio de Janeiro: CONTAG/IBASE.

———. 1985b. *Violência no Campo*. Petrópolis: Editôra Vozes–IBASE.

Candido Filho, José. 1982. *O Movimento Operário: O Sindicato, O Partido*. Petrópolis: Editôra Vozes.

Carrière, Jean, Nigel Haworth, and Jacqueline Roddick, eds. 1989. *The State, Industrial Relations and the Labor Movement in Latin America*. New York: St. Martin's Press.

Carvalho, Marcus Joaquim Maciel de. 1994. Slave Resistance in Pernambuco in the First Half of the Nineteenth Century. Atlanta: Paper presented at the 18th Latin American Studies Association Conference, March.

Cavalcanti, Paulo. 1980. *O Caso Eu Conto Como O Caso Foi Volume 2: Memórias Políticas*. Recife: Editôra Guararapes Limitada.

———. 1986. *Arraes: Breve História de um Governo Popular*. Recife: Editôra Pirata.

Cavarozzi, Marcelo. 1992. Beyond Transitions to Democracy in Latin America. *Journal of Latin American Studies* 24, pt. 3 (October): 665–84.

Centro de Educação Popular do Instituto Sedes Sapientiae (CEPIS). 1985. *Reflexão Sobre a Violência no Campo*. São Paulo: CEPIS–Movimento Sem Terra.

Centro Ecumênico de Documentação e Informação (CEDI). 1985. *Canavieiros em Greve: Campanhas Salarias e Sindicalismo*. São Paulo: CEDI, Cadernos do CEDI 14.

Centro Josué de Castro, Pesquisa Nacional Sobre Estrutura e Representação Sindical. 1983. *Análise das Informações Referentes Aos Estados de Pernambuco e Paraíba*. Recife: Centro de Estudos de Cultura Contemporânea (CEDEC).

Cerqueira, Maria dos Milagres Leite. 1986. *A Ação Sindical dos Trabalhadores Rurais*. Recife: Governo Do Estado de Pernambuco, Secretária de Planejamento, Instituto de Desenvolvimento de Pernambuco.

Chacon, Vamireh. 1968. As Eleições Estaduais Em Pernambuco Em 1966. *Revista Brasileira De Estudos Políticos* nos. 23–24 (July 1967–January 1968): 83–95

Chalmers, Douglas, et al. 1997. *The New Politics of Inequality in Latin America: Rethinking Participation and Representation*. New York: Oxford University Press.

Chaloult, Yves. 1985. *Uma Das Contradições Da Nova República: O Projeto Nordeste*. Brasília: manuscript.

Chauí, Marilena. 1984. Considerações Sobre O Realismo Político. *Desvios 3*. São Paulo: Paz e Terra.

———. 1994. *Convite a Filosofia*. São Paulo: Editôra Atica.

Chiarelli, Carlos Alberto G. 1976. Social Security for Rural Workers in Brazil. *International Labor Review* 113 (March–April).

Chilcote, Ronald H. 1990. *Power and the Ruling Classes in Northeast Brazil: Juazeiro and Petrolina in Transition*. Cambridge: Cambridge University Press.

Chilvers, Lloyd, and Robin Foster. 1981. *The International Sugar Market: Prospects for the 1980s*. London: Economist Intelligence Unit Special Report no. 106.

Coelho, Plínio Augusto. 1986. *Os Anarquistas e As Eleições*. Brasília: Novos Tempos Editôra.

Cohen, Jean, and Andrew Arato. 1992. *Civil Society and Political Theory*. Cambridge: MIT Press.

Cohen, Robin. 1991. *Contested Domains: Debates in International Labor Studies*. London: Zed Press.

Cohen, Youseff. 1982. The Benevolent Leviathan: Political Consciousness Among Urban Workers Under State Corporatism. *American Political Science Review* 76, no. 1: 46–59.

———. 1989. *The Manipulation of Consent: The State and Working-Class Consciousness in Brazil*. Pittsburgh: University of Pittsburgh Press.

Coletivo, Edgar Leuenroth. 1980. *Movimento Operário Brasileiro 1900–1970*. Belo Horizonte: Editora Vega.

Collier, Ruth, and David Collier. 1991. *Shaping the Political Arena*. Princeton University Press.

Comissão Nacional dos Bispos do Brasil (CNBB), Regional Nordeste II, Setor de Pastoral Rural. 1987. *Os Descompassos da Reforma Agrária em 1987—Pernambuco*. Recife: Centro de Estudo e Ação Social, Setor Rural.

Confederação Geral dos Trabalhadores (CGT). 1991. *Mechanisms of Violence in Brazil: A Special Report*. Translated by American Institute for Free Labor Development, Washington, D.C.

Confederação Nacional dos Trabalhadores na Agricultura (CONTAG). 1993a. *Relatório 1993*. Brasília: CONTAG.

———. 1993b. *CONTAG: 30 Anos de Luta*. Brasília: CONTAG.

Córdova, Efrén. 1985. *A Organização Sindical Brasileira e a Convenção 87 da OIT*. Brasília: Ministério do Trabalho–Instituto Brasileiro de Relações do Trabalho.

Costa, Sérgio Armad. 1986. *Estado e Controle Sindical no Brasil*. São Paulo: T. A. Queiroz.

Crone, Patricia. 1989. *Pre-Industrial Societies*. Oxford: Basil Blackwell.

Curtin, Philip D. 1990. *The Rise and Fall of the Plantation Complex*. Cambridge: Cambridge University Press.

Da Fonseca, Gondin. 1962. *Assim Falou Julião*. São Paulo: Editôra Fulgor.

Dahl, Robert A. 1971. *Polyarchy*. New Haven: Yale University Press.

Davis, Diane. 1994. Failed Democratic Reforms in Contemporary Mexico: From Social Movements to the State and Back Again. *Journal of Latin American Studies* 26, pt. 2 (May): 375–408.

De Janvry, Alain, and Elisabeth Sadoulet. 1989. The Political Feasibility of Rural Poverty Alleviation. Berkeley: manuscript.

Demetrius, F. Joseph. 1990. *Brazil's National Alcohol Program*. New York: Praeger.

Diaz, Alvaro. 1993. *Restructuring and the New Working Classes in Chile*. Geneva: United Nations Research Institute for Social Development Discussion Paper no. 47.

Diniz, Eli. 1986. The Political Transition in Brazil: A Reappraisal of the Dynamics of the Political Opening. *Studies in Comparative International Development* 21 (summer): 63–73.

Dunlop, John T. 1988. Is Small Beautiful at the Workplace? *Villanova Law Review* 33, no. 6 (November): 1059–72.

Eckstein, Susan, ed. 1989. *Power and Protest: Social Movements in Latin America*. Berkeley: University of California Press.

Economist Intelligence Unit. 1992. *Brazil Country Profile*. London: Business International Ltd.

———. 1995. *Country Report: Brazil*. 4th Quarter. London: Business International Ltd.

Eisenberg, Peter L. 1974. *The Sugar Industry in Pernambuco, 1840–1910: Modernization Without Change*. Berkeley: University of California Press.

Erickson, Kenneth Paul. 1977. *The Brazilian Corporative State and Working-Class Politics*. Berkeley: University of California Press.

Escobar, Arturo, and Sonia Alvarez, eds. 1992. *The Making of Social Movements in Latin America*. Boulder, Colo.: Westview Press.

Evans, Peter. 1979. *Dependent Development*. Princeton: Princeton University Press.

———. 1989. Predatory, Developmental, and Other Apparatuses: A Comparative Political Economy Perspective on the Third World State. *Sociological Forum* 4, no. 4: 561–87.

Evans, Peter, and John Stephens. 1988. Studying Development Since the Sixties. *Theory and Society* 17: 713–45.

Federação dos Trabalhadores na Agricultura do Estado de Pernambuco (FETAPE). 1988. *Propostas e Reivindacações dos Trabalhadores Rurais da Zona Canavieira do Estado de Pernambuco*. Recife: FETAPE.

Figueiredo, Vilma. 1982. A Questão Agrária e as Estratégias do Governo. In *Brasil em Perspectiva: Dilemas da Abertura Política*, edited by Hélgio Trindade. Porto Alegre: Editôra Sulina.

Figueiredo, Vilma, and João Gabriel Teixeira. 1989. Diferenciação Social e Resposta Sindical as Transformações Tecnológicas na Agricultura Brasileira. *Cadernos de Difusão de Tecnologia* 6 (May–December): 217–35.

Figueiredo, Vilma, João Gabriel Teixeira, and Caetano de Araújo. 1985. Tecnologia Agropecuário: O Parlamento e as Reivindacações dos Trabalhadores Rurais. *Cadernos de Difusão de Tecnologia* 2 (May–August): 247–69.

Finch, H., and B. Munslow, eds. 1984. *Proletarianisation in the Third World: Studies in the Creation of a Labor Force Under Dependent Capitalism*. London: Croom Helm.

Fishman, Robert. 1990a. Rethinking State and Regime: Southern Europe's Transition to Democracy. *World Politics* 40 (April): 422–40.

———. 1990b. *Working-Class Organization and the Return to Democracy in Spain*. Ithaca: Cornell University Press.

Flynn, Peter. 1978. *Brazil: A Political Analysis*. London: Ernest Benn.

Food and Agriculture Organization of the United Nations. 1988. *Potentials for Agricultural and Rural Development*, Annex II: *Rural Poverty*. Rome: FAO.

Forgacs, David, ed. 1988. *An Antonio Gramsci Reader*. New York: Schocken Books.

Forman, Shepard. 1975. *The Brazilian Peasantry*. New York: Columbia University Press.

French, John D. 1988. Workers and the Rise of Adhemarista Populism in São Paulo, Brazil, 1945–47. *Hispanic American Historical Review* 68, no. 1: 1–43.

———. 1991. *The Brazilian Workers' ABC*. Chapel Hill: University of North Carolina Press.

———. 1992. *What Workers Want and What Union Leaders Do: Analyzing a 1961 Diary from São Paulo, Brazil*. Paper presented at the ninth Latin American Labor History Conference, State University of New York, Stony Brook, April 10–11.

Freyre, Gilberto. 1978. *The Masters and the Slaves*. New York: Knopf.

Frieden, Jeffry A. 1991. *Debt, Development, and Democracy: Modern Political Economy and Latin America, 1965–1985*. Princeton: Princeton University Press.

Fundação Jorge Duprat Figueiredo de Segurança e Medicina do Trabalho (FUNDACEN-TRO). 1987. *Cadastro de Acidentes do Trabalho Rural: Estado de Pernambuco*. São Paulo: Ministério do Trabalho.

Furtado, Celso. 1963. Brazil: What Kind of Revolution? *Foreign Affairs* 41 (April): 526–35.

Gacek, Stanley A. 1994. Revisiting the Corporatist and Contractualist Models of Labor Law Regimes: A Review of the Brazilian and American Systems. *Cardozo Law Review* 16 (August): 21–110.

Galloway, J. H. 1989. *The Sugar Cane Industry: An Historical Geography From Its Origins to 1914*. Cambridge: Cambridge University Press.

Garretón, Manuel Antonio. 1988. Problems of Democracy in Latin America: On the Processes of Transition and Consolidation. *International Journal* 43 (summer): 357–77.

Geertz, Clifford. 1984 [1956]. Capital-Intensive Agriculture in a Peasant Society: A Case Study. *Social Research* (spring–summer): 419–36.

Goldszal, Eduardo de Figuereido. 1992. Long-Term Movements of the Terms of Trade of Brazil. Ph.D. diss., New School for Social Research.

Gomes, Angela Maria de Castro, ed. 1980. *Regionalismo e Centralização Política: Partidos e Constituinte nos Anos 30*. Rio de Janeiro: Editôra Nova Fronteira.

Gomes, Angela Maria de Castro, and Maria Celina D'Araújo. 1993. A Extinção do Imposto Sindical: Demandas e Contradições. *Dados* 36, no. 2: 317–51.

Gomes, Gustavo Maia. 1979. Açúcar Em Pernambuco: A 'Crise Permanente' E Diretrizes Para Uma Reabilitação. *Revista Pernambucana de Desenvolvimento* 6 (January–June): 59–74.

Goodwin, Jeff. 1995. *State-Centered Approaches to Social Revolutions: Strengths and Limitations of a Theoretical Tradition*. New York: New School for Social Research–Center for the Study of Social Change, Working Paper no. 216.

Gould, Jeffrey. 1991. *To Lead As Equals*. Chapel Hill: University of North Carolina Press.

Governo do Estado de Pernambuco. 1983. *Programa de Ação Coordenada Para a Melhoria da Produtividade do Setor Agroindustrial Canavieiro do Estado de Pernambuco*. Recife: Secretaria de Planejamento.

———. 1985. *Anuário Estatístico de Pernambuco 1983*. Recife: CONDEPE.

———. 1987a. *Articulação Sócio-Econômica do Estado de Pernambuco*. Recife: CONDEPE.

———. 1987b. *Desempenho da Economia de Pernambuco 1985*. Recife: CONDEPE.

———. 1987c. *Desempenho da Economia de Pernambuco 1986*. Recife: CONDEPE.

Graham, Richard, ed. 1969. *A Century of Brazilian History Since 1865*. New York: Knopf.

Grigg, David. 1992. *The Transformation of Agriculture in the West*. Oxford: Blackwell.

Gryzbowski, Cândido. 1987. *Caminhos e Descaminhos dos Movimentos Sociais no Campo*. Petrópolis: Editôra Vozes.

Guanziroli, Carlos Enrique. 1984. *Política Agrária do Regime Pós-64*. Rio de Janeiro: IBASE.
———. 1985. *Reforma Agrária: Análise do Plano do Governo Sarney*. Rio de Janeiro: IBASE.
Hagopian, Frances. 1990. "Democracy by Undemocratic Means?": Elites, Political Pacts, and Regime Transition in Brazil. *Comparative Political Studies* 23 (July): 147–70.
———. 1993. After Regime Change. *World Politics* 45 (April): 464–500.
———. 1994. Traditional Politics Against State Transformation in Brazil. In *State Power and Social Forces*, edited by Joel Migdal et al., 37–64. New York: Cambridge University Press.
Hagopian, Frances, and Scott Mainwaring. 1987. Democracy in Brazil: Problems and Prospects. *World Policy Journal* (summer):485–514.
Hall, Michael, and Marco Aurélio Garcia. 1989. Urban Labor. In *Modern Brazil*, edited by Michael L. Conniff and Frank McCann. Lincoln: University of Nebraska Press.
Hanagan, Michael. 1994. New Perspectives on Class Formation. *Social Science History* 18 (spring): 77–94.
Handelman, Howard, and Thomas Sanders, eds. 1981. *Military Government and the Movement Toward Democracy in South America*. Bloomington: Indiana University Press.
Hattam, Victoria. 1993. *Labor Visions and State Power: The Origins of Business Unionism in the United States*. Princeton: Princeton University Press.
Heilbroner, Robert. 1985. *The Nature and Logic of Capitalism*. New York: W. W. Norton and Co.
Held, David, et al., eds. 1983. *States and Societies*. New York: New York University Press.
Hewitt, Cynthia. 1969. Brazil: The Peasant Movement of Pernambuco, 1961–1964. In *Latin American Peasant Movements*, edited by Henry A. Landsberger. Ithaca: Cornell University Press.
Hirschman, Albert. 1970. *Exit, Voice, and Loyalty: Responses to Decline in Firms, Organizations, and States*. Cambridge: Harvard University Press.
Hobsbawm, Eric. 1974. Peasant Land Occupations. *Past and Present* 62 (February).
Hoffman, Rodolfo, and Luiz Artur Clemente da Silva. 1986. Contribuição ao Estudo da Conçentração da Produção Agropecuária no Brasil em 1975 e 1980. *Revista de Economia Rural* 24 (April–June): 145–59.
Holanda, Sérgio Buarque de. 1956. *Raízes do Brasil*. Rio de Janeiro: Livraria José Olympio Editôra.
Huizer, Gerit. 1972. *The Revolutionary Potential of the Peasantry in Latin America*. Lexington, Mass.: D. C. Heath.
Humphrey, John. 1982. *Capitalist Control and Workers' Struggle in the Brazilian Auto Industry*. Princeton: Princeton University Press.
Huntington, Samuel P. 1991. *The Third Wave*. Norman: Oklahoma University Press.
Instituto Brasileiro de Análise Socio-Econômico. 1981. *Alguns Dados Sobre a Estrutura Agrária Brasileira*. Rio de Janeiro: IBASE.
———. 1983. *Organização Sindical no Meio Rural*. Rio de Janeiro: IBASE.
———. 1984a. *Agricultura no Brasil: Produção Para Consumo Interno x Produção Para Exportação*. Rio de Janeiro: IBASE.
———. 1984b. *Os Donos da Terra e a Luta Pela Reforma Agrária*. Rio de Janeiro: Editôra Codecri.
———. 1985. *Política Agrária do Regime Pós-64*. Rio de Janeiro: IBASE.
Instituto Brasileiro da Geografia e Economia (IBGE) 1950a. *Censo Agrícola de 1950*. Vol. 2, Tomo 6, Pt. 2a, Pernambuco.

——. 1950b. *Recenseamento Geral do Brasil 1950*. Vol. 17, tomo 1. Censo Demográfico, Pernambuco.

——. 1960. *Censo Agrícola de 1960*. Vol. 2, tomo 6, pt. 1a, Pernambuco, plus volumes on Rio Grande do Sul and Brazil.

——. 1980a. *Censo Agropecuário de 1980*, Pernambuco. Vol. 2, Tomo 3, no. 12, plus volume on Brazil.

——. 1980b. *Recenseamento Geral do Brasil 1980*. Vol. 1, tomo 6, no. 12. Censo Demográfico, Pernambuco.

——. 1985. *Censo Agropecuário de 1985*, Pernambuco. Vol. 27, tomo 2, plus volumes on Rio Grande do Sul (vol. 14), São Paulo (vol. 21), and Brazil.

——. 1987. *Anuário Estatístico 1987*.

——. 1988. *Anuário Estatístico 1988*.

——. 1991. *Anuário Estatístico 1991*.

Instituto do Açúcar e Álcool (IAA), Superintendencia Regional de Pernambuco. 1987. *Quadro Comparativo de Safras*, 1960–1961 to 1986–1987.

——. 1988. *Eficiência da Moagem de Canas, Fabricação de Açúcar e Respectivos Rendimentos Industriais*. Safra de 1987–1988, Final Report.

Instituto Nacional de Colonização e Reforma Agraria (INCRA), Superintendencia Estadual de Pernambuco, Divisão de Projetos de Colonização, Seção de Programação e Controle. 1988. *Areas Obtidas Para Assentamento*. Brasília: INCRA.

International Sugar Organization. 1987. *Annual Report*, 1957–1987.

Jaccoud, Luciana de Barros. 1986. "Na Lei Ou Na Marra . . .": Movimentos Sociais e Crise Política em Pernambuco 1955–1968. Master's thesis, UFPE.

James, Daniel. 1988. *Resistance and Integration: Peronism and the Argentine Working Class, 1946–1976*. Cambridge: Cambridge University Press.

Jatobá, Jorge. 1986. The Labour Market in a Recession-Hit Region: The North-East of Brazil. *International Labor Review* 125, no. 2 (March–April).

Jazairy, Idriss, et al. 1992. *The State of World Rural Poverty: An Inquiry Into Its Causes and Consequences*. New York: International Fund for Agricultural Development–New York University Press.

Jonas, Susanne, and Nancy Stein, eds. 1990. *Democracy in Latin America*. New York: Bergin and Garvin Publishers.

Julião, Francisco. 1962. *Que São As Ligas Camponesas?* Rio de Janeiro: Editôra Civilização Brasileira.

——. 1972. *Cambão—The Yoke: The Hidden Face of Brazil*. Middlesex: Penguin Books.

Kageyama, Angela. 1987. Algumas Características das Categorias de Imóveis Rurais no Brasil em 1978. *Reforma Agrária* 16 (December 1986–March 1987).

Karl, Terry Lynn. 1990. Dilemmas of Democratization in Latin America. *Comparative Politics* 23: 1–21.

Katznelson, Ira, and Aristide Zolberg, eds. 1986. *Working-Class Formation*. Princeton: Princeton University Press.

Kaufman, Robert. 1980. Industrial Change and Authoritarian Rule in Latin America: A Concrete Review of the Bureaucratic-Authoritarian Model. In *The New Authoritarianism in Latin America*, edited by David Collier. Princeton: Princeton University Press.

Keith, Robert G., ed. 1977. *Haciendas and Plantations in Latin American History*. New York: Holmes and Meier.

Kitschelt, Herbert. 1986. Political Opportunity Structures and Political Protest: Anti-Nuclear Movements in Four Democracies. *British Journal of Political Science* 16, pt. 1 (January): 57–85.

Krissman, Fred. 1994. The Transnationalization of the North American FVH Agricultural Sector: Mechanization or "Mexicanization" of Production? Paper presented at the Latin American Studies Association's XVIII Congress, Atlanta, March 12.

Lamounier, Bolívar. 1989. Brazil: Inequality Against Democracy. In *Democracy in Developing Countries: Latin America*, vol. 4, edited by Larry Diamond, Juan Linz, and Seymour Martin Lipset. Boulder, Colo.: Lynne Rienner, 1989.

Lancaster, Roger. 1988. *Thanks to God and the Revolution*. New York: Columbia University Press.

Lavareda, Antônio, ed. 1987. *A Vitória de Arraes*. Recife: M. Inojosa.

Leeds, Anthony. 1964. Brazil and the Myth of Francisco Julião. In *Politics of Change in Latin America*, edited by Joseph Maier and R. W. Weatherhead. New York: Praeger.

———. 1977. Myths and Pathos: Some Unpleasantries on Peasantries. In *Peasant Livelihood*, edited by Rhoda Halperin and James Dow. New York: St. Martin's Press.

Leite, Ronildo Maia. 1987. *A História de um Jornal Que Morreu, Ou Ascensão e Queda de Miguel Arraes*. Recife: Editôra de Pernambuco.

Lenin, Vladimir Ilich. 1982 [1899]. *O Desenvolvimento do Capitalismo na Russia*. São Paulo: Victor Civita.

Lessa, Sonia Sampaio Navarro. 1985. O Movimento Sindical Rural em Pernambuco: 1958–1968. Master's thesis, PIMES, UFPE.

Levine, Robert. 1978. *Pernambuco in the Brazilian Federation*. Stanford: Stanford University Press.

Linhart, Robert. 1980. *O Açúcar e A Fome*. Rio de Janeiro: Paz e Terra.

Lopes, José Sergio Leite. 1978. *O Vapor do Diabo: O Trabalho dos Operários do Açúcar*. São Paulo: Paz e Terra.

Lopez, Luiz Roberto. 1987. *História do Brasil Imperial*. Porto Alegre: Mercado Aberto.

Lothian, Tamara. 1986. The Political Consequences of Labor Law Regimes: The Contractualist and Corporatist Models Compared. *Cardozo Law Review* 7 (summer).

Loveman, Brian. 1976. *Struggle in the Countryside*. Bloomington: Indiana University Press.

MacEwan, Ian. 1988. Transitions from Authoritarian Rule. *Latin American Perspectives* 15, no. 58 (summer): 115–30.

Machado, Gilson, and Guimarães Filho. 1982. *Cana e Açúcar em Pernambuco: Em Busca de Novos Caminhos*. Recife: Editôra Raiz.

———. 1978. *Açúcar e Álcool, Seus Problemas e Sua Importância em Pernambuco*. Recife: Exposição à Escola Superior da Guerra, Sindicato da Indústria do Açúcar no Estado de Pernambuco (SIAEP).

Mainwaring, Scott. 1988. Political Parties and Democratization in Brazil and the Southern Cone. *Comparative Politics* 21, no. 1 (October): 91–120.

Mainwaring, Scott, Guillermo O'Donnell, and J. Samuel Valenzuela, eds. 1992. *Issues in Democratic Consolidation*. West Bend: University of Notre Dame Press.

Mallon, Florencia E. 1978. Peasants and Rural Laborers in Pernambuco 1955–1964. *Latin American Perspectives*, 5, no. 4: 49–70.

Malloy, James M. and Mitchell A. Seligson, eds. 1987. *Authoritarians and Democrats: Regime Transition in Latin America*. Pittsburgh: University of Pittsburgh Press.

Mann, Michael. 1986. The Autonomous Power of the State: Its Origins, Mechanisms, and Results. In *States in History*, edited by John Hall. London: Basil Blackwell.

———. 1993. *The Sources of Social Power*. Vol. 2: *The Rise of Classes and Nation-States, 1760–1914*. New York: Cambridge University Press.

Mansbridge, Jane. 1983. *Beyond Adversary Democracy*. Chicago: University of Chicago Press.

Marks, Gary. 1989. *Unions in Politics*. Princeton: Princeton University Press.

Martin, Scott. 1994. Forward or Backward? Corporatism and Industrial Restructuring in Brazilian Autos. Paper presented at a conference, The Politics of Inequality, Columbia University, March.

Martinez-Alier, Juan. 1977. *Haciendas, Plantations and Collective Farms*. London: Frank Cass.

Martinez-Alier, Verena, and Armando Boito, Jr. 1977. The Hoe and the Vote: Rural Labourers and the National Election in Brazil in 1974. *Journal of Peasant Studies* 4 (April): 147–70.

Marx, Karl. 1967 [1852]. *The Eighteenth Brumaire of Louis Bonaparte*. Moscow: Progress Publishers.

———. 1970 [1867]. *Capital: A Critique of Politial Economy*. Vol 1. London: Lawrence and Wishart.

Maxwell, Kenneth. 1991. The Mystery of Chico Mendes. *The New York Review of Books* 38, no. 6 (March 28).

Maybury-Lewis, Biorn. 1990. The Debate over Agrarian Reform in Brazil. Columbia University Institute of Latin American and Iberian Studies, Papers on Latin America no. 14.

———. 1994. *The Politics of the Possible: The Brazilian Rural Workers' Trade Union Movement, 1964–1985*. Philadelphia: Temple University Press.

McAdam, Doug. 1995. "Initiator" and "Derivative" Movements: Diffusion Processes in Protest Cycles. In *Repertoires and Cycles of Collective Action*, edited by Mark Traugott. Durham: Duke University Press.

Melo, Marcus. 1993. Financiers, Builders, and Bureaucrats: The Rise and Demise of Housing Coalitions in Brazil, 1964–1991. New York: Janey Program on Latin America, New School for Social Research, Working Paper no. 3, April.

Mericle, Kenneth Scott. 1974. *Conflict Regulation in the Brazilian Industrial Relations System*. Ph.D. diss., University of Wisconsin.

———. 1977. Corporatist Control of the Working Class: Authoritarian Brazil Since 1964. In *Authoritarianism and Corporatism in Latin America*, edited by James Malloy. Pittsburgh: University of Pittsburgh Press.

Midlarsky, Manus. 1989. Land Inequality and Political Violence. *American Political Science Review* 83 (June): 587–95.

Migdal, Joel, et al., eds. 1994. *State Power and Social Forces*. New York: Cambridge University Press.

Ministério da Indústria e do Comércio. 1986. *Caracterização Edafo-Climática das Regiões Canavieiras do Brasil: Pernambuco*. Piracicaba: IAA.

Ministério da Reforma e do Desenvolvimento Agrário (MIRAD). 1985. *Proposta Para a Elaboração do 1 Plano Nacional de Reforma Agrária da Nova República*. Brasília.

Mintz, Sidney. 1974a. The Rural Proletariat and the Problem of Rural Proletarian Consciousness. *Journal of Peasant Studies* 1 (April): 291–325.

———. 1974b. *Caribbean Transformations*. Baltimore: Johns Hopkins University Press.

Mir, Luís. 1984. *A Revolução Impossível: A Esquerda e a Luta Armada no Brasil*. São Paulo: Editôra Best Seller.

Moore, Barrington, Jr. 1966. *Social Origins of Dictatorship and Democracy*. Boston: Beacon Press.

Morães, Clodomir. 1970. Peasant Leagues in Brazil. In *Agrarian Problems and Peasant Movements in Latin America*, edited by Rodolfo Stavenhagen. Garden City, N.Y.: Anchor Books.

Morães Filho, Evaristo de. 1952. *O Problema do Sindicato Único no Brasil*. São Paulo: Editôra Alfa-Omega.

Movimento dos Trabalhadores Rurais Sem Terra. 1987. *Assassinatos no Campo: Crime e Impunidade 1964–1986*. São Paulo: Global Editôra.

Muller, Edward N., et al. 1989. Land Inequality and Political Violence. *American Political Science Review* 83 (June): 577–86.

Munck, Gerardo. 1994. Democratic Transitions in Comparative Perspective. *Comparative Politics* 26, no. 3 (April): 355–75.

Navarro, Zander. 1992. Democracy, Citizenship, and Representation: Rural Social Movements in Southern Brazil, 1978–1990. Cambridge, Mass.: unpublished.

Novães, José Roberto. 1987. I Programa Nacional de Reforma Agrária: E o Sonho Acabou? *Cardenos do CEAS* 109 (May–June): 18–28.

Nunberg, Barbara. 1986. Structural Change and State Policy: The Politics of Sugar in Brazil Since 1964. *Latin American Research Review* 21, no. 2.

Nunes Leal, Victor. 1949. *Coronelismo, Enxada e Voto*. São Paulo: Alfa-Omega.

Obregón, Aníbal Quijano. 1967. Contemporary Peasant Movements. In Seymour Martin Lipset and Aldo Solari, eds. *Elites in Latin America*. New York: Oxford University Press.

O'Donnell, Guillermo. 1973. *Modernization and Bureaucratic-Authoritarianism*. Berkeley: University of California Press.

———. 1993. The Browning of Latin America. *New Perspectives Quarterly* 10 (fall): 50–53.

O'Donnell, Guillermo, Philippe C. Schmitter, and Laurence Whitehead, eds. 1986. *Transitions from Authoritarian Rule: Prospects For Democracy*. Baltimore: Johns Hopkins University Press.

Offe, Claus. 1985. *Disorganized Capitalism*. Cambridge: MIT Press.

Oliveira, Clide de Fátima Galiza de. 1984. O Empreiteiro—Elemento Intermediário Na Contratação da Mão-de-Obra Volante na Zona Canavieira Pernambucana. *Boletim Sobre População, Emprego, e Renda no Nordeste* 3, no. 3 (September–December): 285–304.

Page, Joseph. 1972. *The Revolution That Never Was*. New York: Grossman Publishers.

Paige, Jeffrey. 1975. *Agrarian Revolution*. New York: Free Press.

Palmeira, Moacir. 1979. The Aftermath of Peasant Mobilization: Rural Conflicts in the Brazilian Northeast Since 1964. In *The Structure of Brazilian Development*, edited by Neuma Aguiar. New Brunswick, N.J.: Transaction Books.

———. 1989. Modernização, Estado e Questão Agrária. *Estudos Avançados* 3 (September–December): 87–108.

Pandolfi, Maria Lia. 1988. Forças Sociais e Articulações Políticas no Encaminhamento da

Reforma Agrária. Recife: Fundação Joaquim Nabuco, Departamento de Sociologia, manuscript.

Pang, Eul-Soo. 1985. A Requiem for Authoritarianism in Brazil. *Current History*, 84, no. 499 (February): 61–89.

———. 1989. Agrarian Change in the Northeast. In *Modern Brazil*, edited by Michael L. Conniff and Frank McCann. Lincoln: University of Nebraska Press.

Passos, Ana Tereza Bittencourt, and Ahmad Saeed Khan. 1988. Política Agrícola e Desigualdades Econômicas e Sociais do Setor Agrícola Brasileiro. *Revista de Economia e Sociologia Rural* 26 (January–March): 23–38.

Pateman, Carole. 1970. *Participation and Democratic Theory*. Cambridge: Cambridge University Press.

Pearson, Neale J. 1967. *Small Farmer and Rural Worker Pressure Groups in Brazil*. Ph.D. diss., University of Florida.

Pereira, Anthony W. 1989. Fire in the Forest: The Politics of Land in Brazil. *Hemisphere* 1 (Summer): 20–23.

———. 1993a. Agrarian Reform and the Rural Workers' Unions of the Pernambuco Sugar Zone, Brazil, 1985–1988. *The Journal of Developing Areas* 26 (January): 169–92.

———. 1993b. Economic Development, Democracy, and Civil Society in the Third World: The Northeastern Brazilian Case. *Third World Quarterly* 14 (November): 365–80.

———. 1994. *Democratic Change?* New York: New School for Social Research, Center for the Study of Social Change, Working Paper no. 193.

Perruci, Gadiel. 1978. *A República das Usinas*. Rio de Janeiro: Paz e Terra.

Pessoa, Dirceu, ed. 1986. *Política Fundiária no Nordeste*. Vol. 1, Pano de Fundo. Recife: Fundação Joaquim Nabuco, Instituto de Pesquisas Sociais, Departamento de Economia.

Plant, Roger. 1987. *Sugar and Modern Slavery*. London: Zed Books.

Popkin, Samuel. 1979. *The Rational Peasant: The Political Economy of Rural Society in Vietnam*. Berkeley: University of California Press.

Porto, Maria Stela Grossi. 1992. A Tecnologia Como Forma de Violência. Caxambú, Minas Gerais. Paper presented at the Sixteenth National ANPOCs Conference.

———. 1993. *Tecnologia e Violência: Algumas Relações Possíveis*. Caxambú, Minas Gerais: Paper presented at the Seventeenth National ANPOCs Conference.

Prado, Caio, Jr. 1953. *História Econômica do Brasil*. São Paulo: Editôra Brasiliense.

Price, Robert E. 1964. *Rural Unionization in Brazil*. Madison: University of Wisconsin Land Tenure Center Research Paper no. 14.

———. 1965. *The Brazilian Land Reform Statute*. Madison: University of Wisconsin Land Tenure Center Research Paper no. 15.

Przeworski, Adam. 1991. *Democracy and the Market*. New York: Cambridge University Press.

Putnam, Robert. 1993. *Making Democracy Work: Civic Traditions in Modern Italy*. Princeton: Princeton University Press.

Ramos, Pedro, and Walter Belik. 1989. Intervenção Estatal e a Agroindústria Canavieira no Brasil. *Revista de Economia de Sociologia Rural* 27 (April–June): 197–214.

Reis, Palhares Moreira. 1976. Pernambuco e Sua Eleição de 1974. *Revista Brasileira de Estudos Políticos* no. 43 (July): 69–109.

Remmer, Karen. 1989. *Military Rule in Latin America*. Boston: Unman Hyman.

———. 1984. *Party Competition in Argentina and Chile*. Lincoln: University of Nebraska Press.

Ribeiro, Nelson de Figueiredo. 1987. A Reforma Agrária na Constituinte: Uma Opção Pelos Pobres. *Reforma Agrária* 16, no. 3 (December 1986–March 1987).

Ricci, Rudá. 1994. Terra de Ninguém: O Sistema Confederativo Rural em Crise. *Reforma Agrária* 24 (January–April): 5–26.

Rodrigues, Aluísio. 1981. *O Estado e o Sistema Sindical Brasileiro*. São Paulo: Editôra LTR.

Rodrigues, Edgar. 1987. *ABC do Sindicalismo Revolucionário*. Rio de Janeiro: Achiamé.

Roemer, John, ed. 1986. *Analytical Marxism*. Cambridge: Cambridge University Press.

Roseberry, William. 1991. Beyond the Agrarian Question in Latin America. In *Confronting Historical Paradigms*, edited by Frederick Cooper et al. Madison: University of Wisconsin Press.

Rosenberg, Tina. 1991. *Children of Cain: Violence and the Violent in Latin America*. New York: Penguin Books.

Roxborough, Ian. 1979. *Theories of Underdevelopment*. London: The Macmillan Press.

Rubin, Jeffrey. 1994. COCEI in Juchitan: Grassroots Radicalism and Regional History. *Journal of Latin American Studies* 26, pt. 1 (February): 109–36.

Rueschemeyer, Dietrich, Evelyne Huber Stephens, and John D. Stephens. 1992. *Capitalist Development and Democracy*. Chicago: University of Chicago Press.

Sachs, Ignacio, Dalia Maimom, and Mauricio Tiomno Tolmasquim. 1987. The Social and Ecological Impact of "Pró-Álcool." *IDS Bulletin* 18 (January): 39–45.

Saes, Décio. 1985. *A Formação do Estado Burguês no Brasil*. São Paulo: Paz e Terra.

Sandoval, Salvador A. M. 1993. *Social Change and Labor Unrest in Brazil Since 1945*. Boulder, Colo.: Westview Press.

Sarney, José. 1986. Brazil: A President's Story. *Foreign Affairs* 65, no. 1 (fall): 101–17.

Scheper-Hughes, Nancy. 1992. *Death Without Weeping: The Violence of Everyday Life in Brazil*. Berkeley: University of California Press.

Schmitter, Philippe C. 1993. The International Context of Contemporary Democratization. *Stanford Journal of International Affairs* 2 (fall–winter): 1–34.

Schneider, Ben Ross. 1991. *Politics Within the State: Elite Bureaucrats and Industrial Policy in Authoritarian Brazil*. Pittsburgh: University of Pittsburgh Press.

Schwartz, Stuart B. 1985. *Sugar Plantations in the Formation of Brazilian Society*. Cambridge: Cambridge University Press.

Scott, James. 1985. *Weapons of the Weak: Everyday Forms of Peasant Resistance*. New Haven: Yale University Press.

———. 1991. *Domination and the Arts of Resistance: Hidden Transcripts*. New Haven: Yale University Press.

Shafer, D. Michael. 1990. Sectors, States, and Social Forces: Korea and Zambia Confront Economic Restructuring. *Comparative Politics* 22, no. 2.

Sigaud, Lygia. 1979. *Os Clandestinos e Os Direitos*. São Paulo: Livraria Duas Cidades.

———. 1980. *Greve Nos Engenhos*. Rio de Janeiro: Paz e Terra.

———. 1984. Luta Política e Luta Pela Terra no Nordeste. In *Anais do Seminário: Revisão Crítica da Produção Sociológica Voltada Para a Agricultura*, edited by Teresa Sales et al. São Paulo: CEBRAP.

———. 1986. A Luta de Classes em Dois Atos: Notas Sobre Um Ciclo de Greves Camponesas. *Dados* 29, no. 3: 319–43.

Silva, José Gomes da. 1985. *O Debate em Torno da Proposta do 1 PNRA da Nova República: Explicações Necessárias*. Brasília: MIRAD e INCRA.

Skidmore, Thomas E. 1967. *Politics in Brazil, 1930–1964*. Oxford: Oxford University Press.
———. 1988. *The Politics of Military Rule in Brazil, 1964–85*. Oxford: Oxford University Press.
Slater, David, ed. 1985. *New Social Movements and the State in Latin America*. Amsterdam: CEDLA.
———. 1994. Power and Social Movements in the Other Occident: Latin America in an International Context. *Latin American Perspectives* 21, no. 2 (spring): 11–37.
Smith, Robert Freeman, ed. 1966. *Background to Revolution: The Development of Modern Cuba*. New York: Knopf.
Smith, William C. 1987. The Travail of Brazilian Democracy in the New Republic. *Journal of InterAmerican Studies and World Affairs* 28 (winter 1986–1987): 39–74.
Soares, Glaucio, and Maria Celina D'Araújo, eds. 1994. *21 Anos de Regime Militar: Balanços e Perspectivas*. Rio de Janeiro: Editôra da Fundação Getúlio Vargas.
Soares, José Arlindo. 1982. *A Frente Do Recife e O Governo do Arraes*. São Paulo: Paz e Terra.
Spalding, Hobart, et al. 1988. *Working Against Us: The American Institute for Free Labor Development and the International Policy of the AFL-CIO*. New York: North American Congress on Latin America.
Stein, Stanley J., and Barbara H. Stein. 1970. *The Colonial Heritage of Latin America*. Oxford: Oxford University Press.
Stepan, Alfred, ed. 1973. *Authoritarian Brazil*. New Haven: Yale University Press.
Stepan, Alfred, ed. 1989. *Democratizing Brazil*. Oxford: Oxford University Press.
Suits, Daniel B. 1990. Agriculture. In *The Structure of American Industry*, edited by Walter Adams. New York: Macmillan.
Sutton, Alison. 1994. *Slavery in Brazil*. London: Anti-Slavery International, Human Rights Series no. 7.
Tannenbaum, Frank. 1960. *Ten Keys to Latin America*. New York: Vintage Books.
Tarrow, Sidney. 1994. *Power in Movement: Social Movements, Collective Action and Politics*. New York: Cambridge University Press.
Taylor, Kit Sims. 1978. *Sugar and the Underdevelopment of Northeastern Brazil 1500–1970*. Gainesville: University Presses of Florida.
Teixeira, João Gabriel. 1989. Estado, Sindicatos e as Transformações Tecnológicas na Agricultura Brasileira. *Temas Rurais* 2, no. 2 (September–December): 43–55.
Teixeira, João Gabriel L. C., et al., eds. 1991. *Tecnologia Agropecuária e a Organização dos Trabalhadores Rurais*. Brasília: Pax.
Thompson, E. P. 1971. The Moral Economy of the English Crowd in the Eighteenth Century. *Past and Present* 50 (February).
Tilly, Charles. 1978. *From Mobilization to Revolution*. Reading, MA: Addison-Wesley.
———. 1986. *The Contentious French*. Cambridge: Harvard University Press.
———. 1988. Solidary Logics. *Theory and Society* 17: 451–58.
———. 1995. Democracy Is a Lake. In *The Social Construction of Democracy, 1870–1990*, edited by George Reid Andrews and Herrick Chapman. New York: New York University Press.
Tribunal Regional Eleitoral de Pernambuco. 1962. *Resultado Final da Eleição de 1962*. Recife: TRE.
———. 1977. *Relatório das Eleições Municipais de 1976*. Recife: TRE.
———. 1990. *Resultado Final da Eleição Presidencial de 1989, Primeiro e Segundo Turnos*. Recife: TRE.
Troyano, Annez Andraus. 1978. *Estado e Sindicalismo*. São Paulo: Edições Simbolo.

Truda, Leonardo. 1971. *A Defesa da Produção Açucareira*. Rio de Janeiro: Ministério de Indústria e Comércio–Instituto do Açúcar e do Álcool.

Twomey, Michael J., and Ann Helwege, eds. 1991. *Modernization and Stagnation: Latin American Agriculture into the 1990s*. New York: Greenwood Press.

Unger, Roberto Mangabeira. 1990. *A Alternativa Transformadora: Como Democritizar o Brasil*. Rio de Janeiro: Guanabara Koogan.

United Nations. Various dates. *Economic Survey of Latin America and the Caribbean*. Santiago: UN.

———. 1967. *United Nations Statistical Yearbook 1966*. New York: Statistical Office of the UN, Department of Economic and Social Affairs.

United Nations Development Programme. 1994. *World Development Report 1994*. Oxford: Oxford University Press.

———. 1995. *World Development Report 1995*. Oxford: Oxford University Press.

U.S. Department of State. 1988. *Country Reports on Human Rights Practices for 1987*. Report Submitted to the House Foreign Affairs and Senate Foreign Relations Committees. Washington, D.C.: U.S. Government Printing Office.

———. 1989. *Country Reports on Human Rights Practices for 1988*. Report Submitted to the House Foreign Affairs and Senate Foreign Relations Committees. Washington, D.C.: U.S. Government Printing Office.

———. 1994. *Country Reports on Human Rights Practices for 1993*. Report Submitted to the House Foreign Affairs and Senate Foreign Relations Committees. Washington, D.C.: U.S. Government Printing Office.

Valenzuela, J. Samuel. 1989. Labor Movements in Transitions to Democracy: A Framework for Analysis. *Comparative Politics* 21 (July): 445–72.

Venceslau, Paulo de Tarso. 1989. Limpar o Terreno. *Teoria e Debate* 2 (April–June): 62–66.

Ventura, Jorge.1988. A Teia das Articulações: Um Estudo Sobre Estrutura de Poder Interno no Sindicato de Trabalhadorers Rurais de Arcoverde. Master's thesis, UFPE.

———. 1989. A Esperança dos Homens: Sindicato e Assistência Social. Paper prepared for the Fifteenth Congress of the Latin American Studies Association, San Juan, Puerto Rico, September.

Villar, Roberto. 1995. Lacking Jobs and Hope, Landless Gauchos Occupy Farms. *Real Brazil* 1, no. 1 (October–November): 6–8.

Viola, Eduardo, and Scott Mainwaring. 1985. Transitions to Democracy: Brazil and Argentina in the 1980s. *Journal of International Affairs* 38, no. 2 (winter): 193–219.

Walzer, Michael. 1988. The Ambiguous Legacy of Antonio Gramsci. *Dissent* (fall): 444–56.

Weber, Max. 1971. Capitalismo e Sociedade Rural na Alemanha. In *Ensaios de Sociologia*, edited by H. Gerth and C. Wright Mills. Rio de Janeiro: Zahar Editôra.

———. 1978. *Economy and Society*. Vols. 1–2. Ed. Guenther Roth and Claus Wittich. Berkeley: University of California Press.

———. 1979. Developmental Tendencies in the Situation of East Elbian Rural Laborers. *Economy and Society* 8, no. 2 (May): 177–205.

Weffort, Francisco. 1992. Novas Democracias. Que Democracias? *Lua Nova* 27: 5–30.

Weiner, Myron, and Ergun Özbudun, eds. 1987. *Competitive Elections in Developing Countries*. Durham: Duke University Press–American Enterprise Institute.

Welch, Clifford A. 1990. *Rural Labor and the Brazilian Revolution in São Paulo 1930–1964*. Ph.D. diss., Duke University.

Wickham-Crowley, Timothy P. 1992. *Guerrillas and Revolution in Latin America*. Princeton: Princeton University Press.

Wolf, Eric. 1969. *Peasant Wars of the Twentieth Century*. New York: Harper and Row.

Woo, Jung-Eun. 1991. *Race to the Swift*. New York: Columbia University Press.

World Bank. 1987. *Agricultural Mechanization: Issues and Options*. Washington, D.C.

Zolberg, Aristide. 1972. Moments of Madness. *Politics and Society* 2, no. 2 (winter): 183–208.

INDEX